T0383813

Beyond Symbolic Diversity, Equity, and Inclusion

This book extends strategic diversity work beyond internal organization efforts to social engagement and accountability. The book authors contend that organizations should work to achieve social impact across both business and employee. Organizations around the world are committed to increasing the racial diversity of their employees. Simultaneously, there is also greater interest in creating more welcoming and psychologically safe environments for people of color within organizations.

As the workforce demographics shift because of these initiatives, the interests and needs of the employee population have also shifted. This shift presents a challenge for organizations to move beyond symbolic diversity, equity, and inclusion (DE&I) work, of which increasing racial representation is chief, to helping organizations understand how to determine which issues to support of concern, value, and importance to their employees and society.

Essentially, this book, a venture into the field called transorganization development, also moves beyond the traditional view of corporate social responsibility to take the position that businesses have a responsibility to proactive stances on the many challenges facing the world today, including DE&I and accessibility. Many employees today expect their employers to take positions that will lead to making the world a better place.

Beyond Symbolic Diversity, Equity, and Inclusion

Creating a Culture of Enduring Organizational Social Impact

Edited by
William J. Rothwell
Jamie Campbell
Phillip L. Ealy

Routledge
Taylor & Francis Group

A PRODUCTIVITY PRESS BOOK

First published 2024
by Routledge
605 Third Avenue, New York, NY 10158

and by Routledge

4 Park Square, Milton Park, Abingdon, Oxon, OX14 4RN

Routledge is an imprint of the Taylor & Francis Group, an informa business

ISBN: 978-1-032-57509-4 (hbk)
ISBN: 978-1-032-57508-7 (pbk)
ISBN: 978-1-003-43971-4 (ebk)

DOI: 10.4324/9781003439714

Typeset in ITC Garamond Std
by KnowledgeWorks Global Ltd.

William J. Rothwell dedicates this book to his wife *Marcelina*, his daughter *Candice*, his son *Froilan*, his grandsons *Aden* and *Gabriel*, and his granddaughters *Freya* and *Lina*.

Jamie Campbell dedicates this book to his parents *Wilhemena* and *Claude*, his wife *Kimberly*, and his daughters *Grace, Vivian,* and *Lillian.*

Phillip L. Ealy dedicates this book to his wife *Michelle,* and kids *Cain, Phillip,* and *Terrell.*

Contents

12 Step 11: Communicating Your Organization's Social Change Efforts 198

BARBARA HOPKINS

13 Reflecting on the Future Role of Business Social Activism 211

JAMIE CAMPBELL AND PHILLIP L. EALY

Appendix A: Selected Social Impact and Social Change Resources 221

Preface

By William J. Rothwell, Jamie Campbell, and Phillip L. Ealy

What should be the role of organizations in bettering the world? That question has provoked much thought among business leaders, government leaders, philanthropists, and workers. Employers, many of whom have been hard pressed at the time this book goes to press to recruit and retain workers, find that many of today's workers expect their organizations to take proactive stances on the troubling issues confronting people in the world today. They include (but are not limited to) problems with:

- Social justice
- Diversity, equity, and inclusion
- Accessibility
- Income inequality
- Crime
- Drug addiction
- Population growth/decline
- Unemployment
- Climate change
- Gun control
- Healthcare inequities
- Corruption
- Ageism
- Social isolation

Social problems are understood to mean issues that can pose harm to individuals or segments of society.

In our previous book, *Rethinking Organizational Diversity, Equity, and Inclusion: A Step-by-Step Guide for Facilitating Effective Change* (Routledge, 2022), we (the editors and our contributing authors) provided detailed guidance on an effective way for diversity practitioners to implement a Diversity, Equity, and Inclusion (DE&I) program in an organization. But as we completed the book, we realized that it does little good for an organization to formulate and implement a DE&I program internally if the community and society surrounding the organization does not support the principles of DE&I. As a result, we began to research what organizations were doing to improve the conditions of their communities and the larger world of which they are part. That led us to explore social change, social impact, and social action.

It is a topic on which the U.S. public is divided. In a Gallup survey (Marken, 2023), Americans were split on whether businesses should take a public stance on political and social issues—with 48 percent believing they should and 52 percent disagreeing. Younger adults believe their employers should take a stand on social issues more than older ones: 59 percent of those aged 18–29 agree to this compared to 51 percent of those aged 30–44, 41 percent of those aged 45–59, and 43 percent of those aged 60 and beyond. When talent is tough to acquire and retain, employers that wish to attract younger workers are well-advised to take social stances and create a reputation for taking progressive stances on efforts to make the world a better place. As Thompson (2023) writes:

> In a 2021 survey by software company Atlassian, 61 percent of Millennial respondents said they prefer companies that take a stand on social issues. Taking a stand can potentially help companies lower attrition and be intentional about attracting and retaining employees who add an element of diversity to the culture.

Many well-known companies have taken a stand on social issues. They have committed more than merely financial donations (Birch, 2022; Mancilla, 2021; Ripplematch team, 2023).

In Exhibit P-1, we have listed over 20 organizations that are "walking the walk" with their social change efforts. The usual suspects of Nike, Timberland, EY, TOMS, and a few others were left off because these are the known, constantly spoken about companies. Though we have included some that are well known, we wanted to showcase different institutions that individuals may not be as aware of. Which companies do you think should

Organization	Industry	SCM	Address
Ben & Jerry	Ice Cream	Social Justice, Sustainability, Fair Trade	https://www.benjerry.com/values
LEGO	Construction Toy	Sustainability, Child Health/Education	https://www.lego.com/en-us/sustainability
Sprout Social	Social Media/Information	Sustainability	https://sproutsocial.com/
Lemonade	Insurance	Varied by client donation selections	https://www.lemonade.com/giveback
Purely Elizabeth	Holistic Food	Sustainability	https://purelyelizabeth.com/pages/journey
New Belgium Brewing Company	Spirits (Beer)	Sustainability	https://www.drinksustainably.com/
Panasonic	Technology	Social Justice, Education	https://na.panasonic.com/us/social-impact#:~:text=In%20keeping%20with%20these%20core,initiatives%20and%20strategic%20philanthropic%20investments.
BLQK	Coffee	Social Justice	https://blqk.coffee/
Citigroup	Financial Services	Varied	https://www.citigroup.com/global/our-impact
Proctor & Gamble	Packaged Goods	Gender Equity	https://www.pg.co.uk/gender-equality/
Esri	Mapping Technology	Sustainability	https://www.esri.com/en-us/about/sustainability-statement
Salesforce	Cloud-Based Software	Social Justice	https://www.salesforce.com/company/philanthropy/salesforce-foundation/
Thinx	Women's Clothing	Women's Health	https://www.thinx.com/thinx/about-us

Exhibit P-1   Organizations That Engage in Social Change Movements (SCM) *(Continued)*

Organization	Industry	SCM	Address
Squarespace	Website Creation	Social Justice	https://www.squarespace.com/about/diversity-and-inclusion
Tenttree	Eco-Friendly Clothing	Social Justice, Environment	https://www.tentree.com/pages/sustainability-report
CVS	Healthcare	Healthcare	https://www.cvshealth.com/impact/esg-reports/priority-topics.html
Intel	Technology	Social Justice, Education	Corporate Social Responsibility (intel.com)
Signify	Lighting	Socio-Economic	https://www.signify.com/global/our-company/signify-foundation
Warbly Parker	Optometry	Socio-Economic, Healthcare	https://www.warbyparker.com/buy-a-pair-give-a-pair
Art Lifting	Arts	Socio-Economic, Mental Health	https://www.artlifting.com/
One Hope Wine	Spirits (Wine)	Water Purity	https://www.onehopewine.com/impact
cuddle + kind	Pet Care	Socio-Economic, Food Insecurity	https://cuddleandkind.com/pages/our-story

Exhibit P-1 *(Continued)*

have been included? What areas are they engaging in? How did they come to these conclusions?

Understanding how organizations prioritize goals and initiatives around their social change efforts could be as simple as visiting their organizational sites to see how easy their message is to find on their sites. You often can hear companies speak about what they are doing in articles and interviews, but it is often not displayed as a part of the culture. For social change efforts to be successful, both internally and externally, they have to be embedded in the culture of that organization. Hower (2016) gives four tools that can be utilized to see if the talk and the walk match. The most common one is the balanced score card which can be used as a part of your identification of how engaged your organization is in the social change it is speaking about.

It is also important to note that none of these efforts can be seen as silver bullets, many of these efforts are successful because the efforts were given the time to grow, flourish, and adjust as needed. For example, TOMS has adjusted its direction on how it engages its social change efforts, not only because it was good for business but because the efforts could do more in even communities it wanted to support (McDonald, 2021)!

The coming chapters will review companies like Nike, Coke, and others but the few listed below will give an idea of how to engage in social change and efforts. A few of these companies mentioned below are included in the Forbes 500 (P&G, Salesforce, Citigroup, Intel, and Target) for their diversity and business best-in-class diversity efforts.

There are many reasons to care about organizations and their roles in social change.

Employers play a pivotal role in every society. Their voices matter. If they take a stance for or against an issue, their voice can have social impact.

Second, it just makes sense that conditions in the world outside employing organizations affect conditions inside those organizations. Organizations are not closed systems; rather, they are open systems that are dramatically affected by conditions outside their boundaries.

While much has been published about organizational change, less focus has been placed on change happening across organizations (a field of practice called *Transorganization Development* [*TOD*]). This book makes an effort to do that using the principles of Organization Development (OD) (Rothwell et al, 2015).

What role should organizations play in social change? And once organizational leaders decide an organization should play a proactive role in inducing change outside their organizations, what should they do? Should they throw money at social problems and do nothing else? Or should they devote time, money, and effort of the organization to grappling with those social problems?

The Purpose of the Book

This book offers a step-by-step, systematic approach to implementing externally focused social change efforts from inside an employing organization. While many approaches to organizational change could work to help facilitate social change efforts, the editors and contributing authors of this book favor the use of Organization Development (OD). Organization Development is a planned approach to change that relies on behavioral science principles to facilitate—rather than impose or coerce—change.

This book provides readers with a comprehensive, step-by-step approach to implement social change outside an organization from inside an organization.

The Target Audience for the Book

This book is written for anyone who seeks to bring about social change efforts designed to make the world a better place. That would include:

- *DE&I program managers, HR directors and human resource professionals* tasked to facilitate the implementation of DE&I efforts who wish to affect the world outside their organization's boundaries.
- *Managers* and *workers* who participate in change efforts and often help to shape them.
- *Teachers* or *professors* who teach about social change, organizational change, or community development.
- *Consultants* who facilitate social change and social impact change efforts.

The Organization of the Book

This book is organized in a step-by-step approach. It is based on a "Big Picture" model that can help those tasked in an organization to lead or facilitate social change efforts outside their organizations. See Exhibit P-2

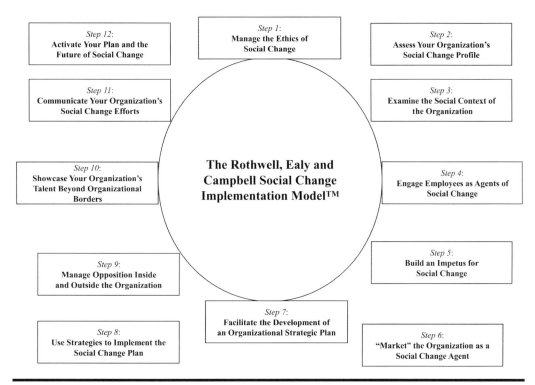

Exhibit P-2   The Rothwell, Ealy and Campbell Social Change Implementation Model™

for a change model that can guide a program facilitator and is also the organizational scheme for this book.

This book opens with this **Preface**, which is intended to summarize the book. An **Acknowledgments** page thanks to contributors. An **Advance Organizer** is designed to help readers assess on which chapters they should focus attention. **Chapter 1**, entitled *"The background: facilitating social and organizational change,"* describes theoretical views about social change. **Chapter 2** looks at the first step in the implementation model and thereby provides the big picture surrounding the ethics of social change. **Chapter 3** reviews Step 2 in the implementation model, which is to assess your organization's social change profile. **Chapter 4**, entitled *"Examining the Social Context of the Organization,"* is the third step of the social change model guiding the book. **Chapter 5** covers Step 4 of the model, which centers on "engaging employees as agents of social change." **Chapter 6**, covering Step 5, is about "building an impetus for social change." **Chapter 7**, reviewing Step 6, discusses how to market the organization as a social change agent. **Chapter 8**, which focuses on Step 7 of the social change implementation model, is entitled "facilitating the development of an organizational strategic plan." Step 8, discussed in **Chapter 9**, is about strategies for implementing a social change plan. **Chapter 10** deals with the critical issue of how to manage opposition to social change efforts surfacing from inside and outside the organization. **Chapter 11** examines ways of showcasing your organization's talent beyond the organization's boundaries, and **Chapter 12** covers the last step in the social change model—which is planning how to communicate about your organization's social change efforts.

This book concludes with **Appendix A**, which lists selected resources to support an organization's efforts to effect social impact and social change, and **Appendix B**, which provides Frequently Asked Questions (FAQs) about social impact and social change.

References

6 Companies that have taken bold stands on Social Issues. JUST Capital. (2023, September 23). https://justcapital.com/news/companies-that-have-taken-bold-stands-on-social-issues/

12 Companies with Amazing Community Support Programs – Comparably. (2020, December 3). https://www.comparably.com/news/12-companies-with-amazing-community-support-programs/

Birch, K. (2022, August 26). 9 Companies taking a stance on political or social issues. *Business Chief.* https://businesschief.com/leadership-and-strategy/9-companies-taking-a-stance-on-political-or-social-issues

Calica, A. (2022, June 16). *59 Companies that give back and make volunteering essential to their culture.* Built In. https://builtin.com/articles/companies-that-give-back

Hower, M. (2016, March 7). *4 Tools to tell if your company is walking the walk on CSR.* GreenBiz. https://www.greenbiz.com/article/4-tools-tell-if-your-company-walking-walk-csr#The%20Multicapital%20Scorecard

Mancilla, A. (2021, October 18). 7 Brands influencing social change. *Hollywood Branded.* https://blog.hollywoodbranded.com/5-brands-influencing-social-change

Marken, S. (2023, January 10). U.S. adults split on companies taking political, social stances. *Gallup.* https://news.gallup.com/opinion/gallup/405656/adults-split-companies-taking-political-social-stances.aspx#:~:text=About%20three%2Dquarters%20of%20each,a%20public%20stance%20on%20issues.

McDonald, S. (2021, April 6). *Toms undergoes its biggest rebrand - inside the company's new business model.* Footwear News. https://footwearnews.com/business/retail/toms-one-for-one-business-model-grassroots-good-1203128043/

Morgan, B. (2023, September 12). *20 Companies that use their profits for social good.* Forbes. https://www.forbes.com/sites/blakemorgan/2021/10/26/20-companies-that-use-their-profits-for-social-good/?sh=df6d38411a84

Perrone, G. (2021, October 12). *30+ Companies with significant volunteer programs - twenty now.* Twenty Now. https://www.twentynow.com/sustainability-initiatives/social/30-companies-with-significant-volunteer-programs/

Ripplematch team. (2023, July 26). 35 Companies with powerful social impact initiatives. *Ripplematch.* https://ripplematch.com/career-advice/companies-with-powerful-social-impact-initiatives-65f368a5/

Rothwell, W. J., Ealy, P. L., & Campbell, J. (Eds.). (2022). *Rethinking organizational diversity, equity, and inclusion: A step-by-step guide for facilitating effective change.* Routledge. https://doi.org/10.4324/9781003184935

Rothwell, W. J., Stavros, J. M., & Sullivan, R. L. (Eds.). (2015). *Practicing organization development: Leading transformation and change* (4th eds.). Wiley.

Sull, D., Turconi, S., & Sull, C. (2020, July 21). *When it comes to culture, does your company walk the talk?* MIT Sloan Management Review. https://sloanreview.mit.edu/article/when-it-comes-to-culture-does-your-company-walk-the-talk/

Thompson, R. (2023, May 26). Should employers take positions on social and political issues? *HR Magazine.*

Acknowledgments

The editors appreciate all those who contributed to this project.

William J. Rothwell wants to express his special thanks to Jamie Campbell and Phillip L. Ealy for their excellent ability to facilitate the contributing authors to meet deadlines, deal with writing issues, and make sure the project was on course. They kept the project on time and on course.

William J. Rothwell
State College, Pennsylvania
November 2023

Jamie Campbell
State College, Pennsylvania
November 2023

Phillip L. Ealy
State College, Pennsylvania
November 2023

About the Editors and Contributors

Editors

William J. Rothwell, PhD, DBA, SPHR, SHRM-SCP, RODC, CPTD Fellow, is President of Rothwell & Associates, Inc. and Rothwell & Associates, LLC (see www.rothwellandassociates.com). He is also a distinguished professor in the Workforce Education and Development program, Department of Learning and Performance Systems, at The Pennsylvania State University, University Park campus. Before arriving at Penn State in 1993, he had 20 years of work experience as a Training Director and HR professional in government and business. He has also worked as a consultant for over 50 multinational corporations–including Motorola China, General Motors, Ford, and many others. His recent books since 2020 include *Accelerated Action Learning* (2024), *Building an Organizational Coaching Culture* (2024), *Mastering the Art of Process Consultation and Virtual Group Coaching Simulation* (2023); *Successful Supervisory Leadership* (2023); *Transformational Coaching* (2023); *Succession Planning for Small and Family Businesses* (2022); *High-Performance Coaching for Managers* (2022); *Rethinking Diversity, Equity, and Inclusion* (2022); *Organization Development (OD) Interventions: Executing Effective Organizational Change* (2021); *Virtual Coaching to Improve Group Relationships* (2021); *The Essential HR Guide for Small Business and Start Ups* (2020); *Increasing Learning and Development's Impact Through Accreditation* (2020); *Adult Learning Basics*, 2nd ed. (2020); and, *Workforce Development: Guidelines for Community College Professionals*, 2nd ed. (2020). He can be reached by email at wjr9@psu.edu and by phone at 814-863-2581. He is at 310B Keller Building, University Park, PA 16803.

Jamie Campbell, PhD, CDE, serves as the Associate Dean for Diversity Enhancement Programs in the Smeal College of Business at The Pennsylvania State University. He has served as a panelist on topics ranging from social justice to students' issues and has been a keynote speaker for various leadership programs. Jamie also serves as an advisor to several student organizations within the Smeal College of Business and mentors graduates of the college working in Fortune 500 companies. He was an inaugural Fellow with the CEO for Racial Equity Fellowship which supports programs for underrepresented persons across the United States. Jamie is also recognized as a Certified Diversity Executive. He is a 1995 graduate of Morehouse College where he obtained his B.A. in Sociology, and completed an M.Ed. in Adult Education and Instruction Education from Central Michigan University in 2003. Jamie is a Ph.D. graduate of the Workforce Education Program with concentrations in Organization Design and Human Resource Development at The Pennsylvania State University. His research focuses on Succession Planning as a form of Crisis Management.

Phillip L. Ealy, PhD, MPS, is a retired United States Army Officer where he spent time coaching, teaching, developing, and facilitating leadership. He works as the coaching coordinator for the Children, Youth, and Families at Risk (CYFAR) grant program. In this role, Phillip trains and develops coaches that work with land-grant universities on implementing government funded programs for local communities. Phillip holds a Ph.D. in Workforce Education and Development with an emphasis in Human Resource Development and Organization Development and a Master of Professional Studies in Organization Development and Change from The Pennsylvania State University and a Bachelor of Science degree in Communications from West Virginia State University. He is a veteran book writer, speaker, and presenter. Phillip has recently co-founded Ealy Hopkins Consulting, LLC.

Contributing Authors

S. Ron Banerjee, MPS, CFS, CLTC, is a financial advisor specializing in the Tax-Exempt Markets for Voya Financial Advisors, Inc. He is a PhD student in Workforce Education and Development and received his Master of Professional Studies degree in Organization Development and Change from The Pennsylvania State University. Ron is a decorated veteran of the

US Navy. He can be reached by email at srb4@psu.edu and by phone at 814-404-8578.

R. Adidi Etim-Hunting is the Director of Diversity, Equity and Inclusion for The Pennsylvania State University's Division of Development and Alumni Relations (DDAR) where she is charged with developing policies, programs, and division wide initiatives. As a director, she carries out the DDAR Strategic Plan and advances its four-part framework of priorities, the recruitment and retention strategies for a diverse workforce, and initiatives to promote a welcoming and inclusive Penn State community. She has presented at national and international conferences, as well as professional development workshops focused on diversity, equity, inclusion, and engagement. She has over a decade of experience in Higher Education administration, student affairs, and academic affairs. She is a Californian and Michigander who deeply values her Nigerian American background. She earned her bachelor's degree from Grand Valley State University in photography, and a master's degree in counseling, adult, and higher education at Northern Illinois and is a PhD student in Workforce Education specializing in Organization Development and Human Resource Development with a concentration in diversity, inclusion, access and equity at The Pennsylvania State University. You can reach her by email at Adidi@psu.edu

Kaitlin Farnan, MBA, is an Instructor in Management at The Pennsylvania State University, Altoona College. Her teaching includes international business, economics, management, and sustainability, and her research focuses on sustainable development of organizations and communities. She has consulted for both for-profit and non-profit companies and has helped students engage in community work and service. Kaitlin comes from an interdisciplinarity background with her Master's in Business Administration from The Pennsylvania State University, and she also holds bachelor's degrees in History and International Politics. Kaitlin is a PhD student in Workforce Education specializing in Organization Development and Human Resource Development at The Pennsylvania State University.

Wayne Gersie, PhD, Wayne Gersie, Ph.D., is the owner and principal of Oasis Strategic Consulting LLC. Dr. Gersie is an expert facilitator and coach in organizational development, inclusive change management practices, and culturally responsive strategic planning. He has a specific focus and experience in assisting organizations to develop enduring equity-responsive strategies and practices to build high-performance 21st-century teams. Dr. Gersie's coaching philosophy facilitates winning outcomes that enhance a sense of belonging for all stakeholders and increase innovation, efficiency, and industry relevance. His coaching is centered on preparing those who have the privilege of influence to lead the way in their organizations through techniques that are inclusive and responsive to the diverse needs and identities of their stakeholders.

Dr. Gersie earned his Ph.D. in Workforce Education and Development, with an emphasis on Human Resource Management, and an MEd in Counselor Education, both from the Pennsylvania State University. Additionally, he holds certificates from the Harvard University Institute for Management and Leadership Education, Cornell University, Center for Creative Leadership in Colorado Springs, Colorado, and the National Association of Diversity Officers in Higher Education's Standards for Professional Practice Institute.

Dr. Gersie is the inaugural Vice President for Diversity and Inclusion at Michigan Technological University. In this role, he works to identify and address organizational and systemic challenges related to diversity, equity, and inclusion on Michigan Tech's campus. This includes developing policies and practices in collaboration with academic colleges and operational areas including human resources, finance, and student and academic affairs with the goal of creating a sense of belonging for all stakeholders. He is also an experienced grant writer and has secured over 15 million dollars in both federal, state, and private grants as principal and co-principal investigator. Prior to Michigan Tech, Dr. Gersie served as the inaugural Chief Diversity Officer at the Pennsylvania State University Applied Research Laboratory.

Barbara R. Hopkins, MS, is an administrator at the Geremanna Community College in Virginia. Her current role involves developing, implementing, and coordinating organizations. During her 20-year career in higher education, she has held multiple leadership positions and participated in projects at the institutional, state-wide, and national levels. Before beginning her tenure in higher education, she had an accounting career, which included owning her own practice. Hopkins has also been highly active in the business community and the public school system. She holds a master's degree in accounting and is working toward a Doctor of Education in Community College Leadership to be an even larger contributor to resolving Community College issues nationwide.

Christina Pettey, MPS, PHR, is a Six Sigma Black Belt specializing in continuous process and organizational improvement. She has over 15 years of experience in Human Resources and continuous improvement working for Bechtel Corporation at the vitrification plant being built to process nuclear waste from Hanford. She specializes in using a blended approach to improve interactions between people and processes. She holds a bachelor's degree in Psychology from the University of Washington and a Master of Professional Studies degree in Organization Development and Change from Penn State University. She is a certified Six Sigma Black Belt and Professional in Human Resources. Her volunteer service includes support for Modern Living Services (assisting developmentally disabled adults) and COLAGE (Children of Lesbians and Gays Everywhere).

Farhan Sadique, MS, is a PhD candidate and recognized student leader in the Learning and Performance System Department at The Pennsylvania State University. Farhan has served as an instructor and guest lecturer in various online courses for Penn State. In addition, he has several years of experience in management, focusing on employee training and development, where he successfully advocated employee career development opportunities. He has co-authored peer-reviewed scholarly journal articles, book chapters, and newsletters; and has presented at conferences in national and international boundaries. Due to his intense research and innovative thinking skills and experience, he has been invited to versatile projects, including an open-source innovation lab for organization development, a state-granted research program on evaluation capacity building of extension educators, transformational coaching methodologies, job satisfaction in stressful working environments for nurses, air-traffic controllers, flight safety trainers, and retail workforce development. Besides pursuing his PhD, he is also leading multiple student and professional organizations, a professional photography service firm, and a personal portfolio in the stock market.

Melissa A. Walker, PhD, is the current Organizational Development Manager for the State of Colorado, and previous Director of the TRIO Training Academy at Penn State University, which provides TRIO specific training and advocacy consulting and training nationwide. During her 12 years at Penn State, she managed five concurrent grant programs which includes three Talent Search, one Educational Opportunity Center, and one TRIO Training program. Melissa still holds a contract position as a Learning Partner at Penn State's Workplace Learning and Performance where she provides diversity, team building, accountability, and leadership training for all personnel. She is the owner of Training and Development Network, where she provides consulting and professional development internationally. She has spent over 15 years working with grant funded educational programs and developing training curriculum for talent development—which include: diversity, leadership, teamwork, and communication. In her 25 years of professional experience, she has run volunteer training programs for domestic violence centers in Santa Ana, CA, and volunteer research and training design for the CA Dept. of Corrections. Melissa has presented at international conferences such as ATD; national conferences such as SHRM (Society for Human Resource Management) and COE; and has been a returning guest panelist for the US Office of Personnel Management (OPM) as an expert in the future of leadership in the United States.

She has a BA in English Literature, a dual master's in education, and a PhD in Workforce Education from Penn State University. She identifies as Autistic and prefers identity first language in her neurodiverse representation. She spends her spare time with her children, her spouse, and her four cats.

Advance Organizer

By William J. Rothwell

Complete the following Organizer before you read the book. Use it to help you assess what you most want to know about social change interventions using a bottom up approach (sometimes called *Transorganization Development*).

The Organizer

Directions

Read each item in the Organizer below. Spend about 10 minutes reflecting on your needs by completing the Organizer. Be honest! Think of how your organization engages with the world outside its boundaries. Then indicate whether you would like to develop yourself professionally to engineer social change and facilitate your organization's efforts to bring about social impact. For each item in the center column, indicate with a *Y* (for Yes), *N/A* (for Not Applicable), or *N* (for No) in the left column whether you would like to develop yourself on that issue or topic. When you finish, score, and interpret the results using the instructions appearing at the end of the Organizer. Then be prepared to share your responses with others you know to help you think about what you most want to learn about externally focused social change interventions. To learn more about one item below, refer to the number in the right column to find the chapter in which the subject is discussed.

The Questions

Circle your Answer below:	I would like to develop myself to:	Chapter in the book response in which the topic is for each covered: item below:
1. **Y** N/A N	Conceptualize a model to guide my organization's efforts to improve the world outside the boundaries of my organization	**1**
2. **Y** N/A N	Reflect on how to manage the ethics of social change and social impact	**2**
3. **Y** N/A N	Assess my organization's social change profile	**3**
4. **Y** N/A N	Be able to examine the social context of my employing organization	**4**
5. **Y** N/A N	Engage employees as agents/ catalysts of social change	**5**
6. **Y** N/A N	Build an impetus for social change	**6**
7. **Y** N/A N	Market the organization as a social change agent/catalyst	**7**
8. **Y** N/A N	Facilitate the development of an organizational strategic plan focused on facilitating social change outside the organization's boundaries	**8**
9. **Y** N/A N	Devise implementation strategies for a social change plan	**9**
10. **Y** N/A N	Manage opposition to the organization's efforts on social change inside and outside the organization	**10**
11. **Y** N/A N	Showcase your organization's talent beyond the organization's borders	**11**
12. **Y** N/A N	Communicate about your organization's social change efforts	**12**
_____ **Total**		

Scoring and Interpreting the Organizer

Give yourself *1 point for each* Y and a *0 for each N or N/A* listed above. Total the points from the Y column and place the sum in the line opposite to the word **TOTAL** above. Then interpret your score:

Score	
12–11 points =	Congratulations! This book is just what you need. Read the chapters you marked Y.
10–9 points =	You have great skills in bringing about social change already, but you also have areas where you could develop professionally. Read those chapters marked Y.
8–5 points =	You have skills in bringing about social change, but you could still benefit from building skills in selected areas.
4–0 points =	You believe you need little development in planning, implementing, and evaluating social change efforts carried out by your organization.

Chapter 1

The Background: Facilitating *Social* and *Organizational* Change

William J. Rothwell

Say the word *change* to sociologists or historians, and they will probably think you mean *social change* affecting everyone. Say the same word *change* to managers, and they may think you mean *change management* (CM) affecting their organizations. Say the same word to human resource professionals, and they may think you mean *organization development* affecting groups or teams. Others in the human resource field may associate the word with *positive change theory*, which is sometimes known as *appreciative inquiry*.

While varied groups may think of change differently, nearly everyone would agree with the ancient Greek philosopher Heraclitus that change is the only constant (Kahn, 1979). Events like the global pandemic, the U.S. financial crisis of 2008, and the terrorist-engineered collapse of the World Trade Center twin towers on 11 September 2001 have prompted immediate, tumultuous change. The 6 January 2020 insurrection in the United States, racial unrest in the wake of videotaped police shootings, social unrest stemming from mask and vaccine mandates and government lockdowns, religious scandals involving priests in the Roman Catholic Church, sporting scandals involving child abuse, and celebrity scandals involving shootings or sexual harassment share a common thread: they all prompt change or calls for change. Some scandals can be verified, and others—such as conspiracy theories like those that spawned the QAnon movement—are fake but still influence what people think.

DOI: 10.4324/9781003439714-1

Not all change is welcome. *Black swan events*, defined as seemingly inconsequential events that then spiral out of control to grow into a complex global phenomenon, have become more common. They can spur massive, global social changes overnight (Taleb, 2007). Black swan events stand as counterpoints to *gray rhino events*, such as demographic change, which are understood to mean predictable changes that can be addressed but that people seem to ignore deliberately (Wucker, 2016).

Few can dispute that the pandemic of 2020–2021 has shaped the future, creating a basis for profound future social change. Studies of past pandemics in history, according to Yale researcher Nicholas Christakis in his book *Apollo's Arrow: The Profound and Enduring Impact of Coronavirus on the Way We Live* (2021), demonstrate that pandemics exert an impact on the future. Christakis believes that the social impact of the virus falls into three phases: (1) what happens during the pandemic, (2) what happens in the immediate aftermath of the pandemic, and (3) what happens long after the pandemic. To Christakis, fewer people will chase more job openings. The result could be a "Roaring 20s" like environment in which people party in celebration after the virus is contained while business opportunities explode in growth. However, the impact of the virus is already being felt as workers demand more flexibility in how and where they work (the work-from-home movement), reconsider whether they wish to work in relatively low-wage jobs with abusive managers (like public school teachers and nurses in the United States), and rethink whether loyalty to any employer is deserved when many employers did not demonstrate loyalty or sensitivity to employees during the pandemic (the Great Resignation).

What is the relationship between social and organizational change? What is social change? What is CM? What is organization development, and what is appreciative inquiry? How are they similar, and how are they different? This chapter explores those similarities and differences. It also explains why you should care about change and about ways the word can be understood.

What Is the Relationship Between *Social* and *Organizational* Change?

Social change is the broader framework (macro or external change) against which change happens inside organizations (micro or internal change). Much has been written about social change (Crutchfield, 2018; Daly & Little, 2010; Midwest Academy Manual for Activists, 2010; Nichols, 2006; Rayner

& Bonnici, 2021; Simon, 2017; Stroh, 2015). Think of it like this: society is like the frame of a picture, and the organization is like the picture itself. What happens to the picture frame influences what happens in the picture. However, the organization only rarely influences the picture frame unless the leaders and people of the organization take proactive steps to do so. While *corporate social responsibility* (CSR) is the label associated with efforts by organizations to upgrade rather than degrade social conditions outside organizational boundaries, mounting evidence exists that organizations like businesses should take a more active role in promoting social change than is typical of CSR (Frynas, 2009). Young people believe that businesses and other social institutions should take a more aggressive role in advocating for social change that affects humanity—such as climate change, social justice, gender equality, and similar issues.

What Is *Social* Change?

Social change was the preoccupation of sociologists of the nineteenth century. They longed for one grand, unified theory that would adequately explain why human civilizations rise, fall, and change. They proposed many theories of social change. Many still have relevance and shape the thinking of decision-makers and policymakers today. Other theories about social change have fallen from favor.

But what is meant by the term *social change*? What are examples of social change? What theories can describe it? How can those theories of social change be used today to engineer social change when needed? This section focuses on answering these questions.

Defining Social Change

Social change is about changing the world. Broadly understood, social change refers to efforts to change assumptions about, and behaviors associated with, what people think is good and bad, right and wrong, and desirable or undesirable. It can generally be understood as changing *values*, meaning beliefs about what is important and how people should act. Social change is really a story about how cultures change (Denison et al., 2012; Freeth, 2018; Johnson, Whittington, & Scholes, 2011; Schein, 2016; Shapiro, 2019; White, 2020). It is about changing the world outside of, but including, the nations, communities, organizations, groups, and individuals composing that world. Kingsley Davis associated social change with only such alterations that affect organizations and the structure and functions of society (Davis & Moore, n.d.). Nisbet (1966) regarded social change as a succession of differences in time within a persisting identity. To Macionis (2010), social change means how culture and social institutions transform.

What Are Social Movements?

Social movements are organized efforts of groups of people to bring about deliberate social change in the values, norms, institutions, culture, relationships, and traditions of society. They also generate new identities or individuals and the groups or organizations to which they hold allegiance. Often, social movements arise from groups of people who feel aggrieved, and they seek to address sources of imbalance. Some social movements arise from those who wish to formulate and pursue the implementation of a compelling dream that represents a better future. Some social movements do both: they tap into grievances but also appeal to a dream of a better future. The civil rights movement in the United States is a good example of a movement that did both, appeal to grievances and a dream of a better future, and Martin Luther King's most famous speech was "I have a dream."

Reflecting on Examples of Social Change Efforts or Movements

Any movement to bring about change in the world, whether it is an organized social movement or merely a small group of interested individuals, is an example of a social change movement.

According to Social Movements (n.d.), an incomplete list of social movements intended to bring about social change includes:

■ Anti-fascism (ANTIFA)
■ Black lives matter
■ Black power movement
■ Chicano movement
■ Children's rights movement
■ Civil rights movement
■ Climate movement
■ Earth First!
■ Free school movement
■ Free software movement
■ Lesbian, gay, bisexual, and transgender (LGBT) social movements

- Human rights movement
- Indigenous peoples movement
- Mad pride (psychiatric social movement)
- March for our lives movement
- Men's rights movement
- Me too movement
- Mothers against drunk driving
- Occupy wall street
- Pro-choice movement
- Pro-life movement
- QAnon
- Right to life
- Time to change
- Women's liberation movement
- Women's suffrage

Most social change efforts are centered on making changes on political issues, economic issues, technology issues, health and safety issues, geographical issues, and more.

Categories of Social Change

Cultural anthropologist Aberle (1966) placed all social change movements into four broad categories. They are as follows:

- Alternative
- Redemptive
- Reformative, and
- Revolutionary

According to Social Movements (n.d.), *alternative social movements* are at the individual level and advocate for minor change; *redemptive social movements* are at the individual level and advocate for radical changes. *Reformative social movements* occur at a broader group or societal level and advocate for minor changes; *revolutionary social movements* occur at a broader group or societal level and advocate for radical changes. Other ways to categorize social movements include the *scope* (reform or radical), *type of change* (innovative or conservative), *targets* (group-focused or individual-focused), *methods* (violent or non-violent), and *range* (local or global).

Aberle organized social movements based on how they answered two key questions: (1) *who wants the change?* and (2) *how much change is advocated?* However, other questions could also be the focus of attention in social change. Such questions would center on what changes to make, when to make the changes, how to make the changes, and how to evaluate results.

Who Leads Social Change?

Sometimes, society's leaders spearhead social change; sometimes, society's leaders oppose the social change sweeping other groups. C. Wright Mills, in his 1956 book *The Power Elite*, contended that average citizens are relatively powerless at the hands of corporate, government, and other institutional leaders who exert enormous influence over social issues. Change often will not occur if prominent citizens and leaders in positions of power do not support it. Leaders include anyone who exercises influence in society. That includes elected leaders, employers, journalists, and many others. According to the Social Change Model of Leadership Development, created in 1993 by the Higher Education Research Institute of UCLA, leaders must begin to work on social change by building their self-awareness and performing in-depth soul-searching before they can change other people. Only then can they live as role models to demonstrate to followers how to live in ways aligned with the social changes they seek.

Social media have broadened the range of people who can exert leadership on social opinions and thus influence social change. The Arab Spring movement in the Middle East demonstrated that social media can mobilize the people and help them focus their efforts to bring about sweeping and dramatic change. Social media empowers people to create "flash mobs for change" that suddenly show up in various locations and protest for the social change that the loosely organized members of the "flash mobs" advocate.

What Causes Social Change?

Various authors and theorists have listed different causes of social change. A partial, but not exhaustive, list of these causes include:

- Technology/inventions
- Borrowing of ideas from other cultures (for example: the "lying flat" movement in China spreading to other nations in the "Great Resignation" sweeping Europe and the United States)

- Social institutions
- Population/demographics
- Environment
- Tension or conflict between one group and other groups (race/gender/ religion)
- Biological factors
- Change in the physical environment—such as climate change and its impact on people
- New ideas in one sphere (such as science) lead to new ideas in other spheres (such as management and religion)
- Economic factors spur changes that lead to social change (such as the cost of child care affecting family decisions about how many children to have)
- Changes in the political environment (who holds power?) can lead to changes in social norms and views
- Psychological factors (how do people feel about themselves and others?)
- Social movements (what are the *cause célèbre* of the times?)
- Legal changes
- Competitive changes
- Natural and manmade disasters

How Long Does Social Change Take?

Social change can take generations (Bodnar, 1999). Social change rarely occurs overnight. The more radical the change is from the status quo, and the more people involved in the social change, the longer it will take. Global change takes longer than national, regional, organizational, local, small group, or individual change.

Is Social Change Accelerating in the World?

According to Hartmut Rosa (2015), social change is accelerating. That creates the basis for the burnout and depression felt by many people today (Rosa, 2015). A survey of 1300 psychological therapists revealed an upsurge of depression during the isolation period caused by the recent pandemic (Parker-Pope, Caron, & Sancho, 2021). However, the impact of the pandemic on suicide rates is controversial, and experts do not agree on whether suicide rates are increasing globally. Making sense of suicide statistics around the world can be a complex endeavor (Appleby, 2021).

How Can Social Change Be Accelerated?

To accelerate social change, address the root causes that drive the change. If social change is caused by such factors as changing technology, changing economic conditions, changing population groups, and so forth, then efforts to build pressure leading to change can be increased by making careful examinations of the impact of these causes and working to intensify them. At the same time, care should also be taken to intensify efforts to weaken the forces resisting change.

Reviewing Theories of Social Change

Many theories have been proposed to describe social change. Among them:

- Deterioration theory
- Cycle theory
- Linear theory
- Deterministic theory
- Marxian theory
- Functional theory
- Evolutionary theory, and
- Chaos or complexity theory

They are briefly described below.

Deterioration Theory

This view suggests that the world is gradually getting worse. The idea, which authorities believe was first proposed by the ancient Greek Hesiod (West, 1966), is that the first age of mankind was the Golden Age. Everything has been in decline since then. The same basic notion is described in the *Bible*, where Adam and Eve fall from grace and the world steadily degenerates. The idea that the world was in a constant state of decline shaped the thinking of Renaissance writers like Shakespeare and others (Levin, 1961).

How does this theory guide social change? While many would say that the theory is outdated because it directly contradicts the assumption that progress is always positive, it drives some efforts to bring about nostalgic change by promising to restore better times. Consider the implications of the simple phrase, "Make America Great Again." Does it not imply a return to a golden age that some would say never existed? Yet a phrase like that has enormous power to motivate political groups and is a rallying cry for those who feel aggrieved.

Cycle Theory

This view of social change suggests that the world proceeds through cycles. This idea, proposed in Hindu sacred scriptures when they describe *yugas* and advocated by such diverse theorists as Spengler (1918 & 1922) and Stuart Chapin (1928), suggests that the world proceeds through cycles of change.

Cycle theory applies to more than social change. Shakespeare wrote about this idea, noting the seven stages of man. Historian Arnold Toynbee, in his famous *A Study of History* (1934–1961) that examined the rise and fall of 26 civilizations, concluded that civilizations "rose by responding successfully to challenges under the leadership of creative minorities composed of elite leaders" (Toynbee, 2014). Authors Erikson (1963) and Sheehy (2006) have more recently written about individual life transitions—essentially predictable stages of individual life by age category. They thought all individuals progress through the same basic stages of life and must overcome specific challenges that arise from the individual's lifecycle stage. A similar idea was formulated by Havighurst (1972), who wrote about learning challenges encountered by individuals at different stages in the lifecycle. Appeals to helping individuals overcome those lifecycle stages would motivate individuals to learn. Tuckman (1965) proposed a four-stage lifecycle for all small groups or teams, and Nolan (1979) proposed a six-stage model to describe the lifecycle of information technology in organizations—from less to more sophistication. The stages (or cycles) indicate what should be the focus of management at each stage.

How does this theory guide social change? It suggests that individuals and civilizations progress through predictable lifecycle stages. Social change should be aligned with the predictable needs in each stage or cycle of an individual, team, work group, organization, industry, nation, or *zeitgeist* of humanity.

Linear Theory

According to the linear theory of social change, popularized by the work of Comte (1968–1970) and Spencer (1851), humankind is developing in a linear fashion. Progress is always positive, meaning the future is always better than the past. The assumption that progress is always positive is directly opposed to the deterioration theory, which suggests that each succeeding stage of humankind is worse than the one immediately preceding it.

How does this theory guide social change? It is simple. Plans made today can be carried out with confidence since the future will be like the past. Long-range planning is based on this assumption. While modern business leaders tend to hedge their bets by making more than one assumption about the future—and that leads to the use of scenario planning—linear theory can still be found represented in many strategic plans. Once an initial strengths, weaknesses, opportunities, and threats (SWOT) analysis is conducted, leaders choose *one* grand strategy. Unfortunately, global conditions are changing so quickly that there is a distinct tendency in modern organizations to reduce the duration (time horizon) of a strategic plan to one year or less.

Deterministic Theory

Deterministic theory, popular among modern sociologists, posits that social change occurs based primarily on economic factors. Authors Sumner (1883) and Keller (1975) regarded social change as a result of economic relationships dominating social relationships. Other thinkers emphasize religious affiliation's role in history, and they regard social change as a product of religious influence (Frazer, 1890; Sorel, 1921).

How does this theory guide social change? Generally suggesting a pessimistic view of the human condition, it posits that individuals are shaped by socioeconomic factors surrounding their birth, upbringing, education, and so forth. Breaking out of the conditions imposed by birth can be a daunting challenge, though not impossible. Determinists believe that individuals can change their social conditions through sheer hard work and determination. The same view would apply to efforts to formulate and implement social change.

Marxian Theory

Marxist theory, based on the writings of Karl Marx, regards social change in history as a function of class conflict as different strata of society jockey for power and influence. In more recent times, Marxist theory has gradually given way to so-called *critical research theory and practice.*

How does this theory guide social change? While many versions of critical research or critical theory exist, one way to conceptualize it is as follows (Rothwell & Sullivan, 2005):

- Describe the *ideology* (How do people believe the society, organization, or group should function?)
- Identify situations, events, or conditions that conflict with the ideology (What is happening?)
- Identify individuals or groups desiring progressive change (Who wants to challenge the ideology and/or actual situations to create an impetus for progressive change?)
- Confront proponents of the ideology with situations, events, or conditions that dramatize that the ideology is not always followed consistently
- Use conflict to empower the creation of a new ideology or action steps to correct the inconsistency
- Help the group establish a timetable for change
- Implement the change
- Ask the group members to monitor the change, identifying opportunities for continuous improvement as necessary

Functional Theory

Society for functionalists is akin to the human body. Each component of society is like a body part. Body parts and organs cannot exist in isolation; rather, they function together systematically. Originally, functional theory was proposed by the influential sociologist Emile Durkheim (Hinkle, 1976). Social change can be regarded as a response to tensions within society and is meant to alleviate those tensions.

How does this theory guide social change? It would focus on the role of institutions in preserving the status quo or bringing about social change. How does each institution within society regard specific social issues? Trying to change the positions of those institutions would be a practical application of functional theory in engineering social change. For instance, target the courts, the legislatures, educational institutions, and the executive leaders in government; identify and target the leading employers; target the leading influential opinion leaders of society; and sway them to the side of a social change. All those steps would be a functionalist view of how to engineer social change.

Evolutionary Theory

Evolutionary theory moves beyond functional theory and cyclical theory to propose that social change occurs gradually and incrementally. Complexity emerges from simple beginnings. Influenced by Charles Darwin, evolutionists regard society as changing over time as biological organisms do. The strong dominate the weak, and the strong gradually render the weak extinct. So, too, changes happen in social settings, according to social Darwinists. An important and implicit assumption of all evolutionary theories of social change is that progress always leads to the betterment of the human condition, an idea rejected by advocates of deterioration theory.

How does this theory guide social change? How does evolutionary theory guide social change? One approach to using evolutionary theory is to identify what individuals or groups/institutions have greatest power in the social setting. Then, try to change the stance of those leading individuals and groups to align with desired social change. Doing that will render the efforts of common citizens largely ineffectual if they advocate against the change.

Chaos or Complexity Theory

In recent years, the physical sciences have exerted much influence on thinking in the social sciences. *Chaos theory*, which posits that what appears to be random events in the universe actually have a larger pattern that is not immediately detectable to humans, has been reinterpreted in the social sciences as *complexity theory* or what some call *complex adaptive systems* (Turner, Baker & Morris, 2018).

It is difficult to reduce complexity theory to a set of easy steps to follow when focusing on social change. However, patterns emerge from interactions, and those interactions that appear to be randomized actually form a pattern. By this logic, managing change is akin to working with patterns.

For leaders, working with complexity theory means being flexible and adapting to rapidly changing events and dynamic interactions. Being a manager is like being the leader of a jazz ensemble, and managing change is like organizing the patterns of interactions that occur in jazz.

How does this theory guide social change? One way is to encourage flexibility and permit individuals and groups seeking social change to self-organize as they wish. Social media provide one way to organize quickly and martial resources and people to action in flexible ways. Do not assume leaders must guide change; rather, create ways for groups to self-organize on social media and use other methods (such as Communities of Practice) to implement social change.

The Role of Emotion in Social Change

When managers or decision-makers think of change, they often begin with a rational approach. They start with logic. Their emphasis is on finding solid reasoning by which to justify change. Described another way, it means "thinking with the head."

But many social change movements begin with emotion, which can also be regarded as "feeling with the heart." While reasoning is good—and nobody is saying it is not—appeals to the head alone will rarely work. It is also necessary to appeal to the heart—that is, appeal to emotions and sometimes to emotions regarding self-interest. Storytelling can be powerful, providing heartbreaking examples of how current events hurt individuals or groups.

What emotions drive change? Eckman (1999) identified six major emotions that drive humans. They are as follows:

- Happiness
- Sadness
- Fear
- Disgust
- Anger
- Surprise

Ekman found these six major emotions could be used individually or collectively to inspire change. Some researchers argue fear or anger is the most powerful of all emotions; others argue that love is really the most powerful. A research study based on 70 million tweets on Chinese social media giant Weibo found that anger is the most powerful emotion (English, 2013). Dingfelder (2007), reporting on brain imaging research conducted by Arthur Aron, found that love is the most powerful emotion. Note that political leaders often appeal to fear or anger; religious leaders often appeal to love.

While it may not be clear what emotion is the most powerful—anger, fear, or love—appeals to these emotions can have a major impact when motivating people to change.

Models Guiding Social Change Efforts

Many books and articles have been written about how to facilitate, design, or engineer social change. Many people, it would seem, are preoccupied with what it takes to change the world. Among them are (1) the Social Change Model of Leadership Development, (2) Roger's diffusion theory, and (3) other social change models. There are other models to guide social change. It is worthwhile to remember that these models are intended to drive change outside organizations in the broader community or in society and not so much inside organizations.

The Social Change Model of Leadership Development

The Social Change Model (SCM) has broad appeal to social groups looking for ways to bring structure to their activism. The approach is based on seven Cs. They are (Astin & Astin, 1996):

- *Consciousness of self*: Build awareness of self and others
- *Congruence*: Be authentic and genuine with others to inspire trust. Make sure actions follow the values espoused by the group or social movement
- *Commitment*: Be engaged. Demonstrate what motivation looks like
- *Collaboration*: Be willing to work with others (Steil, 2017). Cooperate. Place group efforts over individual pride or need for recognition
- *Common purpose*: Work with a willingness to participate with others
- *Controversy with civility*: Harness the power of creative conflict without allowing it to turn people against each other
- *Citizenship*: Be willing to work to benefit the whole group or social movement and not just for oneself or one's own team

These seven Cs can help shape and organize social movements of any kind. There is a possible eighth C that can also provide guidance for all others. That is *change*. It can shape and give meaning to all other Cs.

Rogers' Diffusion Theory

Diffusion is about how change—such as new technology or even new ideas—spreads throughout society. E. M. Rogers' diffusion theory is one view of how new ideas or technology create the basis for social change.

To Rogers, the introduction of novelty in social settings leads to the gradual adoption of the change by different groups. They are as follows:

- *Innovators*: Willing to take risks for the chance to get huge returns, innovators are eager to try out new ideas and new technology. They hope to reap the rewards and outsmart competitors.
- *Early adopters*: Not as open to risk as innovators, early adopters see the potential for gains and will try out new approaches, new ideas, and new technology based on the experience they see that innovators gained from their efforts.
- *Early majority*: Members of this group watch the experience of early adopters, who have higher social status as opinion leaders. However, members of the early majority category will try out new ideas based on what they believe the payoffs will be.
- *Late majority*: Members of this group are less influential than the members of the previous groups. However, they have watched the gains they saw the previous groups secure by using the new approach or technology. They accept the innovation after many others have tried it out and have proven that it works.
- *Laggards*: Last to accept new ideas or approaches, laggards tend to be skeptics of change and want to see overwhelming evidence that a new idea or technology will secure the payoffs promised. They are often skeptics who regard any change with suspicion.

Rogers' theory has generally been supported by research. However, it is not always easy to apply. To use it, change agents must classify people into the five groups and then use different strategies with members of each group to gain support for change. Each group will require different approaches to facilitate the diffusion of innovation.

Other Social Change Models

Other models to guide social change or social design have been proposed. Some are practical—such as this one:

- Decide what angers you
- Learn more about the issue
- Team with others who share similar reasons to be angry
- Guide the group to learn even more about the issue

- Develop a plan for social change by working with others
- Ask for help and resources from those with selfish reasons to help you
- Spread the word, communicating far and wide, about the need for social change
- Establish social networks with decision-makers to stay in touch as action to bring about change is planned and carried out
- Celebrate small wins as they occur
- Sustain the change energy over time

While sustaining the social change effort over time is difficult, activists should take continuous steps to learn, listen, read, write, volunteer, donate, talk, empathize, and vote to support the change they advocate. They should work to energize the social change effort by:

- Attracting philanthropy to provide resources to support social change
- Tapping community and economic development efforts to support social change
- Building a group of people to vote and work on political efforts to support social change
- Building informal associations, online and onsite, to support social change
- Placing advertisements in mass media and in personal interactions to build awareness about the social movement espoused
- Choosing leaders who set examples through their words and deeds to demonstrate what social change looks like
- Supporting and conducting community-based research about the social change issue
- Supporting advocacy efforts about social change in all forms
- Organizing supporters at the grassroots from the community, region, nation, and globe
- Encouraging charitable donations to support social change
- Encouraging volunteers to donate their time and effort to the social change movement
- Planning and carrying out highly visible social protests to raise public and media awareness of the social change issue(s)
- Building community groups to support social change
- Encouraging businesses founded to address problems associated with social change (social entrepreneurship)
- Measuring the results of the efforts to address social change and communicating that information to donors and other relevant groups

What Strategies Can Be Used to Formulate and Implement Successful Social Change Efforts?

Follow the strategies for social change in Ebrahim's (2019) book on measuring social change, which include:

- *Focus on a niche*: Meet one social need at a time to bring about social change. Example: provide food service for the homeless. The homeless have many needs. Food is but one, and providing it meets a niche need.
- *Focus on an integrated strategy*: Coordinate a sequence of related services to meet different needs at the same time. For example, provide food service while also providing clothes for the homeless. The two may be related but are different needs. Food is the most basic requirement. Dress comes in second but is still important. Two groups or charities could coordinate their efforts to offer both services, but the two charities are actually working in concert.
- *Focus on an emergent strategy*: Cause and effect relationships may be complex in social change situations where there is a need to offer help when conditions are complicated. Roll out different services over time to meet present and growing/emergent needs. Develop different measures of impact, depending on the service. For example, serving people experiencing homelessness is a worthy goal. However, many homeless face mental health challenges that may complicate efforts to get them food, clothing, and shelter. So, an emergent strategy would be to determine whether mental health services or food and clothing are a priority service and then act.
- *Focus on an ecosystem strategy*: In this example of social change strategy, conditions are complex. Needs are many. Multiple organizations must collaborate to meet a complex set of requirements. An example is meeting all the needs of the homeless. One organization may provide food; one organization may provide clothing; one organization may provide housing; one organization may provide mental health counseling; one organization may provide medical services; and so forth. Taken together, this group of different but related social support groups achieve synergy because their combined efforts are greater than the sum of their individual parts. It is thus called an ecosystem strategy because it involves managing the entire ecosystem surrounding the homeless.

What Is *Organizational* Change?

Organizational change focuses on the inner workings of organizations. Some change is imposed from outside organizations. Other changes inside organizations result from leadership change, reorganizations, new technology, new policies, and much more. Change inside organizations is often handled through CM, organization development, or appreciative inquiry. This part of the chapter will address those topics.

What Is CM?

What is meant by the term *change management*? Why is CM usually regarded as internally focused to organizations? What models can guide it? How can those models of CM be applied? This section focuses on answering these questions.

Note that social change, as described in the previous section of this chapter, focuses on bringing about change *outside* organizations. However, CM, organization development, and appreciative inquiry tend to focus on bringing about change *inside* organizations. They can overlap. However, it is important at the outset of this section to emphasize this distinction between change inside (internal) and outside (external) organizations.

What Is Meant by CM?

CM has four possible meanings. CM has been the focus of much attention (Fusch et al., 2020).

First, the term can refer to marketing efforts by large consulting companies. For those organizations trying to persuade managers to hire their firms to offer consulting on how to carry out change effectively, the term is a general label for any change effort that the client organization may need help with.

Second, the term can refer to any change. Humans can generally be changed through *coercion* (force them to behave a certain way on pain of punishment), *persuasion* (offer them incentives to behave in a certain way), *leadership change* (provide new supervisors), *policy or legal change* (change what the organization or the nation requires and then punish those who do not comply), *dialectic change* (use conflict to drive change and discover truth), and *normative re-educative change* (show people a better way by "living it" and changing the unspoken norms that guide group behavior).

Third, the term can refer to efforts to implement one consistent change model or approach to govern all organization projects. In this sense, project management and CM are synonymous. First, the organization considers existing change models. Then, the organization's leaders select one. Third, everyone in the organization is trained on how to use the model. Then, all change projects are managed consistently in compliance with the change model.

Fourth, the term can apply to adopting a unified, prescriptive model of what the organization should look like. Many such models exist. For instance, managers may choose the Malcolm Baldrige National Quality Award criteria (Kendall & Bodinson, 2016). Then, they manage the organization to bring it into alignment with that model, trusting that such a change effort will lead to creating a corporate culture that fosters quality. Similar criteria exist for other desirable corporate cultures—such as high performance (Aldrich, 2020; Bingham & Dusin, 2018; Richman & Kirlin, 2015), high involvement (Lawler, 1986), high retention (Pulver, 2021), high engagement (Bowles & Cooper, 2012; Miller, 2019), and even outstanding change management (Association of Change Management Professionals, 2014).

In the fourth approach, leaders follow a step-by-step model. They:

- *Step 1*: Select a desired corporate culture (*What should be?*).
- *Step 2*: Compare the existing culture to the desired culture (*What is?*).
- *Step 3*: Identify the measurable gaps between Steps 1 and 2.
- *Step 4*: Brainstorm strategies to close the gaps.
- *Step 5*: Devise action plans to close the gaps.
- *Step 6*: Implement the action plans while monitoring results.
- *Step 7*: Evaluate the change effort during implementation, making course corrections as needed.

It is best if the desired corporate culture has been researched such that organizations aligned with the characteristics of that desired culture are effective and represent proven quality, productivity, engagement, involvement, retention, or whatever the targeted culture is meant to provide.

Why Is CM Usually Regarded as Internally Focused?

While there is nothing to prohibit organizational leaders from applying popular CM approaches to change the nation, society, or community outside their firms, leaders generally focus on CM internally. About 70 percent of organizational change efforts fail to achieve the measurable goals that management set for them. Managers focus on what they are rewarded for doing. Usually, they are not rewarded for achieving measurable changes in society; rather, they are rewarded for achieving business results for one organization. That is why most of the time, CM models and theories are internally focused on meeting organizational production or performance targets. For most managers, making a profit trumps changing the world.

What Models Guide CM?

Many models have been applied to CM (Sharma, 2019). It would require too much space to review them all here. However, important models that are worth knowing about include Kotter's model and Prosci's ADKAR model. Both can be the basis for that third definition of CM—that is, a consistently developed model for all organizational change efforts.

The steps in Kotter's (2012) model are well-known and self-explanatory:

- Create a sense of urgency
- Build a guiding coalition
- Form a strategy vision and initiatives
- Enlist a volunteer army
- Enable action by removing barriers
- Generate short-term wins
- Sustain acceleration
- Institute change

The steps in the Prosci ADKAR model may require training. However, they are generally (Hiatt, 2006):

- **A**wareness
- **D**esire
- **K**nowledge
- **A**bility *and*
- **R**einforcement

Each model implies a project planning approach to change. The standards associated with good XM efforts are heavily influenced by best practices in project planning (Association of Change Management Professionals, 2014).

How Can Models of CM Be Applied?

CM models guide project plans to implement change. An important advantage of using CM is that it reduces the unpleasant anxiety that managers and workers feel when they are unsure of where change efforts are heading. By using CM models on which everyone has been trained, uncertainty is reduced but not eliminated.

What Is Organization Development (OD) and Appreciative Inquiry (AI)?

What is meant by the term organization development (OD)? appreciative inquiry (AI)? What theories can describe them? This section focuses on answering these questions.

What Is Meant by Organization Development (OD)?

The web is full of definitions for Organization Development. However, OD differs from CM. In CM, the change helpers (consultants or managers) typically play project managers. They set change targets; they establish milestones and deadlines; they assign responsibilities; and they create and monitor change project budgets. However, OD is not like that. Generally, OD develops project plans based on what managers and workers agree are organizational problems to be solved. It requires active participation and genuine decision-making involvement from all stakeholders affected by a change. In OD, solutions, action plans, and evaluation strategies are developed by the managers and workers and not by outside experts or by managers alone. OD professionals play the role of facilitators, asking questions and helping the group members agree on what to do, how to do it, and how to measure it.

Mainstream OD is often divided between diagnostic OD and dialogic OD (Bushe & Marshak, 2015). In *diagnostic OD*, OD practitioners work with stakeholders to diagnose the organization's problems; in *dialogic OD*, change initiatives emerge from collaboration in continuing dialogues. Those dialogues can occur in retreats, meetings, hallway conversations, or anywhere where stakeholders congregate. Change occurs because of creating new narratives and new storylines about the organization.

What Is Meant by Appreciative Inquiry (AI)?

Appreciative Inquiry (AI) is a new approach in OD. Instead of starting with perceived problems and perceived solutions, which is typical of mainstream OD, AI begins by identifying the organization's strengths. Then, managers and workers are guided through a facilitated process by which they dream of a future in which they leverage their present strengths to maximum advantage. This approach is typically strengths-based (Rath & Conchie, 2009).

What Theories Guide OD and AI?

Traditional OD is guided by Kurt Lewin's Action Research Model. One way to describe it is that the OD practitioner should (Rothwell et al., 2015):

- Help the client organization's members pinpoint the problem to be solved.
- Collect information about organizational problems, feeding them back to stakeholders to secure broad agreement on problems and the priorities of what problems to solve first.
- Collect information about solutions to the problems, feeding back that information to agree on solutions and the priorities of what solutions should be implemented first.
- Collect information about action plans to implement the priority solutions, getting involvement from managers and workers.
- Implement the change effort, facilitating efforts to monitor the execution of the action plans.
- Evaluate the change effort on a continuing basis and facilitate decisions by the stakeholders to change the change goals if conditions change.

Note that this approach differs from traditional CM or from expert-driven approaches to change. It is also different from social change theories.

Appreciative Inquiry is a new approach to OD. However, it bears many similarities to the traditional OD approach because managers and workers are involved at every stage and make key decisions. AI consultants, like their traditional OD counterparts, are facilitators rather than experts imposing unwelcome ideas on unwilling clients. In AI, OD consultants help stakeholders of the organization (Cooperrider, Whitney & Stavros, 2008):

- Define what are the key strengths of the organization
- Discover stories that demonstrate those strengths
- Dream of a better future where the strengths are maximized and leveraged
- Design action plans to realize the dream
- Deliver results by implementing the action plans

How Are Social Change, CM, OD, and AI Related?

Social change, CM, OD, and AI are related because they all seek change.

Social change seeks change in society; CM, OD, and AI are usually focused on change in organizations. However, nothing prohibits using social change models in organizations or using CM, OD, or AI models directed toward changing society.

How Are Social Change, CM, OD, and AI Different?

Social change efforts are usually undertaken to rectify grievances or perceived imbalances. As one example, the Black Lives Matter movement seeks to address excessive, unfair police violence and racism. That effort assumes a problem exists and seeks to rectify it. However, most organizational change efforts are not directed to address grievances; rather, they are carried out to increase profits, maximize productivity, and help the organization achieve measurable targets.

Why Should You Care About Social Change, CM, OD and AI?

So what? Who cares about social change, CM, OD, and AI?

Generally, anyone who wants to improve the world, their organizations, and their jobs or lives should care about social change, CM, OD, and AI. These change approaches are the means to the end of improvements in social or organizational conditions. Knowledge of social change and other ways to bring about change, like CM, OD, and AI, can increase the chance that change efforts will succeed.

Chapter Summary

This chapter focused on defining such terms as social change, CM, organization development, and appreciative inquiry. Social change is the broader framework (macro or external) against which change happens inside organizations (micro or internal). Think of it like this: the social condition is like the frame of a picture, and the organization is like the picture. What happens in the frame can, and does, influence what happens inside the picture. However, the organization only rarely influences the picture frame unless the leaders and people of the organization take proactive steps to do so, moving beyond traditional views of CSR to take a more activist stance in social change. The chapter concluded with an explanation as to why you should care about these differences.

References

Aberle, D. (1966). *The peyote religion among the Navaho.* Aldine.

Aldrich, B. (2020). *Winning the talent shift: Three steps to unleashing the new high performance workplace.* Wiley.

Appleby, L. (2021). What has been the effect of covid-19 on suicide rates? *Thebmj.* https://www.bmj.com/content/372/bmj.n834

Association of Change Management Professionals (ACMP) (2014). *Standards of change management.* ACMP.

Astin, H., & Astin, A. (1996). *A social change model of leadership development guidebook version III.* The National Clearinghouse of Leadership Programs, University of California at Berkeley.

Bingham, S., & Dusin, B. (2018). *Creating the high performance workplace: It's not complicated to develop a culture of commitment.* Indie Books International.

Bodnar, J. (1999). How long does it take to change culture? Integration at the U.S. Naval Academy. *Armed Forces and Society.* https://doi.org/10.1177/00953 27X9902500206

Bowles, D., & Cooper, C. (2012). *The high engagement work culture: Balancing me and we.* Palgrave-Macmillan.

Bushe, G., & Marshak, R. (2015). *Dialogic organization development: The theory and practice of transformational change.* Berret-Koehler.

Chapin, F. (1928). *Cultural change.* The Century Company.

Christakis, N. (2021). *Apollo's arrow: The profound and enduring impact of coronavirus on the way we live.* Hachette.

Comte, A. (1968–1970). *Œuvres*. (Vol 11). Anthropos.

Cooperrider, D., Whitney, D., & Stavros, J. (2008). *Appreciative inquiry handbook: For leaders of change* (2nd ed.). Berrett-Koehler.

Crutchfield, L. (2018). *How change happens: Why some social movements succeed while others don't*. Wiley.

Daly, J., & Little, J. (Eds.). (2010). *Social network theory and educational change*. Harvard Education Press.

Davis, K., & Moore, W. E. (n.d). *Some principles of stratification [by] Kingsley Davis and Wilbert E. Moore*. Bobbs-Merrill.

Denison, D., Hooijberg, R., Lane, N., & Lief, C. (2012). *Leading culture change: Aligning culture and strategy*. Jossey-Bass.

Dingfelder, S. (2007). More than a feeling: New research suggests love may be a drive as primal as thirst or hunger. https://www.apa.org/monitor/feb07/morethan.html

Ebrahim, E. (2019). *Measuring social change: Performance and accountability in a complex world*. Stanford Business Books.

Eckman, P. (1999). Basic emotions. In T. Dalgleish & M. Power (Eds.), *Handbook of cognition and emotion* (pp. 45–60). Wiley.

English, N. (2013, September 24). Anger is the internet's most powerful emotion. USA Today. https://www.usatoday.com/story/news/nation/2013/09/24/anger-internet-most-powerful-emotion/2863869/

Erikson, E. (1963). *Childhood and society* (2nd ed.). W. W. Norton & Co.

Frazer, G. (1890). *The golden bough*. (Vol. 11). Macmillan Press.

Freeth, P. (2018). *Change magic: The evolutionary approach to organizational change* (3rd ed.). CGW publishing.

Frynas, J. (2009). *Beyond corporate social responsibility*. Cambridge University Press.

Fusch, G. E., Ness, L., Booker, J. M., & Fusch, P. I. (2020). People and process: Successful change management initiatives. *Journal of Social Change, 12*, 166–184.

Havighurst, R. (1972). *Developmental tasks and education*. McKay.

Hiatt, J. (2006). *ADKAR: A model for change in business, government, and our community*. Prosci Research.

Hinkle, R. (1976). Durkheim's evolutionary conception of social change. *The Sociological Quarterly, 17*, 336–346.

Johnson, G., Whittington, R., & Scholes, K. (2011). *Exploring strategy: Text and cases* (9th ed.). Pearson Education.

Kahn, C. (1979). *The art and thought of Heraclitus: Fragments with translation and commentary*. Cambridge University Press.

Keller, S. (1975). *Uprooting and social change: The role of refugees in development*. Manohar Book Service.

Kendall, K., & Bodinson, G. (2016). *Leading the Malcolm Baldrige way: How world-class leaders align their organizations to deliver exceptional results*. McGraw-Hill.

Kotter, J. (2012). *Leading change*. Harvard Business Review Press.

Lawler, E. (1986). *High-involvement management: Participative strategies for improving organizational performance*. Jossey-Bass.

Levin, H. (1961). *The myth of the golden age in the Renaissance.* Indiana University Press.

Macionis, J. J. (2010). *Social problems.* Prentice Hall.

Midwest Academy Manual for Activists (2010). *Organizing for social change* (4th ed.). The Forum Press.

Mill, C. (1956). *The power elite.* Oxford University Press.

Miller, M. (2019). *Win the heart: How to create a culture of full engagement.* Berret-Koehler.

Nichols, A. (2006). *Social entrepreneurship: New models of sustainable change.* Oxford University Press.

Nisbet, R (1966). *The sociological tradition.* Basic Books.

Nolan, R. (1979, March-April). Managing the crisis in data processing. *Harvard Business Review.* 115–126. https://cir.nii.ac.jp/crid/1571980073975396608.

Parker-Pope, Caron, C., & Sancho, M. (2021). *The New York Times.* https://www.nytimes.com/interactive/2021/12/16/well/mental-health-crisis-america-covid.html

Pulver, C. (2021). *I love it here: How great leaders create organizations their people never want to leave.* Page Two.

Rath, T., & Conchie, B. (2009). *Strengths based leadership: Great leaders, teams, and why people follow.* Gallup.

Rayner, C., & Bonnici, F. (2021). *The systems work of social change: How to harness connection, context, and power to cultivate deep and lasting change.* Oxford University Press.

Richman, R., & Kirlin, B. (2015). *The culture blueprint: A guide to building the high performance workplace.* Culture hackers.

Rogers, E. (2003). *Diffusion of innovations* (5th ed.). Simon and Shuster.

Rosa, H. (2015). *Social acceleration: A new theory of modernity.* Columbia University Press.

Rothwell, W., & Sullivan, R. (Eds.) (2005). Models for change. In W. Rothwell & R. Sullivan (Eds.), *Practicing organization development: A guide for consultants.* (pp. 39–80). 2nd ed. Pfeiffer.

Rothwell, W., Sullivan, R., Kim, T., Park, J., & Donahue, W. (2015). Change process and models. In W. Rothwell, J. Stavros, & R. Sullivan (Eds.), *Practicing organization development: Leading transformation and change.* (pp. 42–59). Pfeiffer.

Schein, E. (2016). *Organizational culture and leadership* (5th ed.). Jossey-Bass.

Shapiro, B. (2019). *Facts don't care about your feelings.* Creators publishing.

Sharma, K. (2019). 10 proven change management models in 2021. *Whatfix.* https://whatfix.com/blog/10-change-management-models/

Sheehy, G. (2006). *Passages: Predictable crises of adult life.* Random House.

Simon, M. (2017). *Real impact: The new economics of social change.* Bold Type Books.

Social Movements. (n.d.). https://courses.lumenlearning.com/boundless-sociology/chapter/social-movements/

Sorel, G. (1921). *De l'utilité du pragmatisme.* Paris. https://shorturl.at/fhU03

Spencer, H. (1851). *Social statics: Or, the conditions essential to human happiness specified, and the first of them developed.* John Chapman.

Spengler, O. (1918 & 1922). *The decline of the west.* Alfred A. Knopf.

Steil, G. (2017). *The collaboration response: Eight axioms that elicit collaborative action for a whole organization a whole community a whole society.* CreateSpace Independent Publishing Platform.

Stroh, D. (2015). *Systems thinking for social change: A practical guide to solving complex problems, avoiding unintended consequences, and achieving lasting results.* Chelsea Green Publishing.

Sumner, W. (1883). *What social classes owe to each other.* Harper & Brothers.

Taleb, N. (2007). *The black swan: The impact of the highly improbable.* Penguin.

Toynbee, A. (1934–1961). *A study of history.* Oxford University Press.

Toynbee, A. (2014). Encyclopædia Britannica online academic edition. *Encyclopædia Britannica.* Retrieved 6 April 2014.

Tuckman, B. (1965). Developmental sequence in small groups. *Psychological Bulletin, 63,* 384–399.

Turner, J., Baker, R., & Morris, M. (2018). Complex adaptive systems: Adapting and managing teams and team conflict. In Ana Alice Vilas Boas (Ed.), *Organizational conflict.* Intechopen. https://doi.org.10.5772/intechopen.69420

West, M. (1966). *Hesiod: Theogony.* Oxford University Press.

White, D. (2020). *Disrupting corporate culture: How cognitive science alters accepted beliefs about culture and culture change and its impact on leaders and change agents.* Productivity Press.

Wucker, M. (2016). *The gray rhino: How to recognize and act on the obvious dangers we ignore.* St. Martin's Press.

Chapter 2

Step 1: Managing the Ethics of Social Change

Kaitlin Farnan

Case Study: South Africa

During the 1980s in South Africa, debates and social movements grew in the country around the apartheid policies of the South African government. The laws within the country, as they stood, made it illegal to employ and mix races in factories. While the country was split on the issues with strong voices on both sides, foreign-based multi-national corporations within the country were in a tough spot. Per international law, when operating in a foreign country, a business must abide by the laws of the host country. Specifically, for U.S.-based companies, they had to decide how to handle that legal imperative to separate races in their operations in South Africa given the dynamics back home in the United States and when it was just two decades after the Civil Rights Movement of the 1960s. Many individuals in South Africa, in the United States, and around the world called for businesses to take a stand against this racial inequality. Businesses had to decide if they were going to abide by the laws in South Africa angering customers in several markets or take a stand and please customers but potentially anger the government and risk their business in a foreign market. The law was clear on what businesses had to do, but for many people, the law represents only part of the equation, with ethics shaping another major component. Many businesses were left having to consider their position, which often came down to questions of

    DOI: 10.4324/9781003439714-2

what is our role as a business within a country and what is our obligation to the people in the communities we serve.

Businesses have been answering variations on these questions for many millennia. Some even point back to the days of Ancient where the code of Hammurabi (circa 1750s BC) included aspects of what businesses needed to do in response to certain elements. While this code is most famous for its "eye for an eye" style justice, there were elements related to business that consider responsibilities in business to other individuals (Hammurabi, 2008). The code of Hammurabi was a legal code, and some consider the law as the bare minimum of what someone must do. It was not until the First Industrial Revolution and the start of the 19th century that the idea of businesses instead of trades, and concepts like unemployment were even a common thought. The First Industrial Revolution changed dynamics in the United States, United Kingdom, and parts of Europe as people who flocked to cities to work for factories became employees who could be hired or fired at any time. People at this time were considered a resource just like timber or cloth. Workplace safety was often a concern for the employee, not the employer. If workers were injured and could not do their jobs, they were replaced (Workman's Compensation did not come until later). If they were sick, then they worked or didn't earn a wage. Laborers started to work together to demand more rights and unions started to form.

The early 20th century movements of unionization in the United States brought about ideas that businesses had an obligation to workers to provide for some elements of safe working environments and weekends off, pivoting away from the idea that businesses gave you money for labor and nothing more. In 1913, a government more modern than that of Ancient Babylon started to turn to the law again in response to these social pushes. President Taft signed legislation that created the U.S. Department of Labor. This new role marked a unique shift as workers now had a seat in the U.S. cabinet and a major voice in government. Taft, though, was not a fan of this move even though he signed the legislation. His concern encompassed much of the thoughts on business at the time; he was concerned that it would reduce efficiency (MacLaury, 1998).

While President Roosevelt took steps to offer jobs and welfare in the wake of the Great Depression, much of that was not meant to last, but to just get the country through the Depression. After World War II, the idea of unemployment being a major government concern evolved with the return of millions of soldiers from war. While many thought they could simply return to jobs they left, many women did not want to leave the workforce as they took jobs while the men were away. This situation shifted societal thought away from the idea that it was just an individual's issue with finding employment. Over the next few decades union power grew and peacetime brought expansion to the United States and many countries around the world. Expectations shifted.

Moving forward a couple of decades, the debate was raging about the role of a business in society when, in September 1970, famed Nobel Prize winning economist Milton Friedman wrote a large article in the *New York Times* stating that the only ethical thing for a business to concern itself with is increasing profits for shareholders. In Friedman's argument, the rest was the concern of the government (Friedman, 1970). This article brought the debate to the forefront, bringing with it the idea of *corporate social responsibility* (CSR) to a larger focus in society. This focus shifted the conversation away from businesses just being focused on profit and efficiency to businesses having more social responsibility. Over the next 50 years, governments, businesses, communities, and individuals would take major positions on both sides of the argument.

Today, the debate still rages. Recent years have seen business taking part in politics with donations, sponsoring commercials on social movements and issues, and releasing statements on current events and politics. We have seen companies faced with new governmental policies when they take a stance on political issues in the United States. Some companies have been voicing support for, or against, social movements related to race, gender identity, sexual orientation, women's rights, and more. However, other companies have stayed silent on these issues. Among all this debate, some have applauded businesses for taking a stance on social issues; others have stated it is not the role of a business to be involved in social issues. That leaves businesses stuck between opposing arguments.

This book is written as an applied way for businesses to think through their role and potential actions that they want to take with regard to social change. The chapters in this book are written for those who are doing the work of bringing about social change initiatives to organizations around the world. It is meant to be a manual that can be used to walk you through step-by-step considerations, and actions with usable tools in each chapter to help you get started. The chapters that follow will cover the model introduced in the Preface of this book and embedded, step by step, in this book's Table of Contents.

The first place we will start with, though, is the root of many of these debates: ethics.

What Does the Research Say?

Ethics

Ethics is a subject not many like to discuss but is at the heart of most of the debate around the role and obligation of a business. Many of the arguments for or against a business getting involved with social change center on what people view as the obligations of a business to different stakeholders. Friedman's claim, which some now call the *Friedman Doctrine*, surrounded a view of ethics that business had an ethical obligation restricted to its shareholders. It is a limited view of ethical obligation to just one group—those with an ownership stake in a company. Those on the other end of the spectrum of the role of a business believe that businesses have an obligation to consider anyone who could be a stakeholder—that is, anyone who could be impacted by the actions or decisions of a business. That line of thought just extends to consider their viewpoints—not act to please. As anyone in business knows, it is not possible to please everyone. So, if business leaders start off knowing they will anger some they will not be surprised when they do. The question is: who will business actions anger, and what will that impact?

If we consider the case from the introduction, GM had to consider things like the impact of angering citizens opposed to apartheid, the impact of disobeying the law in a foreign country, and what it would mean to take a stand against a law in a foreign country to the employees and business. Friedman would argue they just had to do whatever would make a profit for the shareholders, and they had to obey the law. So, if it was more profitable to anger those opposed to apartheid but stay in South Africa obeying the law, then that is what they should do. However, if the result of potentially losing customers in many markets for staying and participating in apartheid reduced profits, then they should leave. Again, Friedman did not think businesses should "take a stand" so we will not explore that option. Those on the other end of the spectrum would argue to consider the potential impacts on anyone who could be impacted by those decisions which might include more exploration than just what is listed above.

So how do business leaders know which stakeholders and what impacts to consider?

Theory

There are many different ethical paradigms, theories, and decision-making models out there, and most major companies around the world have some mandatory annual ethics training. This training often revolves around what the company leaders think is ethical and not ethical to do. That slant makes the training sound more like rules and regulations. Getting into the ethical debate on these issues usually requires more thought on uncomfortable ideas—such as if the business takes a stand on an issue and loses tax-exempt status, that cost could force the organization to lay off several workers. If the business must lay off workers to take a stand on an issue, then the workers will lose their health benefits and salaries—their livelihoods. Is it morally right to do that? Should business leaders hurt some to potentially help many?

Several common ethical paradigms exist that can answer "yes" to that last question. The *utilitarian paradigm* states that one should maximize the good to as many as possible. Therefore, if you potentially help many, even though you are hurting a few if it is for the greater good, the business is warranted to take this action. The *justice paradigm* states that business actions can lead to harm, but business leaders should try to balance the harm faced by the workers with benefits. The *moral rights paradigm* also indicates it is ethical if a business takes a stand to provide people with their basic human rights. Kantian ethics, though, indicates that employees should not be treated as a means to an end. So, in Emmanuel Kant's eyes, business leaders are in the wrong when they do that. They should look for ways to take a stand that does not use employees as a way out of financial challenges. The problem is that there are many views on ethics.

So, who is right? While many academics and theorists like to debate one theory versus another, that is not commonly where businesses end up. Those making business decisions usually come down to a combination of balancing what the shareholders think, what the C-suite thinks, what customers think, and in some cases, what the company's employees think. It can be a difficult decision to think through if a business should get involved in a social cause. There are more than just those three questions that business leaders should ask. However, there are several basic steps business leaders can take to do some basic ethical checks before involving an organization in social change (see Exhibit 2-1).

Exhibit 2-1   Basic steps in deciding to involve an organization in social change.

Putting It Into Practice

When business leaders are considering their role in a social issue–their CSR, or corporate social justice–they should consider several aspects (illustrated in graphic #). These aspects can be thought of as a step-by-step process to consider the ethics.

Step One: Articulate Organizational Values

First, consider the company and leader values: *How can the organization's existing mission, values, and organizational culture inform the decision? How does that align with the issue(s) at hand?* It is easy to get into dangerous waters by taking a stand on a cause when it goes against the mission, existing culture, or the existing values of the business. Brands have had issues both internally and externally when they have taken up a cause or a stance with misalignment. Most infamously Gillette released a commercial about toxic masculinity playing off their old tagline "the best a man can get." However, it was quickly seen as fake or just capitalizing on a social wave when people looked back at previous Gillette campaigns where the company had women in skintight, very low-cut outfits with the company name printed across the "seat" area or print ads for men's razors only featuring female models posing on couches. Additionally, the company has commonly come under fire for what is known as the "pink tax" where women's items such as razors cost more even though they are the same product that is used by men. The ethics here for many did not line up as the company seemed to be practicing the same issues they condemned in their own ad.

Contrast this with Nike, a company that took a stand with their representative Colin Kaepernick. Nike in this instance is being used as an example of a company that did have alignment in what the business was doing and stood by it. This use is not to say Nike is in general a benchmark in good business ethics. For this one case where the company took a stand, we can also cite cases where Nike failed in social change with respect to pregnant athletes. Like most people and businesses there is a history of successes and failures in social action. We are going to focus on just one instance here for the sake of an example for this process as they took one aspect of it to a new level.

Nike brought Kaepernick in as a spokesperson at the height of the controversy surrounding his actions of kneeling during the national anthem at professional football games. This controversy garnered attention on social media, network news, and many other news outlets. Nike has historically espoused free speech. Bringing him into commercials by the company prompted the organization to take a stand on a social issue related to race, social change, and free speech. However, this stance aligned with the company, its history of free speech and race, and its stated values.

Does that mean that Gillette could never take a stand on gender issues as Nike did? No, they could have taken steps to demonstrate that, for the organization, it was part of a broader change in values, having the data to say the pink tax issue was gone, apologizing for previous ads, or showing more gender equality in their operations and marketing. Then, they could have reduced the ethical misalignment and issues. The issue for Gillette was not that the company took a stand; rather, it was that ethically for consumers watching the advertisement it seems disingenuous based upon the companies' actions, demonstrated values, and culture. Note: future chapters in this book will deal with how to integrate social change efforts into business strategy and operations.

The Nike example was not without controversy. Many people faulted Nike for being disrespectful to the country and to veterans who fought for the flag as they stood by their decision to hire Kaepernick. Additionally, while Nike has stood strong on racial support in sports, they have faced controversy with gender such as with several female runners. When some find alignment others may find fault. This brings us to the second ethical question a business needs to ask: *how committed is the organization to the cause or issue?*

Step Two: Hold Steadfast to Values

Is the organization willing to stand firm in the face of losses and objections from consumers, employees, and shareholders? This step is where Nike took things to a new level. Nike was fully committed to taking that stand and stood by the decision. When people started burning their Nike shoes and apparel as a protest, the company came out with a social media campaign with directions on how to burn those items safely, or better yet to donate them to homeless veterans who commonly need shoes and socks. The company was willing to stand by its decision as freedom of speech was part of what they were standing for from the start. Therefore, how could they not allow their own detractors to have free speech?

Contrast that with another recent example. Budweiser had a trans individual as a spokesperson in a promotion advertisement on social media site Tik Tok where the influencer, Dylan Mulvaney, gained fame. When the backlash came in from the video, with social media protests and videos just like the Nike case, the company distanced itself from Mulvaney and stated advertisements in the future would just be about more mundane topics like sports (Holpuch, 2023). Ironically, the promotional video Mulvaney made was about a Budweiser promotion for March Madness. Budweiser now faced a second wave of anger from the LGBTQIA+ community, with Mulvaney herself condemning the lack of support from Budweiser (Holpuch, 2023). The community they were trying to support with the original spokeswoman felt the company did not really believe in their cause and was giving in to hate. Between the two Nike came out on top here again as they were committed to their cause. Nike lost some customers and received backlash in the process but stood by their decision and ethical values. Budweiser, on the other hand, lost consumers on both sides of the issue: first when they took the stand, and then when they reversed their decision. As founder of international social responsibility consulting and marketing firm, Republic of Everyone, Ben Peacock advises: if you are not willing to stand by your choice and those values amidst backlash you could end up angering a larger group by reversing course, be sure you consider how committed you are to your stance before you take one (Peacock, 2023). Future chapters in this book will talk about how to deal with internal and external entities that exert influence on your social change efforts. The book provides specific tools to handle those relationships.

Step Three: Incorporate Values into Behaviors

Be sure the organization acts in an ethical way: consider if you have the manpower for the extra duties that may be required. Often people will be willing to take on extra duties if they believe in the cause but long term that can lead to burnout. Acting to be ethical in an unethical way has a high degree of irony in it. Does the workforce of your organization have the skills in your workforce to perform the actions the organization espouses? If the business goal is to engage with diverse groups of people, does the organization have trained/qualified diversity equity, and inclusion individuals to lead that effort? The final thing to consider here is the assessment or review of the actions and how things are going. Often people look at changes in this respect as a linear process, but it is more circular where you review and find where to make changes, go back to previous steps, and adjust as necessary as GM demonstrated in their changing position over time.

Chapter Summary

To summarize this chapter, let's examine how this chapter aligns with business ethical actions. Think again about how GM ended up in their situation from the introduction. First, the company did not have the strong values at the time to take strong stances. Second, organizational leaders were not willing to take a strong stance. In fact, what they did aligns more with the Friedman Doctrine. They were praised by many at the time for doing so since they pulled out of South Africa during the controversy. But in the early 2000s GM was sued by individuals who were victims of crimes during the apartheid time at the hands of law enforcement as GM sold products to those very police forces. So, for the original 1980s part of the case, they followed the Friedman Doctrine which negated the next few steps. GM settled the lawsuit with a strong statement that today diversity and respect matter to the company. Today, they are willing to stand by their values, pay the money, and admit past wrongdoings. Today, they checked their values and found alignment for step 1, were willing to stand by that decision and pay money, and tried to do it in an ethical way. It was a case that dragged on over several decades.

References

Friedman, M. (1970, Sept. 30). A Friedman doctrine: The social responsibility of business is to increase its profits. *The New York Times*. https://www.nytimes.com/1970/09/13/archives/a-friedman-doctrine-the-social-responsibility-of-business-is-to.html

Hammurabi, (2008). The Code of Hammurabi (King, W. L. trans.). The Avalon Project, Yale Law School (original work published ca. 1750s B.C.E.).

Holpuch, A. (2023, June 23). Behind the backlash against Bud Light. *The New York Times*. https://www.nytimes.com/article/bud-light-boycott.html

MacLaury, J. (1998). A brief history: The U.S. Department of Labor. U.S. Department of Labor. https://www.dol.gov/general/aboutdol/history/dolhistoxford

Peacock, B. (2023, May 28). *How leaders lead* [Lecture]. Penn State University. https://youtu.be/u8KKGXzGiS8

Chapter 3

Step 2: Assessing Your Organization's Social Change Profile

Wayne Gersie

Case Study: Implementing Environmental Assessments

Bill was recently hired as the manager for Diversity, Equity, Inclusion, and Belonging (DEIB) at a mid-sized manufacturing company in the suburbs of a large Midwest city. The primary impetus for creating this administrative position came from climate surveys and feedback. Secondarily, the company experienced unwanted attention in regional reporting due to some incidents related to racist and sexist behaviors. This led a group of employees to file a class-action sexual harassment lawsuit. The national coverage of the murder of George Floyd was the ultimate accelerant to create Bill's new position.

Bill will be part of the company's senior leadership team and will report directly to the CEO. As the inaugural manager for DEIB, Bill is expected to serve as a thought leader for all things DEIB. (The same principles affecting DEIB will also affect other social change efforts in which organizations try to effect change in the world outside their organizational boundaries.) This includes a primary role of training and coaching along with ongoing climate assessments. His charge is to be part of a systemic and organization-wide strategic approach to promote and effectuate DEIB initiatives, supported and implemented in collaboration with the company board, senior leadership, levels of management, and employees.

DOI: 10.4324/9781003439714-3

He holds a terminal degree in industrial psychology, and he has held positions progressing from entry-level to senior leadership over 25+ years. He is expected to review and analyze all artifacts and information he can glean from the company's previous DEIB efforts and then subsequently chart the course forward.

Company Description

ABC Manufacturing is a large to midsize company. The company designs, develops, and manufactures small electronic parts for the automobile industry. The company has one location with a manufacturing plant and company headquarters. The company has 1,200 plus employees across six subdivisions. The management team includes 50 or more mid-level and executive leaders. Most employees live within 50 miles of work. A significant age gap exists in years of service between those with less than five years of service and those with 20+ years of service. The company has experienced significant attrition due in part to retirements while seeing an increase of mostly Millennial and Gen Z new hires. Finally, over recent years, the demographic makeup of the company has moved from predominantly white males to a 51 percent to 49 percent male-to-female ratio. ABC's operating budget is roughly $300 million dollars.

Bill's First 100 Days

One of Bill's immediate responsibilities is to develop a plan to execute the next climate assessment. To prepare for this task, Bill spent his first six months on a listening and learning tour. He met with stakeholders at all levels of the organization, ranging from entry-level machinists to C-Suite executives to collect anecdotes and attitudes and gain an informal understanding of the company's SC profile. Another important task towards gaining sufficient understanding was to review and analyze the climate survey conducted a few years prior.

During his listening and learning tour, Bill noticed that he got different, sometimes conflicting feedback about the survey's impact on stakeholders and the environment. Some stakeholders, mostly at the executive level, argued that the survey was too expensive and that some employees used the published findings to shame leadership. Others, mostly employees who felt marginalized, argued that nothing had been done with the first survey results to improve the climate or to make meaningful changes.

Some complained to Bill that promises were broken and that an immediate follow-up survey was long overdue. There were also whispers that leadership did not want to conduct another survey because they feared the results would remain unfavorable and that they had no plan for addressing climate concerns anyway.

Bill learned from the chief legal officer that his new employer is under investigation for other potential civil violations. He also learned there were at least three open EEOC investigations (Equal Employment Opportunity Commission, the chief federal enforcement arm of the Civil Rights Act) in addition to two more that had recently settled and one in mediation. Alarmingly, the undercurrent of fear about retaliation seemed more than confirmed when Bill found that several "disgruntled" employees were identified by name and prominently featured in company brochures and videos, materials that had been created early in the hiring process.

The company recorded two consecutive years of record losses, and part of the picture was related to their climate issues. Coming out of the recent pandemic, the company has had a difficult time meeting goals for hiring a diverse workforce. "Water cooler conversations," sometimes stated openly and out loud, revealed that the company was known for a lack of receptiveness to concerns from those in underrepresented groups, a reputation that greatly diminished its ability not only to retain current employees but also to recruit them as well. At the launch of the survey, employees received an email announcing the launch and prizes were promised as an incentive for participation. The survey was administered over a two-month window. When the window closed, 19 percent of all employees had completed the survey. Administrators noticed that a higher percentage of survey respondents were entry-level employees. During Bill's review, he realized that the second-highest percentage of respondents had selected the "do not wish to disclose" choice for demographic information for job title. Bill also noticed that the participation rate was in the single digits for Blacks and Latinos. In addition, women had a 30 percent lower participation rate than men.

The key findings indicated that 92 percent of respondents found the work environment "favorable" and "welcoming." Respondents from marginalized groups and several respondents that did not disclose demographics found their work environment "hostile" and "unwelcoming." Some disclosed instances of sexism, sexual harassment, sexual assaults, homophobia, and racism. Some of these respondents indicated that they planned to leave the company due to hostility and the lack of response by administrators.

Case Study Wrap-Up: Post Planning

Following administration and assessment, Bill's next steps involved post-planning initiatives. Identifying areas for improvement seemed to be the obvious priority, but sustaining areas where the organization was doing well was also one of Bill's top priorities. Some action items fell flat, and the "grapevine chatter" about how the new assessment "didn't work" was quelled with intentional and proactive communications about ongoing efforts.

Bill conducted ongoing focus groups, inviting subsets of stakeholders from all levels of the organization and all demographic groups. He was able to specifically include some key employees who were most vocal on social media so these employees did not feel marginalized. This improved morale and restored some confidence. Bill also ensured that their feedback was incorporated into revised action items and consistently communicated about the progress with the steps.

As expected, the process was not linear and setbacks occurred, but employees could see that their opinions mattered and that Bill was sincere and purposeful in working towards improvements. The organization had given Bill ample administrative authority to be an effective DEIB leader, and it paid off.

The primary focus of this chapter is to familiarize readers with the process of comprehensive assessment strategies. Social Change (SC) assessments are used to gain an understanding of organizational climate, culture, and current fit regarding its SC profile, while EAA (EAS) gauges employee attitudes and motivations. These assessments are interrelated: specifically, this chapter discusses how a consideration of SC is crucial when assessing employees' attitudes in the process towards obtaining accurate and complete information about employees' motivations and behaviors. This chapter will culminate by *guiding practitioners through a process of assessing an organization for its current social profile and employee attitudes in a manner that is culturally responsive and representative of all its stakeholders*.

In addition, this chapter will dive into the extensive pre- and post-planning that is equally important in ensuring a continuing impact of your initial assessment. Practitioners and leaders will learn how to prepare their organization for a Culturally Responsive and Equity Minded (CREM) assessment process that elicits an appetite for participation and trust in those who will be assessed, and which translates into a high response rate from critical voices. Readers will learn proven approaches and practices for assessing the views, attitudes, and sentiments of stakeholders at all levels of the organization. We will also discuss strategies to engage those who may be skeptical of the process due to experiences. We will further present a triangulated assessment that is inclusive while avoiding a one-size-fits-all approach to assessing climate and employee attitudes. Last, we will discuss what to do post-survey to ensure its results remain relevant and effective long after the assessment is complete.

What Does the Research Say?

The History and Advances of Assessing Organizational Environments

SCA and EAA have a rich history dating back to the early 20th century when researchers began studying social phenomena such as urbanization and industrialization (Lippitt, Fox, & Dutt, 1969). Initially, the focus was on identifying the effects of SCs on society, broken down initially into how they affect individuals and communities. Eventually, this led social psychologists and researchers to expand their focus to understanding the impact of social and cultural factors on individuals and whole organizations (Cameron & Quinn, 2006).

The momentum for pioneering what was then called "employee attitude testing" was triggered by strikes during World War I that came with the draft and accompanying labor shortages and increased production demands. Strikes compelled companies to move away from focusing solely on actions and behaviors to employee attitudes regarding their work environment, and researchers observed that emotions can affect work performance and production. It became apparent that favorable workplace attitudes would improve employee relations and loyalty. There was a collective understanding that wartime highlighted the value of tracking employee attitudes and uncovering key drivers that ultimately led to higher profit margins.

Over time, employee-attitude assessments became more sophisticated, reflecting changes in work and the increasing complexity of modern organizations (Smith, 2018). Eventually, EAAs evolved to focus on a broader range of issues, including workplace culture, leadership, and organizational communication.

One of the earliest and most influential studies was the Hawthorne Studies, conducted by Elton Mayo and his colleagues at Harvard University (Roethlisberger & Dickson, 1939). Their results had a profound impact and challenged the traditional view that productivity solely depended on individual ability. Instead, they suggested that social and psychological factors played a significant role in worker productivity. The Hawthorne Studies ushered in a focus on industrial and organizational psychology, fostering the development of the human relations movement. (Robbins, Judge & Millett, 2020).

Social psychology researchers advanced their methods with more sophisticated tools for assessing employee attitudes and behaviors. The Likert Scale became one of the most widely used tools (Papalia, Feldman, & Martorell, 2016). The work of J. David Houser, an educational psychologist and a pioneer of employee attitude testing, explained that employee attitudes can inform personnel policies and practices.

Understanding the benefit of employee attitude testing and assessments, the National Industrial Advisory Board encouraged its use, widely reporting a 250 percent jump in productivity in companies that utilized attitude surveys by 1947. Examples of early survey methods include printed questionnaires, directive interviews, and unguided interviews. One of the best examples of the impact of industrial and organizational advances was when the United States Army Research Branch conducted Soldier Surveys to record the opinions of roughly half a million soldiers on topics ranging from food quality to confidence in leadership.

In the 1950s and 1960s, social scientists developed ever more sophisticated methods of SCA, such as the use of surveys and statistical analysis. One influential approach was the SC Impact Assessment (SCIA), designed to measure the impact of SC programs on the attitudes and behaviors of individuals and communities (Lippitt, Fox, & Dutt, 1969). In the 1960s and 1970s, SCA and EAA became more widely used in organizations as a way of understanding the impact of social and cultural factors on organizational effectiveness. These assessments were used to measure employee satisfaction, organizational culture, and the effectiveness of organizational change initiatives (Cameron & Quinn, 2006). One of the most influential models in this area is the Organizational Culture Assessment Instrument (OCAI), developed by Cameron and Quinn in the 1980s.

Today, SCA and EAA continue to be important tools for understanding the attitudes and behaviors of employees and the impact of social and cultural factors on organizational effectiveness. The latest developments in this area include the use of artificial intelligence and machine learning to analyze large datasets of employee attitudes and behaviors, providing more accurate and nuanced insights into the complex dynamics of organizations.

As the workplace continues to evolve, the importance of these assessments is likely to grow, highlighting the need for continued research and development in this field.

Social Change Assessment Defined

Social change refers to altering and hopefully advancing societal structures, behaviors, and attitudes to create a more equitable and just society. According to McLeod (2018), SC can occur at various levels, including individual, community, institutional, and societal. It can manifest through various means, such as legislation, technological innovations, grassroots movements, and cultural shifts. SC is often driven by social movements, which are collective efforts aimed at challenging and transforming the existing social order (Gamson, 1990). These movements can range from those that seek to address specific issues, such as civil rights or environmental justice, to those that aim to transform social, economic, and political structures.

One of the most significant features of SC is its ability to challenge and transform power dynamics within society. As argued by Giddens (1979), SC can redistribute resources, opportunities, and privileges, and it can challenge and transform existing power structures. This process of power redistribution is often contested, as those who benefit from the existing power structures may resist and attempt to maintain their privileged position (Foucault, 1980). To challenge and transform the basis behind power, SC movements often use collective action and advocacy, along with promoting ever-changing concepts of what is equitable and just.

Specific to organizational development, Social Change Assessment (SCA) evaluates the impact of an organization's actions, policies, or programs on the social, economic, and environmental aspects within a community or broader society, of which their workforce is a subset. SCA is more outward facing, whereas the employee attitude and perception assessment is more inward facing, but both aspects are crucial to systematic and comprehensive assessment. Examining how indicators such as administrative actions, policies, or programs impact SC may help us understand the influence SC (or its lack thereof) has on employee attitude and sense of belonging.

Another aspect of SCA allows for an analysis of the effects an organization's activities and reputation have on the local and broader community from whom they are recruiting talent. The analysis identifies areas for improvement and suggests strategies to create positive changes. SCA can also help organizations effectively align their policies and practices with their values and goals. Doing so results in improved reputation and addresses sustainability concerns as demographics and overall values evolve, all directed towards realizing the benefits of diversity when done well and intentionally.

According to Hesselbein and Goldsmith (2009), SCA is a critical component of effective organizational management and leadership. Both qualitative and quantitative data collection uncover the social impact of an organization's activities, programs, or policies, and it guides strategic planning toward key performance goals. The assessment should be inclusive of perspectives from all stakeholders, including customers, employees, suppliers, regulators, and the broader community.

Methods for Conducting SC Assessment

Organization management and leadership are now beholden to all levels of identified stakeholders to maximize their ability to respond to broader societal changes. It involves analyzing the social impact of an organization's activities, identifying areas for improvement, and developing strategies to respond positively to SC. The *Social Impact Assessment* and *Theory of Change* frameworks are two methods that can conduct SCAs.

The Social Impact Assessment (SIA) framework is a systematic, four-stage process for identifying and assessing the social, economic, and environmental impact of an organization's activities. The four stages of SIA are scoping, impact analysis, mitigation, and monitoring and evaluation (Vanclay, Esteves & Franks, 2015).

The Theory of Change (TOC) framework helps organizations to articulate the changes they seek to achieve and the strategies they will use to achieve them. The TOC framework involves developing a logic model that describes the inputs, activities, outputs, outcomes, and impact of an organization's programs or policies (Anderson & Mullen, 2016).

Approaches to SC Assessment

There are several approaches to SCA, each with its unique strengths and limitations. One common approach is the ***participatory approach***, which emphasizes the involvement of all stakeholders. This approach assumes that stakeholders have valuable insights and experiences, including their voices about the assessment process, that can inform the assessment and enhance its validity, especially as a mechanism for buy-in from employees (Cornwall

& Jewkes, 1995). Participatory approaches to SCA have been used in contexts like community development, health promotion, and environmental management (Chambers, 1994). The participatory approach is useful for assessing complex and multifaceted social issues where input from diverse perspectives is essential for developing effective, comprehensive solutions (Cornwall & Jewkes, 1995).

Another approach is the ***evidence-based approach***, which emphasizes the use of rigorous scientific methods to evaluate the impact of social programs, policies, or interventions. This approach uses experimental or quasi-experimental designs to measure the effectiveness of interventions (Shadish, Cook & Campbell, 2002). The evidence-based approach is highly valued for its rigor and objectivity, but it may overlook essential criteria, and it may be limited by diminished emphasis on diverse perspectives or the broader social context in which the intervention takes place (Cousins & Leithwood, 2013).

A third approach to SCA is the ***systems approach***, which emphasizes the interconnectedness and complexity of social issues. This approach recognizes that social problems are not isolated or discrete but are part of broader systems and networks of relationships (Meadows, 2008). The systems approach involves mapping and analyzing the interactions between different components of a social system, such as the relationships between individuals, organizations, policies, and the environment (Meadows, 2008). The systems approach drills down to the root causes of social issues, understanding the dynamics of SC and developing comprehensive and sustainable solutions (Senge, 2006).

SCA is a complex and multifaceted process that requires careful consideration of multiple perspectives and approaches. The participatory approach emphasizes stakeholder involvement, the evidence-based approach emphasizes scientific rigor, and the systems approach emphasizes complexity and interconnectedness. Depending on the context and the topic surrounding the social issue being assessed, one or more of these approaches may be appropriate and effective.

The Broader Context of Implementing SC Assessment Within Organizations

Research has shown that SCA is important in globalization and the increasing value being placed on DEIB initiatives in the workforce. As both the talent pool and organizations become more diverse, they face the challenge of managing a workforce with a variety of cultural backgrounds, values, and beliefs. SCA can help organizations understand the impact of these differences and develop strategies to manage diversity and balance employee needs effectively. Jackson and Ruderman (1999) found that organizations that implemented diversity management programs based on SCA had higher levels of employee satisfaction, commitment, and productivity.

SCA can also help organizations identify opportunities for innovation and growth. Sustained input from diverse voices acts as a formal mechanism for understanding the changing needs and expectations of customers, employees, and other stakeholders. Informed organizations can develop new products and services, gain bigger market shares, and recognize novel areas of strengths and ideas in their talent pool. SCA can also help organizations identify emerging trends and technologies that can be leveraged toward competitive advantages.

Employee Attitude Assessment Defined

EAA measures the overall mindset of employees. Attitudes can affect productivity, morale, job satisfaction, and turnover. An effective attitude assessment provides insight into employee attitudes about aspects of the organization such as job duties, compensation, management style, and the overall work environment. These assessments are typically conducted through surveys or questionnaires, and the data are valuable for improving employee satisfaction and performance (Landy & Conte, 2016).

Approaches to Employee Attitude Assessment

Different approaches to EAA are available, ranging from surveys and questionnaires to in-depth interviews and focus groups. While each method has its unique benefits and drawbacks, the optimal approach ultimately depends on the research objectives and context in which the assessment is conducted.

The self-report questionnaire is especially useful for assessing attitudes related to specific work-related topics, often using job satisfaction and organizational commitment indicators (Barrick & Mount, 1991). Despite their widespread use, self-report questionnaires have limitations. Employee responses may reflect biases and the qualitative data collected in the instrument may not fully capture the complexity of attitudes.

In addition to surveys, ***observation methods*** are also a viable option for evaluating employee attitudes. These methods use a trained observer to conduct ***behavior coding*** and log ***critical incident techniques*** to ascertain objective information about employee behavior and attitudes. These data can help managers make better decisions about performance evaluation and training requirements (Pinder & Harlos, 2001). Observation methods can be time-consuming and therefore, the organization's willingness to undertake this approach may be limited.

A third approach to EAA is ***implicit measures***, such as the Implicit Association Test (IAT). These measures can provide valuable insight into employees' unconscious attitudes towards work-related topics such as DEIB and job satisfaction, according to Greenwald et al. (2009). Regardless, implicit measures have been criticized for their reliability and validity. Some argue that implicit measures may not always accurately reflect an individual's true attitudes since they are based on indirect and often automatic responses. Implicit measures may not be suitable for assessing complex attitudes. Finally, attitudes that are not strongly held may not be assessed well with implicit measures. These points limit its use as a comprehensive tool.

The Intersection of SC and Employee Attitude Assessment

Given this background, this chapter defends the focus that organizational psychology places on the intersection of SC and EAA. As society becomes increasingly diverse, organizations are adapting to ensure that the workplace culture is inclusive and equitable for all employees. Ignoring these factors may affect the bottom line, especially as companies compete with others who are intentional in their recruitment, retention, and product development areas. Research has shown that organizations that prioritize DEIB initiatives have a more engaged and satisfied workforce (Cox & Blake, 1991).

One of the main challenges to conducting EAAs on DEIB issues is ensuring that the assessment tools are culturally sensitive and relevant to the diverse experiences of employees (Mallette & Wilson, 2019). Organizations must also ensure they focus on post-assessment action items and sincerely address any identified issues (Pless & Maak, 2004).

Assessments are crucial to guide improvements in job satisfaction, motivation, and productivity, but it is equally important to consider the broader context of SC when conducting such assessments. For instance, employees who highly value flexible working hours may prioritize this goal above everything else. Thus, if an organization does not offer flexible hours, employees who are otherwise satisfied may still express a negative attitude toward the organization. Therefore, an assessment with no way to prioritize employee values and beliefs may come to incomplete and inaccurate conclusions. Assessing attitudes in isolation may not provide a complete picture of employee motivations and behaviors.

Broader SCs can influence employees' expectations of their workplace. For instance, societal changes, such as increasing awareness of gender and racial equality, have led to employees' expectations for more DEIB in the workplace. Assessing employees' attitudes without considering their changing DEIB expectations may result in organizations failing to meet those expectations, which can lead to negative attitudes and behaviors.

Methods for Integrating SC Assessment into Employee Attitude Assessment

SC's impact on employee attitudes suggests the need to integrate SCA into EAA methods. One approach is to use surveys that measure attitudes towards SC alongside traditional employee attitude surveys. According to Krammer, Kammerlander, & Schondelmayer (2019), such surveys can assess employees' beliefs, attitudes, and behaviors related to SC, diversity, and inclusion. The goal is to use these surveys to identify areas where they need to better align their SC efforts.

Another method for integrating SCA into EAA is to use **focus groups and interviews**. These methods allow employees to express their opinions and experiences related to DEIB in a more personal and in-depth manner. Additionally, the qualitative data may provide themes within the feedback that guide the organization's SC efforts and initiatives.

A third, newly available approach is to use social media analysis. Social media platforms like LinkedIn, Twitter, and Facebook provide a wealth of data that can be mined to assess employee attitudes towards SC. According to Li, Lu & Liu (2020), social media analysis can help organizations understand their employees' sentiment towards SC. Social media is filled with telling voluntary and sometimes anonymous employee interactions that can reflect how employees feel about the organization's SC initiatives (see Exhibit 3-1).

Putting It Into Practice

Step One: Include Diverse Voices in Assessment Planning

We discussed how it is crucial to include a representative perspective from all levels of the organization when conducting an SC and employee satisfaction assessment. Including representatives from all levels of the organization is paramount for a few reasons.

First, it communicates that employees at every level have valuable insights and experiences that can contribute to understanding and improving the organizational climate. Everyone, regardless of their position, brings a unique perspective shaped by their role, responsibilities, and interactions

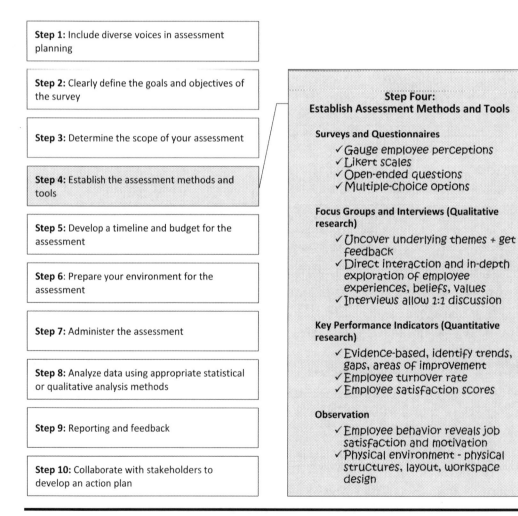

Step 1: Include diverse voices in assessment planning

Step 2: Clearly define the goals and objectives of the survey

Step 3: Determine the scope of your assessment

Step 4: Establish the assessment methods and tools

Step 5: Develop a timeline and budget for the assessment

Step 6: Prepare your environment for the assessment

Step 7: Administer the assessment

Step 8: Analyze data using appropriate statistical or qualitative analysis methods

Step 9: Reporting and feedback

Step 10: Collaborate with stakeholders to develop an action plan

Step Four:
Establish Assessment Methods and Tools

Surveys and Questionnaires
- ✓ Gauge employee perceptions
- ✓ Likert scales
- ✓ Open-ended questions
- ✓ Multiple-choice options

Focus Groups and Interviews (Qualitative research)
- ✓ Uncover underlying themes + get feedback
- ✓ Direct interaction and in-depth exploration of employee experiences, beliefs, values
- ✓ Interviews allow 1:1 discussion

Key Performance Indicators (Quantitative research)
- ✓ Evidence-based, identify trends, gaps, areas of improvement
- ✓ Employee turnover rate
- ✓ Employee satisfaction scores

Observation
- ✓ Employee behavior reveals job satisfaction and motivation
- ✓ Physical environment - physical structures, layout, workspace design

Exhibit 3-1   Putting assessments into practice.

within the organization. By incorporating voices from all levels, the assessment gains a more comprehensive understanding of the organization's challenges and opportunities.

Second, intentionally including diverse voices communicates the organization's commitment to creating an inclusive environment. Inclusion provides a platform for individuals from different backgrounds, identities, and perspectives, and this first step helps foster a sense of belonging and empowerment. It shows marginalized or underrepresented groups that their voices and needs are important, and it ensures that the assessment captures a wide range of perspectives, ultimately leading to more accurate and effective SC strategies.

Step Two: Clearly Define the Goals and Objectives of the Survey

When conducting surveys, OD professionals charged with leading survey implementation must clearly define its purpose, identify issues it aims to address, establish the goals it seeks to achieve, and ensure that the survey objectives are well thought out and align with the organization's overall strategy and vision. With an overall goal of organizational maturity related to DEIS, this step sets the following assessment goals.

Understanding the Current State of Affairs

As a precursor to SC, organizations must clearly understand the prevailing internal attitudes, beliefs, and behaviors to effectively strategize and plan. Surveys can gather data on various indicators, such as employee satisfaction, engagement, perceptions of leadership, workplace culture, diversity and inclusion, and attitudes towards various social issues. These data provide a baseline for identifying strengths and areas that require attention and improvement.

Assessing the Current Status of Organizational SC Profile

Understanding where an establishment is on its journey to becoming a CREM organization can inform decision-making, resource allocation, and, ultimately, aspirational goals. An evidenced-based climate evaluation can assess where your organization falls in relation to its DEIS goals. Evaluation gives leadership a more objective baseline than anecdotal information and sets the stage for a strong commitment to monitoring and improvement. An evaluation can demonstrate organizational commitment if leveraged correctly.

Addressing Specific Issues

Step two also includes the ability to address specific climate issues. Surveys can help identify pain points, challenges, and areas of concern. For example, an organization may notice a decline in employee morale or increased turnover rates, which could indicate underlying issues with work-life balance, job satisfaction, or communication. Also, when surveys shed light on prevailing attitudes towards marginalized groups, discrimination, or social inequalities, the data can develop targeted interventions, policies, and initiatives to address these issues.

Setting Organizational Goals and Vision Related to DEIS

Surveys are the key tool for setting goals and objectives. Once the issues are identified and prioritized, institutions can establish specific goals and objectives to drive change and improvement. For instance, an organization aiming to enhance employee engagement may set a goal to increase overall engagement scores by a certain percentage within a specified timeframe. Similarly, a society striving for social justice may set objectives to reduce discrimination or increase awareness and acceptance of diversity. These goals and objectives provide a roadmap for change and serve as benchmarks for assessing progress.

Step Three: Determine the Scope of Your Assessment

When implemented appropriately, assessments can be used in a range of settings to identify gaps and facilitate actions to improve organizational DEIS goals. Critical strategies for an effective needs assessment require not only representative stakeholders, per step one, but also depth and breadth in the assessment as outlined below:

Molar Versus Focused Climate Assessments

When assessing organizational SC, multiple organizational climates may exist and can be measured on multiple scales. Each multiple climate is subject to assessment. In broad terms, there are two categories of climate assessment, and step two will help you decide if you need a molar or focused climate assessment.

Molar climate assessments measure the overall positive (or negative) sense of the work environment and its effect on employees across the full breadth of an organization and/or in its subsets. Focused climate assessments can involve more elaborate models and measure aspects of climate relevant to specific areas of concern. Examples include the climate surrounding safety, ethics, performance, customer service, and innovation. An assessment seeking to measure the state of DEIS (culturally responsive needs assessment) in an organization and its progression toward CREM would be considered a form of focused climate assessment.

Step Four: Establish the Assessment Methods and Tools

When determining the SC profile and assessing current employee attitudes, several methods and tools are available.

Surveys and questionnaires can provide valuable insights into employee attitudes. These tools can include Likert scales, open-ended questions, and multiple-choice options. By analyzing responses, organizations can gauge employee satisfaction, engagement, and perceptions of SC initiatives.

In addition, qualitative research methods such as **focus groups and interviews** can offer a deeper understanding and context to SC and employee attitudes. These methods allow for direct interaction and in-depth exploration of employee experiences, beliefs, and values. Through focus groups, employees can openly share their thoughts and suggestions, while interviews provide an opportunity for one-on-one discussions. These qualitative approaches enable organizations to uncover underlying issues and themes while gaining valuable feedback.

Key performance indicators (KPIs) are another valuable tool that can provide quantitative data on organizational progress. Examples of relevant KPIs include employee turnover rates, diversity and inclusion metrics, employee satisfaction scores, and participation rates in SC initiatives. By regularly tracking these indicators, organizations can identify trends, gaps, and areas of improvement. This data-driven approach ensures that SC efforts are evidence-based and allows for monitoring the effectiveness of interventions.

And finally, **observation** is another powerful method for determining SC and assessing employee attitudes. In popular culture, the TV show

"Undercover Boss" is a fun, informal example. The disclaimer is that any observation must follow an ethical approach as outlined by company policies and professional organizations' human subjects research protocols. Observation is the process of carefully observing individuals and their interactions within a specific context. In SC, SC, observation can uncover patterns and trends that reflect evolving societal norms, values, and practices. Observations can detect the emergence of new behaviors, beliefs, or social structures.

Observation is an effective tool for assessing **employee attitudes**. By observing employee behavior, body language, and interactions with their colleagues and supervisors, valuable insights can be gathered about their job satisfaction, motivation, and overall engagement. Observing how employees respond to changes, challenges, or new initiatives can provide a deeper understanding of their attitudes and perceptions.

Beyond observing individuals, observation of the **physical environment**, comprising the physical structures, layout, and design of a workspace, can offer valuable insights into prevailing social dynamics and employee perceptions, including clues about the degree of inclusivity, collaboration, and adaptability within the workplace. For example, an open and flexible workspace design with ample areas for teamwork and interaction might suggest a culture that values collaboration and innovation. However rigid, compartmentalized workspaces might indicate a hierarchical and less inclusive organizational structure. Further, the lack of nursing rooms, gender-neutral bathrooms, and meditation spaces can communicate a lack of commitment to DEIS.

Step Five: Develop a Timeline and Budget for the Assessment

Developing a timeline and budget for an SC and EAA process requires careful planning and consideration of various factors. Two key tasks need to be completed in this process. The first step is creating an effective **timeline**. The second is creating a final **budget** for the process.

When creating an assessment **timeline**, break down tasks and set deadlines. The established project objectives outlined in Step Two above will guide decisions about how to separate tasks and determine success in achieving them. The timeline will include plans for implementing specific activities, such as conducting surveys, analyzing data, and implementing new policies. The timeline will also address the assignments of team members with realistic deadlines for each task. The assessment team should also consider any tasks beyond the control of the unit (such as work done by an outside consultant) or potential bottlenecks that may affect the timeline.

A well-developed timeline also includes intermediate and extended timelines that provide for successive iterations of the assessment. One common mistake is a lack of planning beyond the initial assessment. This misstep leads to delays in the next iteration of the assessment and can result in suspicion about lack of follow-up, which can be magnified by what may now seem reactive rather than proactive planning. This delay makes it difficult to determine if the action plans generated after the initial assessment had their intended impact. We recommend that the timeline extend through at least 3 iterations with room to include possible micro/pulse assessments in between.

Step Five is also the time to address resource allocation, an estimate of costs, and ultimately, the final **budget**. Some of the common resources for consideration are personnel, technology, materials, and external consultants. After resources are identified, research and identify any potential costs, such as survey software, data analysis tools, and training programs. Budgeting follows this comprehensive cost analysis, including careful consideration that the allocated resources align with the project's objectives and timeline. Regularly monitor and track the budget throughout the process to make necessary adjustments and avoid any unexpected financial constraints. Following these steps, you can develop a well-structured timeline and budget.

Step Six: Prepare Your Environment for the Assessment

Communication Strategy to Encourage Participation

Step 6 explores buy-in and how to use a well-planned communication strategy to effectively promote an SC and employee satisfaction assessment to stakeholders to ensure active participation. Begin by crafting a clear and concise message that highlights the survey's purpose and its significance in driving positive SC and enhancing employee satisfaction. Stress that the survey is an opportunity for everyone to voice their opinions and contribute to a better work environment that enables a comprehensive understanding of your organization's current strengths and areas needing improvement. Communicate that participation is essential to help the organization move beyond anecdotes and reactive policy creation. Sharing potential benefits, such as improved employee engagement, enhanced productivity, organizational accountability, and a stronger ability to proactively identify and address potential issues, will optimize participation. Next, utilize multiple communication channels such as email, social media platforms, and organizational notice boards to reach a diverse audience. Develop engaging content, including infographics, videos, and testimonials to generate interest and encourage participation. Finally, clearly outline the steps to access the survey, providing direct links or instructions on where to find it.

Seek Input and Feedback

Seek input and feedback from stakeholders when implementing a SC profile and EAA. This approach enhances engagement and participation. One method is to hold focus groups or individual meetings with stakeholders to discuss their thoughts, concerns, and expectations. Actively listen to their perspectives and encourage open dialogue to create a safe space for sharing feedback. Additionally, consider distributing surveys or questionnaires to gather more comprehensive input. These surveys should be designed to gather specific feedback on the assessment process, its effectiveness, and any potential improvements. Acknowledge and appreciate the input received and demonstrate a commitment to incorporating suggestions into the implementation process. By involving stakeholders, you can foster a sense of ownership and collaboration, leading to a more successful implementation of the SC profile and EAA.

Address Any Concerns or Questions Raised

When implementing an SC profile and EAA, establish open channels of communication with stakeholders, such as regular meetings, email updates, and dedicated feedback sessions. Demonstrate empathy regarding their concerns, questions, and perspectives, especially by taking appropriate action based on their suggestions. Provide clear and concise explanations of the purpose, methodology, and benefits of the assessment to address any misconceptions or uncertainties. Additionally, offer opportunities for stakeholders to participate in the planning and decision-making process, allowing them to contribute their ideas and suggestions. Be responsive and prompt in addressing individual concerns, providing personalized support when needed. Transparency is key; share relevant information about the assessment, including its objectives, expected outcomes, and potential impact on employees and the organization. Provide progress reports and updates to keep stakeholders informed and engaged throughout the implementation process. By addressing concerns and questions proactively and maintaining open lines of communication, stakeholders feel heard, valued, and actively involved, fostering a positive environment for SC and employee growth.

Ensure Data Confidentiality and Anonymity

When implementing an SC profile and EAA, ensuring data confidentiality and anonymity is imperative. To achieve this goal, first, ensure that all data collected is stored securely in encrypted databases. Second, any personally identifiable information should be anonymized or removed from the dataset. Additionally, restrict data access using strict controls and user authentication. Access should be granted only to authorized personnel who require it for analysis. When reporting the results, aggregated and anonymized data should be presented, ensuring that individual responses cannot be linked back to specific employees. Finally, establish clear data protection and privacy policies, educate employees on the importance of confidentiality and anonymity, and ensure compliance with relevant data protection regulations. Conduct regular audits to assess the effectiveness of confidentiality measures. By following these steps, organizations can uphold data confidentiality and anonymity, fostering trust and promoting ethical practices in the implementation of SC profiles and EAAs.

Step Seven: Administer the Assessment

During the administration of the assessment, continue to monitor participation rates and analyze the data regularly. Pay attention to any disparities in participation among different demographic groups. If you notice lower participation rates among underrepresented groups, take proactive steps to encourage their involvement. To promote participation among underrepresented groups, implement targeted outreach strategies. Engage with diversity and inclusion groups, employee resource networks, or affinity groups to raise awareness about the survey. Tailor your communication to resonate with different demographics and highlight the relevance of their perspectives. Send periodic reminders to those who have not yet completed the survey, emphasizing the importance of their input. When possible, personal messages may even work well to increase engagement.

Step Eight: Analyze Data Using Appropriate Statistical or Qualitative Analysis Methods

Identify Trends and Patterns

Interpreting the results of an assessment involves carefully analyzing the data and identifying emerging patterns or trends. After establishing the key metrics and indicators, such as overall job satisfaction, work-life balance, organizational culture, and employee engagement, the data can be examined through methods like statistical analysis, visualization techniques, and comparative studies. By looking for patterns or trends, you can identify consistent themes or variations across different groups or time periods. For example, there is a positive correlation between SC initiatives and employee satisfaction. Additionally, patterns may emerge regarding specific factors that contribute to employee dissatisfaction, such as lack of career development opportunities or poor communication channels. By interpreting the results and identifying these patterns or trends, organizations can gain valuable insights to inform strategic decision-making and take targeted actions.

Compare Data to Established Benchmarks

It is crucial to identify and define relevant benchmarks. Benchmarks can include processes established by industry standards, best practices, or specific targets set by the organization. In addition to processes, you may wish to benchmark your outcomes with those of other organizations, but care should be taken here because no two organizations are the same. Outcomes mediocre for Company A might be excellent for Company B due to the differences in their organizational development.

Once benchmarks are identified, the next step is to determine the data or metrics to assess outcomes. Several steps can be taken to ensure a comprehensive evaluation. This point goes beyond survey or interview analysis to performance indicators and other relevant measures. The collected data would then be compared to the predetermined thresholds of success for outcomes measurement.

If your actual outcomes fall short of your projected outcomes, you shouldn't be too concerned, especially if your survey is mainly being used to establish baselines. If it is a follow-up survey after climate interventions have taken place, perhaps your projected outcomes were too ambitious, or your interventions were inadequate. You may need to modify your projected outcomes or your intervention plan for the next iteration of the assessment.

Consider both the overall outcomes and any disparities or variations across different dimensions, such as different demographics or specific subunits of the organization.

Finally, the findings should be communicated effectively to key stakeholders, providing insights into the extent to which the initiatives or assessments have lagged, met, or exceeded the established outcome measures. This information can help inform future decision-making and improvements in SC efforts and employee satisfaction initiatives.

Develop a Framework to Evaluate Organizational Maturity Stage for SC

The next step is to systematically gauge the organization's maturity for SC and employee satisfaction assessment. A clear framework or set of criteria defines what maturity looks like for the organization and includes an evaluation of the organization's alignment with social impact goals, stakeholder engagement, and sustainability practices. Figure One provides an example of a framework that can assess the organizational SC profile as well as the employee attitudes toward DEIS. This framework should be a basis for evaluating the organization's policies, practices, and initiatives. In addition, employee satisfaction data was gathered from feedback through surveys, interviews, and focus groups to gauge their perceptions of workplace culture, job satisfaction, and overall engagement. These data should be analyzed and compared against industry standards or internal targets to identify areas for improvement. Again, care should be taken in comparing your outcomes with industry standards because your organization is not at the same place in its organizational development as others. However, this step can inform you about your own organizational development, which can be used for planning purposes. Valuable insights into the organization's progress can be obtained by regularly reviewing and updating these evaluations, ultimately facilitating continuous growth toward SC and enhanced employee satisfaction.

Step Nine: Reporting and Feedback

Prepare a Comprehensive Report Summarizing the Assessment Findings

Step Nine details a structured approach for preparing a comprehensive report to summarize the findings. The report should effectively communicate key insights and recommendations, beginning with an executive briefing that summarizes the assessment objectives, methodology, and major findings. The executive summary should capture the main points and be easily digestible for stakeholders. The full report should then delve into the detailed assessment findings, clearly presenting the data and analysis with both qualitative and quantitative findings. Include graphs, charts, and visual representations. The report should also highlight any significant trends, patterns, or themes. After reporting on the findings, the report should detail the analysis and interpretation of the results, identifying strengths, weaknesses, opportunities, and threats. Remember the broader context of SC and employee satisfaction, linking any insights to relevant theories, frameworks, or industry benchmarks. Finally, the report should focus on actionable recommendations. These recommendations should be specific, measurable, attainable, relevant, and time-bound (SMART). Consider the potential impact on SC and employee satisfaction and provide strategies for improvement or areas that require further attention. The report's conclusion should summarize key points and emphasize the importance of addressing the findings to drive positive change.

Communicate the Results to Stakeholders

When communicating the results of an SC and employee satisfaction assessment to stakeholders, clarity will ensure effective understanding and engagement. Start by organizing the information in a logical and coherent manner, highlighting the implications of the key findings. Use plain language and avoid jargon to enhance accessibility for a diverse audience. The visual aids included in the report can also convey complex data in a simplified manner. A concise summary of the assessment's purpose, methodology, and limitations can bolster credibility and context, with clear articulation of positive outcomes and areas of improvement. Continue to foster a sense of transparency by opening up discussion to questions, concerns, and feedback from stakeholders. Last, communicate regular updates and progress reports to maintain stakeholder engagement and demonstrate ongoing commitment.

Step Ten: Collaborate with Stakeholders to Develop an Action Plan

Developing an action plan is the last step of the process, and it comes from a thorough analysis of the assessment findings, highlighting key areas of concern and potential opportunities for improvement. Next, prioritize the identified issues based on their significance and feasibility of implementation. At this point it is important to engage stakeholders by presenting recommendations in a clear and concise manner, emphasizing the potential impact on SC and employee satisfaction. Encourage open dialogue and collaboration to ensure all stakeholders have a voice during the process of establishing implementation priorities. From there, develop specific and measurable goals moving forward that align with desired outcomes. Break down these goals into actionable steps and assign responsibilities to individuals or teams. Remember to use your timeline to track progress and ensure accountability. Finally, continuously monitor and evaluate the effectiveness of the action plan, adjusting as needed to ensure its successful implementation and long-term impact on SC and employee satisfaction. Regular communication with stakeholders throughout the process is vital to maintain their support and engagement. In chapter seven, we will build on this approach by presenting key steps for developing a strategic plan for SC in an organization (see Exhibit 3-2).

STEP #____	STEP #____	STEP #____
Step Name	**Step Name**	**Step Name**
Action sequence named above, steps listed below	*Action sequence named above, steps listed below*	*Action sequence named above, steps listed below*
☐	☐	☐
☐	☐	☐
☐	☐	☐
☐	☐	☐
☐	☐	☐
☐	☐	☐
☐	☐	☐
☐	☐	☐
☐	☐	☐
☐	☐	☐
☐	☐	☐
☐	☐	☐

Exhibit 3-2   Putting assessment into practice toolkit.

Chapter Summary

This chapter's major goal was to familiarize readers with the process of thorough assessment methodologies. Social Change (SC) assessments are used to get an understanding of an organization's environment, culture, and present fit with respect to its SC profile, whereas EAA (EAS) assessments are used to analyze employee attitudes and motivations. This chapter addressed how a consideration of SC is critical for measuring employees' attitudes in the process of getting accurate and full information about employees' motives and behaviors. This chapter concluded by directing practitioners through a process of measuring an organization's current social profile and employee attitudes in a culturally relevant and representative manner of all stakeholders. Furthermore, this chapter delved into the substantial pre- and post-planning that is essential in guaranteeing the long-term impact of your first assessment.

References

Anderson, A. K., & Mullen, P. M. (2016). Evaluating SC: A theory-of-change approach. *Journal of Extension, 54*(2), 1–7.

Barrick, M. R., & Mount, M. K. (1991). The big five personality dimensions and job performance: A meta-analysis. *Personnel Psychology, 44*(1), 1–26.

Bennett, M. J. (1993). Towards ethnorelativism: A developmental model of intercultural sensitivity. In R. M. Paige (Ed.), *Education for the intercultural experience.*

Bourke, J., & Dillon, B. (2018). The diversity and inclusion revolution: Eight powerful truths. *Deloitte Review, 22*, 82–95.

Cameron, K. S., & Quinn, R. E. (2006). *Diagnosing and changing organizational culture: Based on the competing values framework.* John Wiley & Sons.

Cavanagh, K., Varela, J., & Armenta, A. (2021). Measuring organizational diversity, equity, and inclusion: A review of Best practices. *Workforce Management, 100*(1), 54–63.

Chambers, R. (1994). The origins and practice of participatory rural appraisal. *World Development, 22*(7), 953–969.

Christensen, C. M., & Overdorf, M. (2000). Meeting the challenge of disruptive change. *Harvard Business Review, 78*(2), 67–76.

Cornwall, A., & Jewkes, R. (1995). What is participatory research? *Social Science & Medicine, 41*(12), 1667–1676.

Cousins, J. B., & Leithwood, K. A. (2013). Current empirical research on evaluation capacity building. In *Handbook of practical program evaluation* (pp. 465–492). John Wiley & Sons.

Cox, T., & Blake, S. (1991). Managing cultural diversity: Implications for organizational competitiveness. *Academy of Management Executive*, 5(3), 45–56.

Greenwald, A. G., Poehlman, T. A., Uhlmann, E. L., & Banaji, M. R. (2009). Understanding and using the implicit association test: III. Meta-analysis of predictive validity. *Journal of Personality and Social Psychology*, 97(1), 17–41.

Harrison, T. M., & Huberman, M. A. (2019). *Qualitative data analysis*. Sage Publications.

Hesselbein, F., & Goldsmith, M. (2009). *Leader to Leader Institute: SC assessment*. Wiley.

Jackson, S. E., & Ruderman, M. (1999). *Diversity in work teams: Research paradigms for a changing workplace*. American Psychological Association.

Koustelios, A. D., Bagiatis, K., & Tsigilis, N. (2021). The role of diversity and inclusion practices in employees' job satisfaction and turnover intentions, *Journal of Business Research*, 128, 244–253, https://doi.org/10.1016/j.jbusres.2021.02.019

Krammer, S., Kammerlander, N., & Schondelmayer, A. (2019). The effect of diversity climate on employees' attitudes: An organizational perspective. *Journal of Business Research*, 98, 365–375.

Landy, F. J., & Conte, J. M. (2016). *Work in the 21st century: An introduction to industrial and organizational psychology* (5th ed.). Wiley.

Li, Y., Lu, Y., & Liu, J. (2020). Employee attitude towards corporate social responsibility: A study of social media sentiment analysis. *Technological Forecasting and SC*, 154, 119985.

Lippitt, R., Fox, R., & Dutt, N. (1969). *Social change impact assessment: A guide to SCIA*. Holt, Rinehart and Winston.

Mallette, L. A., & Wilson, M. G. (2019). A review of diversity and cultural competency training for organizational leaders: Implications for best practices in health care. *Journal of Healthcare Leadership*, 11, 109–121.

McAdam, D., Tarrow, S., & Tilly, C. (2001). *Dynamics of contention*. Cambridge University Press.

McLeod, S. (2018). SC. Simply psychology.

Meadows, D. H. (2008). *Thinking in systems: A primer*. Chelsea Green Publishing.

Meyer, J. W. (2010). World society, institutional theories, and the actor. *Annual Review of Sociology*, 36, 1–20.

Papalia, D. E., Feldman, R. D., & Martorell, G. (2016). *Experience human development* (13th ed.). McGraw-Hill Education.

Pinder, C. C., & Harlos, K. P. (2001). Employee attitudes and organizational performance: An historical perspective and review of the literature. In C. L. Cooper & I. T. Robertson (Eds.), *International review of industrial and organizational psychology* (Vol. 16, pp. 193–246). Wiley.

Pless, N. M., & Maak, T. (2004). Building an inclusive diversity culture: Principles, processes and practice. *Journal of Business Ethics*, 54(2), 129–147.

Robbins, S. P., Judge, T. A., & Millett, B. (2020). *Organizational behavior* (18th ed.). Pearson.

Roccas, S., Klar, Y., & Liviatan, I (2006). The impact of culture and SC on work values. *Journal of Psychology, 140*(5), 421–437.

Roethlisberger, F. J., & Dickson, W. J. (1939). *Management and the worker.* Harvard University Press.

Schneider, A. L., Teske, P., & Mintrom, M. (1995). *Public policy: Theories, models, and concepts.* Duxbury Press.

Senge, P. (2006). *The fifth discipline: The art and practice of the learning organization.* Doubleday/Currency.

Shadish, W. R., Cook, T. D., & Campbell, D. T. (2002). *Experimental and quasi-experimental designs for generalized causal inference.* Houghton Mifflin Company.

Smith, J. (2018). The evolution of assessment tools in workforce settings. *Journal of Applied Psychology, 104*(3), 345–357. https://doi.org/10.1037/apl0000243

Vanclay, F., Esteves, A. M., & Franks, D. M. (2015). Social impact assessment: The state of the art. *Impact Assessment and Project Appraisal, 33*(1), 58–69. https://doi.org/10.1080/14615517.2012.660356

Weber, M. (2015). *The protestant ethic and the spirit of capitalism.* Routledge. (Original work published 1904).

Chapter 4

Step 3: Examining the Social Context of the Organization

Christina Pettey

Case Study: Nike

Organizations interested in creating social impact need to begin by understanding the organization's current impact on their own employees. The American Sociological Association has cited research that shows "corporate culture may affect individual-level decision-making in common ways." This means the social context within an organization spreads from employees out into their families and from those individuals into communities. This chapter explores how to assess the current social context of an organization—how words and actions are interpreted and what behaviors are valued.

In the fall of 2018, Nike released an advertising campaign to celebrate the 30th anniversary of their slogan "Just do it." The campaign featured NFL quarterback Colin Kaepernick, who had recently made headlines by kneeling during the national anthems during the 2016 season in protest of racial injustice and police brutality. After the 2016 season, Kaepernick never played in the NFL again. Nike's ad shows a monochromatic close-up of Kaepernick's face overlaid by the statement, "Believe in something. Even if it means sacrificing everything." Nike's executives knew that the ad would reach a highly polarized audience. They researched the expected response of their target audience, and they took a calculated risk to highlight Kaepernick's social activism (Cohen, 2020).

DOI: 10.4324/9781003439714-4

This isn't the only time Nike's advertising team has taken a stance on social issues (Tyler, 2018). The year prior they had released an "Equality" campaign with prominent black athletes promoting equal opportunity both in sports and in the world (Campaigns of the World, 2017). In 2020 after the murder of George Floyd, Nike posted a video (Nike, 2020) of statements in white letters on a black background, following the Black Lives Matter design. The text reads, "For once, don't do it. Don't pretend there's not a problem in America. Don't turn your back on racism. Don't accept innocent lives being taken from us. Don't make any more excuses. Don't think this doesn't affect you. Don't sit back and be silent." In 1995, they released an ad featuring runner Ric Muñoz, who was openly gay and HIV-positive. Nike has taken on gender in sports with the "If you let me play" ad campaign in 1995 and again in 2012 on the anniversary of Title IX.

While many companies want to take a stance on social issues as Nike does, not every organization is prepared to weather the response that will come externally. While some of Nike's ability to speak out relates to the strength of the company's market position, much of it is related to how well the company is internally prepared to support this activism and ensure that their actions align with their public statements about promoting diversity and inclusion.

The primary focus of this chapter is to assist readers in identifying the best assessment strategies for understanding their organization's climate by understanding the characteristics of Culturally Responsive and Equity Minded Leadership and Organizations and Leaders and how these characteristics are a prequel to developing an effective culturally responsive assessment of the workplace environment. Specifically, readers can identify key factors and barriers that influence the achievement of Culturally Responsive and Equity Minded Organizations and Leadership. Next, readers can identify and develop crucial assessment strategies that provide the representative context of organizational climate. Readers learn proven techniques and practices for assessing the views, attitudes, and sentiments of stakeholders at all levels of the organization.

What Does the Research Say?

Definition of Social Context

Social context can be thought of as the lens we look through when taking in information and processing it. It impacts our perceptions, feelings, interpretations, and reactions. In 2001 the American Journal of Public

Health published a letter referencing an increased interest in how social environments influence health. They proposed a definition for "social environment":

> Human social environments encompass the immediate physical surroundings, social relationships, and cultural milieus within which defined groups of people function and interact. ... Social environments can be experienced at multiple scales, often simultaneously, including households, kin networks, neighborhoods, towns and cities, and regions. Social environments are dynamic and change over time as the result of both internal and external forces.
>
> **(Barnett & Casper, 2001)**

Since then, the concepts of social environment and social context have been researched across fields as diverse as behavioral therapy, public health, public policy, criminal behavior, communication, environmental science, and education.

Impact of Social Context on Diversity and Inclusion Efforts

Frame the social context through the moral lens of the organization. Riley and Burke (1995) referred to a "shared meaning structure" that develops within small groups as a tool for interpretation of verbal and non-verbal communication. Burke et al., (2009) found connections between social context and individual behaviors in healthcare decisions.

Looking from a moral lens, Butterfield, Treviño, and Wier (2000) point out that individual moral awareness impacts behavior, and for this text, the individual equals the organization. Carter (2010) points out that behavior is not only impacted by the individual's morals, but that group membership is also an important input into the behavioral outcome.

Dillard, Rigsby and Goodman (2004) proposed a theory for creating changes in an organizational context, which can better position the organization to support the ability for the organization to impact social issues. As the complexity of social issues requires partnerships between many groups and organizations, Sakarya et al. (2012) measured how social enterprise and business could come together to benefit the organization and for extracurricular community involvement in various situations.

They found that engagement in social change practices has done tremendous wonders for the morale of the organization. While a single organization cannot significantly affect a widespread social issue, they found that they did "create[d] changes in the lives of individuals and families and thus affected the community and institutions." Their efforts also improved relationships between the company and the community in which the organization resides.

To push this thought further, Rest (1986) and Forte (2005) sought to examine how individuals move from moral awareness to moral actions. Rest proposed a four-stage process based on the below-modified steps:

1. Awareness
2. Judgement
3. Recognition of intent
4. Engagement

We propose a similar approach that can be used for assessment of the organization's readiness for action. When reviewing a process for engaging in social change, based on researched information, these initial steps can be taken to support engaging the organization in social change:

1. Research the Social Issue
2. Discuss with various Resource Groups
3. Create a position of engagement
4. Define what action should look like
   a. Engage in community action
   b. Create sustainable actions

Other examples are presented in this chapter of how these steps can be carried out within the organization to secure proper engagement.

Putting It into Practice

For organizations wanting to expand their impact on diversity and inclusion in society, it is critical to understand the organization's internal social context. Organizations are part of a bigger social system that is shaped by social norms, values, and beliefs. By understanding and shaping its own social context, an organization can contribute to broader societal changes.

For example, an organization that prioritizes diversity and inclusion can serve as a model for other organizations in the same industry or sector. This can lead to a gradual shift in industry norms and practices, which can contribute to a broader shift in society toward greater diversity and inclusion. As more organizations adopt similar practices, they can collectively work toward reducing social inequalities and promoting greater inclusivity in society.

An organization that prioritizes diversity and inclusion in its internal social context can also influence its external stakeholders such as customers, suppliers, and community members. By demonstrating a commitment to diversity and inclusion, an organization can attract more diverse stakeholders and foster stronger relationships with the broader community. This can lead to positive brand recognition and reputation, which can further contribute to societal changes toward greater diversity and inclusion.

Determining whether an organization's internal social context will support positively influencing external diversity and inclusion efforts requires a comprehensive assessment of the organization's culture, policies, practices, and leadership. This can be done through auditing policies and practices, assessing leadership commitment, measuring employee engagement, and reviewing external relationships. Use the tool shown in Exhibit 4-1 to document your findings as you assess your organization's social context.

Step One: Review for Characteristics of Culturally Responsive and Equity Minded Leadership

It is important for organizational leadership to be a part of shaping the social context for diversity and inclusion because they play a critical role in creating and sustaining a culture of diversity, equity, and inclusion within their organizations.

Organizational leadership sets the tone for the organization's culture and values, and their actions and behaviors are often emulated by others within the organization. By promoting diversity and inclusion (or other social issues), organizational leadership can create a culture that values and celebrates diversity and fosters an environment where all employees feel valued and included. Organizations that promote diversity and inclusion often have applicants drawn to the company because of their culture, helping increase successful recruiting. Organizational leadership committed to diversity and inclusion or other social issues can enhance the organization's reputation and brand.

Step 1: Review for characteristics of culturally responsive and equity minded leadership	
Assess leadership behaviors related to accountability, resources, support of scope, and external statements.	
Areas of misalignment	**Action plan**

Step 2: Conduct a diversity and inclusion audit	
Review policies and procedures, recruitment and hiring practices, compensation and benefits, and employee retention.	
Areas of misalignment	**Action plan**

Step 3: Assess leadership commitment	
Review the organization's mission and values, how leaders communicate internally, their level of involvement in the change effort, the organization's historical success with change efforts, and gather feedback from employees.	
Areas of misalignment	**Action plan**

Step 4: Measure employee satisfaction and engagement	
Collect feedback from employees regarding areas of improvement, progress toward goals, effectiveness of initiatives, and areas of strength.	
Areas of misalignment	**Action plan**

Step 5: Review external partnerships and collaborations	
Review partnership criteria, partner demographics, partner policies and practices, the impact of current partnerships, and stakeholder feedback.	
Areas of misalignment	**Action plan**

Exhibit 4-1   Internal assessment for social context.

Use this tool as a guide to walk through areas of your organization's social context, identify areas that do not currently align with your desired impact, and begin action plans for those areas.

Conversely, if leadership actions are not in alignment with the espoused values of diversity and inclusion, employees in the organization will interpret that the statements are only lip service and not actual expectations within the organization.

1. *Accountability*: Organizational leaders have the responsibility and authority to hold people accountable for their actions and behaviors related to diversity and inclusion. They must establish clear expectations and consequences for behaviors that are not aligned with the organization's values and ensure that all employees are held to the same standards. This includes holding managers accountable for upholding these expectations and consequences in their groups.
2. *Resources*: Leadership should provide the resources and support necessary for diversity and inclusion efforts to succeed. They can allocate funding, provide training and development opportunities, and establish policies and practices that promote equity and social justice.
3. *Scope support*: They should provide time and support for managers and employees participating in training or service activities that align with diversity and inclusion efforts.
4. *External statements*: Any external statements made by organizational leaders should reflect the company's commitment to diversity and inclusion. Within the industry and their own social circles, leaders should use their influence to advocate for diversity and inclusion issues, partner with community organizations, and contribute to thought leadership on social justice issues.

Step Two: Conduct a Diversity and Inclusion Audit

Comprehensively review the organization's policies, practices, and culture to identify any areas that may pose barriers to diversity and inclusion. This audit can help identify any unconscious biases or practices with disparate impact that need to be addressed.

Begin by defining the audit's scope, including the areas of the organization that will be assessed. Collect data through surveys, focus groups, interviews, or document reviews. Then analyze the data to identify patterns and trends related to diversity and inclusion in the organization. This can involve looking at data related to employee demographics, diversity training, and diversity and inclusion initiatives.

1. *Policies and procedures*: Review written policies and procedures, particularly personnel policies and procedures, for disparate impact on certain groups. Look for policy language or regular practices that affect different people in different ways,

2. *Recruitment and hiring practices*: Collect data on the organization's diversity and inclusion practices, policies, and culture. This can be done through surveys, focus groups, interviews, and document reviews.

3. *Compensation and benefits*: Analyze the data to identify patterns and trends related to diversity and inclusion in the organization. This can involve looking at data related to employee demographics, diversity training, and diversity and inclusion initiatives.

4. *Employee retention*: Identify any gaps or areas for improvement in the organization's diversity and inclusion practices, policies, and culture. This can involve looking at areas such as recruitment and hiring practices, employee retention, and the effectiveness of diversity and inclusion training.

Step Three: Assess Leadership Commitment

Evaluate the level of commitment of the organization's leadership to diversity and inclusion efforts, both formally and informally.

1. *Review the organization's mission and values*: Review the organization's written value statements to determine if they align with the change you are proposing. Look for any statements or commitments related to diversity, equity, and inclusion, and determine if they are reflected in the organization's actions.

2. *Observe how leaders communicate internally*: Observe how leaders communicate about the change. Look for clear and consistent messaging about the importance of the change and how it aligns with the organization's mission and values. Pay attention to whether leaders are actively promoting the change or simply going through the motions.

3. *Evaluate the level of involvement*: Evaluate the level of involvement of leaders in the change effort. Look for signs that leaders are engaged in the effort, such as participating in planning meetings, allocating resources, and setting goals and objectives.

4. *Review the organization's track record*: Review the organization's historical success with similar changes. Look at past initiatives related

to diversity, equity, and inclusion, and evaluate the level of commitment and follow-through by leaders.

5. *Gather feedback from employees*: Gather feedback from employees about leadership commitment to the change effort. Use surveys, focus groups, or interviews to gather feedback on how leaders are communicating about the change and whether they are supporting it.

Step Four: Measure Employee Satisfaction and Engagement

Collect feedback from employees about their experiences with diversity and inclusion in the workplace. This feedback can provide insights into the effectiveness of the organization's diversity and inclusion efforts and help identify areas for improvement. Asking for employee feedback on diversity and inclusion efforts can also increase employee engagement and involvement in the change process. By giving employees a voice and showing that their feedback is valued, organizations can build trust and foster a culture of inclusion.

1. *Identify areas of improvement*: Employee feedback can help to identify areas where the organization's diversity and inclusion efforts may fall short. For example, employees may provide feedback about a lack of diversity in hiring or promotion practices, or they may report experiencing discrimination or harassment.
2. *Measure progress*: Employee feedback can help to measure progress toward diversity and inclusion goals. By asking employees about their perceptions of the organization's culture, policies, and practices, organizations can track progress over time and identify areas where additional efforts may be needed.
3. *Assess effectiveness of initiatives*: Employee feedback can also provide insight into the effectiveness of specific diversity and inclusion initiatives. For example, an organization may implement unconscious bias training and gather feedback from employees to assess whether the training was effective in promoting awareness and reducing bias.
4. *Identify areas of strength*: Employee feedback can also help to identify areas of strength in the organization's diversity and inclusion efforts. For example, employees may provide positive feedback about the organization's commitment to promoting diversity and inclusion or about specific initiatives that have been effective.

Step Five: Review External Partnerships and Collaborations

Evaluate the organization's external partnerships and collaborations to determine whether they align with the organization's commitment to diversity and inclusion.

1. *Review partnership criteria:* Review the criteria used to evaluate potential partnerships and collaborations. Look for criteria related to diversity, equity, and inclusion, such as a commitment to promoting diverse leadership or a track record of supporting underrepresented communities.
2. *Examine partner demographics:* Examine the demographics of the organization's current partners. Look for partners that reflect the diversity of the communities the organization serves and those with a track record of promoting diversity and inclusion.
3. *Assess partner policies and practices:* Assess the policies and practices of potential partners. Look for partners that have policies and practices that align with the organization's values, such as anti-discrimination policies, inclusive hiring practices, and diverse leadership.
4. *Evaluate the partnership's impact:* Evaluate the impact of the partnership on diversity and inclusion efforts. Look for partners with a proven track record of promoting diversity and inclusion and with measurable outcomes related to their efforts.
5. *Solicit feedback from stakeholders:* Solicit feedback from stakeholders, such as employees, customers, and community members, about the organization's partnerships and collaborations. Use surveys, focus groups, or interviews to gather feedback on whether the partnerships align with the organization's diversity and inclusion goals.

Next Steps

Based on the findings of the reviews of these four areas, develop an action plan to address any gaps or areas for improvement in the organization's internal social context. The action plan should include specific goals, strategies, and timelines for achieving greater diversity and inclusion both internally and externally. Metrics for long-term monitoring should also be established.

If your organization's internal social context is strong, it is more likely to support external social change efforts and contribute to a more equitable and inclusive society. You can leverage your organization's internal social context by utilizing the relationships, resources, and expertise within the organization to promote diversity and inclusion in the broader community.

Look for opportunities to partner with community organizations working to promote diversity and inclusion in the community. By building relationships with these organizations, organizations can leverage their expertise and resources to develop programs and initiatives responsive to the needs of the community. This might include encouraging employees to volunteer and engage in community service activities that promote diversity and inclusion, which will help employees develop a better understanding of the needs and experiences of diverse communities and can help build relationships with community members and organizations. Leverage the expertise of employees to promote thought leadership on diversity and inclusion issues. By encouraging employees to publish articles, speak at conferences, and participate in other thought leadership activities, organizations can increase their visibility and influence in the community.

Implement the action plan and monitor progress toward achieving the goals and objectives. This can involve conducting follow-up audits, surveys, and focus groups to monitor progress and identify areas for further improvement. Remember that cultural changes take time and often progress in small ways. It will be important to regularly review the initial targets and assess whether additional action should be taken to continue progress or realign toward the goals.

Chapter Summary

Beginning by assessing your organization's internal social context will ensure that external efforts to create social impact will be supported and enhanced by the organization's leadership and employees. This is an ongoing process that requires continuous assessment, feedback, and improvement to ensure that the organization remains committed to diversity and inclusion.

- Organizations leaders are looking to support social justice efforts must consider their internal social context before taking the next steps.
- Culturally responsive and equity-minded leadership is required for a strong social context that will support external social efforts.
- Assessments of your organization and those involved will help you understand how to prepare your organization and improve the social context.

References

Barnett, E., & Casper, M. (2001). A definition of "Social environment". *American Journal of Public Health*, *91*(3), 465.

Burke, N. J., Joseph, G., Pasick, R. J., & Barker, J. C. (2009). Theorizing social context: Rethinking behavioral theory. *Health Education & Behavior*, *36*(5_suppl), 55S–70S. https://doi.org/10.1177/1090198109335338

Butterfield, K. D., Treviño, L. K., & Weaver, G. R. (2000). Moral awareness in business organizations: Influences of issue-related and social context factors. *Human Relations*, *53*(7), 981–1018.

Campaigns of the World. (2017, February 15). *Nike | Equality* [Video]. YouTube. https://www.youtube.com/watch?v=DWsUrMfDaG4&t=85s

Carter, M. J. (2010). Examining the Social Context in Identity Theory. UC Riverside. ProQuest ID: Carter_ucr_0032D_10200. Merritt ID: ark:/13030/m56q1z2b. https://escholarship.org/uc/item/8nd0t970

Cohen, S. (2020, May 31). 'For once, don't do it': The powerful idea behind Nike's new Anti-Racism Ad. *Forbes*. https://www.forbes.com/sites/sethcohen/2020/05/30/for-once-dont-do-it---the-powerful-idea-behind-nikes-new-anti-racism-ad/?sh=527bb9042fdb

Dillard, J. F., Rigsby, J. T., & Goodman, C. (2004). The making and remaking of organization context: Duality and the institutionalization process. *Accounting, Auditing & Accountability Journal*, *17*(4), 506–542. https://doi.org/10.1108/09513570410554542

Forte, A. (2005). Locus of control and the moral reasoning of managers. *Journal of Business Ethics*, *58*, 65–77, https://doi.org/10.1007/s10551-005-1387-6

Nike [Nike]. (2020, May 29). Let's all be part of the change [Video attached]. Twitter. https://twitter.com/Nike/status/1266502116463370241

Rest, J. R. (1986). *Moral development: Advances in research and theory*. Praeger.

Riley, A., & Burke, P. J. (1995). Identities and self-verification in the small group. *Social Psychology Quarterly*, *58*, 61–73.

Sakarya, S., Bodur, M., Yildirim-Öktem, Ö., & Selekler-Göksen, N. (2012). Social alliances: Business and social enterprise collaboration for social transformation. *Journal of Business Research*, *65*(12), 1710–1720. ISSN 0148-2963, https://doi.org/10.1016/j.jbusres.2012.02.012.

Tyler, J. (2018, September 7). Nike's Colin Kaepernick ad isn't the first time the brand's commercials have made a social statement. *Insider*. https://www.businessinsider.com/nike-ads-make-social-statements-2018-9

Chapter 5

Step 4: Engaging Employees as Agents of Social Change

Melissa Walker

Case Study: The Salesforce—A New Model of Philanthropy

In the bustling heart of San Francisco, Salesforce has been redefining corporate philanthropy. Founded on the belief that businesses can be powerful platforms for social change, Salesforce introduced the 1-1-1 model of philanthropy. This innovative approach commits 1% of the product, 1% equity, and 1% of employees' time to community service.

Salesforce's philanthropy extends beyond mere donations. Employees are encouraged to volunteer, and the company supports various community initiatives, from education to homelessness. The impact is twofold: communities benefit from the resources and expertise, and employees find a deeper connection to their work and purpose.

Unilever: Sustainability as a Business Strategy

Unilever's journey towards social impact takes a different path. With its Sustainable Living Plan, Unilever aims to make sustainable living commonplace. The plan focuses on improving health and well-being, reducing environmental impact, and enhancing livelihoods.

Unilever's commitment to sustainability is not a side project but an integral part of its business strategy. From sourcing raw materials responsibly to reducing waste in production, every aspect of the business aligns with the broader social and environmental goals. The result is a brand that

DOI: 10.4324/9781003439714-5

stands for more than just consumer goods; it represents a commitment to a better future.

The Intersection: Two Paths, One Goal

While Salesforce and Unilever have distinct approaches, they share a common goal: leveraging business as a force for good. Salesforce's model emphasizes community engagement and personal connection, turning employees into ambassadors of change. Unilever focuses on systemic change, integrating sustainability into the fabric of its business operations.

The Problem Statement

The stories of Salesforce and Unilever illuminate the intricate relationship between employee engagement, corporate social justice (CSJ), and organizational success. How can companies foster a culture of engagement that aligns with social justice principles without compromising profitability? How can they empower employees as agents of positive change while maintaining alignment with broader business objectives? How can they innovate in the realm of CSJ without alienating traditional stakeholders?

These questions are not theoretical musings but urgent dilemmas for contemporary organizations. The answers require a profound understanding of each organization's unique context, culture, and goals, particularly in the domains of employee engagement and CSJ.

In the following chapter, we will probe these questions, gleaning insights from the real-world experiences of Salesforce and Unilever. We will explore the latest research, offer practical tools, and delineate actionable steps that organizations can follow to navigate this multifaceted terrain. From enhancing employee engagement to embracing CSJ, we will reveal the strategies that can transform businesses into catalysts for meaningful social change.

What Does the Research Say?

Corporate Social Responsibility (CSR)

Definition and Evolution

Corporate social responsibility (CSR) encompasses the economic, legal, ethical, and discretionary expectations that society has of organizations. Carroll's Pyramid of CSR (1991) provides a framework for understanding the different dimensions of CSR, from economic responsibilities to philanthropic efforts.

Strategic Importance

The evolution of CSR from a peripheral concern to a strategic priority reflects broader shifts in societal values and expectations (Garriga & Melé, 2004). Companies like Salesforce have integrated CSR into their core business strategies, recognizing its importance in building trust and reputation.

Global Perspectives

CSR practices vary across cultures and regions, reflecting different social norms, regulations, and stakeholder expectations. Research has explored the challenges and opportunities of implementing CSR in different contexts, including emerging markets (Visser, 2008).

Corporate Social Justice (CSJ)

Definition and Evolution

CSJ encompasses the economic, legal, ethical, and discretionary expectations that society has of organizations (Porter & Kramer, 2011). It goes beyond traditional CSR by focusing on systemic change and addressing underlying social inequalities (Senge et al., 2006). This approach recognizes that organizations have a responsibility not only to contribute positively to society but also to actively work towards social justice (Freeman et al., 2010). It emphasizes collaboration, transparency, and a commitment to long-term, sustainable change (Kaplan & Minton, 2012).

Diversity, Equity, and Inclusion (DEI)

Importance of DEI

DEI has become a central focus for many organizations, reflecting a growing awareness of the importance of diversity in driving innovation and performance (Cox, 1994; Herring, 2009).

Challenges and Opportunities

Research has explored the challenges and opportunities of creating inclusive workplaces. Topics include the role of leadership (Nembhard &

Edmondson, 2006), the impact of unconscious bias (Greenwald & Krieger, 2006), and the importance of organizational culture (Cox & Blake, 1991).

Case Studies

Companies like Unilever have implemented comprehensive DEI strategies, focusing on recruitment, retention, development, and engagement. These efforts reflect a commitment to creating a diverse and inclusive workplace that reflects the broader community.

Organization Development (OD)

Introduction to OD

Organization Development (OD) is a dynamic field that focuses on improving organizational effectiveness and employee well-being. It encompasses a wide range of practices, theories, and methodologies aimed at enhancing organizational performance.

Historical Perspective

Kurt Lewin's change management theory laid the foundation for modern OD practices (Lewin, 1947). Since then, various models and frameworks have emerged, such as Action Research, Appreciative Inquiry, and the Burke-Litwin Model (Cummings & Worley, 2014).

OD Interventions

Research has explored various OD interventions, including team building, leadership development, and organizational culture change. These interventions are designed to address specific organizational challenges and promote positive change.

Integration of CSR, CSJ, and DEI

The integration of CSR, CSJ, and Diversity, Equity, and Inclusion (DEI) into OD practices reflects a growing recognition of the importance of social and ethical considerations in organizational success.

Sustainability and Environmental Stewardship

Triple Bottom Line Approach

Sustainability goes beyond environmental concerns to include social and economic dimensions. The triple bottom-line approach emphasizes the interconnectedness of economic, social, and environmental goals (Elkington, 1997).

Sustainable Business Practices

Research has explored various sustainable business practices, including green supply chain management, eco-innovation, and sustainable marketing (Porter & Kramer, 2011).

Corporate Examples

Companies like Unilever have embraced sustainability, integrating it into their business strategies and operations. Their Sustainable Living Plan is a notable example of a comprehensive approach to sustainability that aligns with business goals.

Ethical Leadership and Governance

Ethical Leadership

Ethical leadership is critical to building trust and credibility in organizations. Research has explored the role of ethical leadership in shaping organizational culture (Brown, Treviño & Harrison, 2005) and its impact on employee behavior and performance (Treviño et al., 2003).

Governance Structures

The importance of governance structures in ensuring accountability and transparency has been a focus of research (Aguilera & Cuervo-Cazurra, 2004). Effective governance involves clear roles, responsibilities, and oversight mechanisms.

Corporate Scandals and Lessons Learned

The examination of corporate scandals, such as Enron and Volkswagen, has provided valuable insights into the importance of ethical leadership and governance. These cases highlight the potential consequences of ethical failures and the importance of robust governance structures.

The Intersection of OD, CSR, DEI, and Sustainability

Holistic Approach

The convergence of OD, CSR, DEI, and sustainability represents a holistic approach to organizational development and social impact. Scholars like Senge et al. (2008) have explored how organizations can become "learning organizations," continually adapting and evolving in response to social, environmental, and economic challenges.

Integration and Complexity

The integration of CSR, DEI, and sustainability into OD practices reflects a recognition of the complexity and interconnectedness of these issues. It requires a multidisciplinary approach that draws on insights from various fields, including management, psychology, sociology, and environmental science.

Conclusion

The literature on OD, CSR, CSJ, DEI, and sustainability offers a rich and multifaceted perspective on the challenges and opportunities facing organizations today. It highlights the importance of a holistic approach, recognizing the interconnectedness of social, environmental, and economic considerations. The experiences of companies like Salesforce and Unilever provide real-world examples, but the broader research landscape offers insights and guidance that can be applied across industries and contexts.

In the next section, we will explore how these insights can be put into practice, offering a step-by-step approach to implementing strategies that align with these principles.

Putting into Practice: Engaging Employees as Agents of Social Change

Step One: Understanding the Importance of Employee Engagement

1. **Recognize Employee Potential:** Acknowledge that employees are not just workers but potential change agents who can drive social transformation. Employees are the lifeblood of any organization, and their potential extends far beyond their job descriptions. They are individuals with unique perspectives, values, and passions that can be harnessed to drive meaningful social change. Recognizing this potential means seeing employees not merely as workers but as agents of transformation who can contribute to broader societal goals.

   Example: A company that encourages employees to volunteer in community projects not only fosters a sense of purpose but also leverages the diverse skills and passions of its workforce to make a tangible impact in the community.

2. **Align with Organizational Values:** Ensure that social change initiatives align with the organization's core values and mission, as seen in Salesforce's philanthropic efforts.

   Alignment with organizational values is crucial for the success of any social change initiative. When employees see that their efforts toward social change are in harmony with the company's mission and values, they are more likely to feel a sense of ownership and commitment.

   Example: Salesforce's 1-1-1 Model of Philanthropy: Salesforce, a global leader in CRM, has integrated philanthropy into its business model through the 1-1-1 approach. This model dedicates 1% of the product, 1% of equity, and 1% of employees' time to community service. By aligning social change initiatives with its core values, Salesforce has created a culture where employees are engaged in philanthropic efforts, contributing to causes they care about.

3. **Key Takeaways:**
   - **Empowerment:** Recognizing employees as change agents empowers them to take initiative and contribute to social change in meaningful ways.
   - **Alignment:** Ensuring that social change efforts align with organizational values creates a cohesive and supportive environment

where employees feel connected to the company's broader mission.

- **Engagement:** Fostering a culture of engagement in social change initiatives leads to increased job satisfaction, loyalty, and a positive impact on both the organization and society.

4. **Conclusion**

   Understanding the importance of employee engagement in social change is foundational to creating a culture where employees are motivated and empowered to contribute to societal transformation. By recognizing their potential and aligning social change initiatives with organizational values, companies like Salesforce (2021) have demonstrated that employee engagement is not just a buzzword but a strategic approach to leveraging human capital for the greater good.

Step Two: Creating a Culture of Engagement and Social Justice

1. **Foster a Sense of Purpose:** Help employees connect their daily work with broader social goals, such as sustainability, diversity, and community engagement.

   Creating a culture where employees feel a connection between their daily tasks and broader social goals fosters a sense of purpose and meaning. When employees understand how their work contributes to sustainability, diversity, or community engagement, they are more likely to be motivated and committed to their roles.

   Example: A company that emphasizes environmentally sustainable practices in its operations can help employees see how their individual efforts contribute to a larger goal of protecting the planet. This connection between daily tasks and broader social goals fosters a sense of purpose and engagement.

2. **Encourage Volunteerism and Community Involvement: Create opportunities for employees to volunteer and engage with local communities, as practiced by Unilever.**

   Encouraging employees to volunteer and engage with local communities not only benefits society but also enriches the workplace culture. By providing opportunities for community involvement, organizations can help employees develop new skills, build relationships, and feel a sense of accomplishment.

   Example: Unilever's Community Engagement Programs:
   Unilever, a multinational consumer goods company, has been a leader

in encouraging volunteerism and community involvement. Through various programs and partnerships, Unilever provides opportunities for employees to engage in projects that align with its commitment to sustainability, health, and well-being. These initiatives not only make a positive impact on communities but also foster a culture of social responsibility within the organization.

3. **Key Takeaways:**
   - **Purpose-Driven Culture:** Helping employees connect their work with broader social goals creates a purpose-driven culture where individuals feel a sense of meaning and fulfillment.
   - **Community Engagement:** Encouraging volunteerism and community involvement enriches the workplace culture and allows employees to contribute to causes they care about.
   - **Alignment with Corporate Values:** By aligning engagement and social responsibility initiatives with corporate values, organizations can create a cohesive and supportive environment that reflects their commitment to social good.

4. **Conclusion**

   Creating a culture of engagement and social responsibility is not just about implementing programs or initiatives. It's about fostering a sense of purpose, encouraging community involvement, and aligning these efforts with the organization's core values. Companies like Unilever have shown that a strategic approach to engagement and social responsibility can lead to a more fulfilled and engaged workforce, contributing positively to both the organization and society.

Step Three: Developing Psychological Safety

1. **Foster an Inclusive Environment: Create a workplace where employees feel safe to express their ideas, concerns, and identities without fear of judgment or retaliation.**

   An inclusive environment is one where all employees, regardless of their background, feel valued and respected. By fostering a culture of inclusion, organizations can create a safe space where employees feel comfortable expressing their ideas, concerns, and identities.

Strategies:

- **Diverse Representation:** Ensure that diverse perspectives are represented at all levels of the organization.

- **Inclusive Policies:** Implement policies that support flexibility, work-life balance, and the unique needs of different employee groups.
- **Supportive Leadership:** Encourage leaders to actively promote inclusivity and demonstrate empathy and understanding.

2. **Encourage Open Dialogue: Promote open and honest communication, allowing employees to discuss complex issues related to social change, identity, and intersectionality.**

   Open dialogue is essential for addressing complex and sensitive issues related to social change, identity, and intersectionality. By promoting open communication, organizations can create a space where employees feel empowered to share their thoughts and experiences.

Strategies:

- **Regular Forums:** Create regular forums or town halls where employees can discuss important topics openly.
- **Clear Communication Channels:** Establish clear channels for communication, ensuring that employees know how and where to express their thoughts.
- **Active Listening:** Encourage leaders and managers to practice active listening, validating employees' experiences and perspectives.

3. **Address Microaggressions and Bias: Implement training and policies to recognize and address subtle forms of discrimination and bias that can undermine psychological safety.**

   Microaggressions and subtle biases can have a significant impact on psychological safety. By recognizing and addressing these issues, organizations can create a more respectful and supportive environment.

Strategies:

- **Training Programs:** Implement training programs to educate employees about microaggressions and biases, and how to address them.
- **Clear Policies:** Establish clear policies that define unacceptable behaviors and provide guidelines for addressing them.
- **Support Systems:** Create support systems for employees who experience or witness microaggressions, ensuring that they have resources and avenues for reporting and addressing these issues.

4. **Conclusion**

   Developing psychological safety is a multifaceted process that requires intentional effort and commitment. By fostering an inclusive environment, encouraging open dialogue, and addressing microaggressions and bias, organizations can create a workplace where employees feel safe and empowered to engage as agents of social change. This approach aligns with the broader goals of engaging employees in social responsibility and creating a culture that supports diversity, equity, and inclusion.

Step Four: Exploring the Intersectionality of CSJ and Identity

1. **Recognize Diverse Perspectives: Understand that employees' identities and experiences shape their perspectives on social change and CSJ.**

   Employees' unique identities and experiences significantly influence their views on social change and CSJ. Recognizing and valuing these diverse perspectives can lead to more inclusive and effective CSJ initiatives.

Strategies:
- **Employee Surveys:** Conduct surveys to understand employees' perspectives on social change and CSJ, considering factors such as cultural background, gender, and personal values.
- **Inclusive Planning:** Involve employees from diverse backgrounds in the planning and execution of CSJ initiatives.
- **Ongoing Dialogue:** Maintain ongoing dialogue with employees to continuously understand and adapt to their evolving perspectives.

2. **Align CSJ Initiatives with Employee Identities: Create CSJ initiatives that resonate with diverse employee identities, such as gender, race, disability, and sexual orientation.**

   CSJ initiatives that resonate with employees' diverse identities can create a stronger sense of connection and engagement. By aligning CSJ efforts with the unique identities of employees, organizations can foster a more inclusive and impactful approach to social change.

Strategies:
- **Tailored Initiatives:** Design CSJ initiatives that reflect the specific interests and identities of different employee groups.

- **Collaborative Partnerships:** Partner with community organizations that align with the diverse identities and values of employees.
- **Transparent Communication:** Clearly communicate how CSJ initiatives align with and support diverse employee identities.
3. **Embrace Complexity:** Acknowledge that the intersection of CSJ and identity is complex and multifaceted, requiring nuanced approaches and continuous learning.

   The intersection of CSJ and identity is a complex and multifaceted area that requires a nuanced approach. Embracing this complexity means acknowledging there are no one-size-fits-all solutions and that continuous learning and adaptation are essential.

Strategies:

- **Continuous Education:** Provide ongoing education and training on the complexities of CSJ and identity, encouraging a deeper understanding and critical thinking.
- **Adaptive Strategies:** Develop adaptive strategies that can evolve with the changing landscape of CSJ and the diverse identities within the organization.
- **Reflective Practice:** Encourage reflective practice, allowing employees and leaders to continuously assess and refine their approach to CSJ and identity.

4. **Engaging Employee Resource Groups (ERGs)**

   ERGs, which are often organized around shared characteristics or experiences, can provide valuable insights into the needs and perspectives of diverse employee groups.

Strategies:

- **Collaborative Planning:** Involve ERGs in the planning and execution of CSJ initiatives to ensure alignment with the interests and identities of diverse employee groups.
- **Feedback Mechanism:** Use ERGs as a channel for continuous feedback on CSJ initiatives, ensuring that they remain relevant and effective.

5. **Foster a Culture of Inclusivity:**

   A culture of inclusivity creates a safe and welcoming environment where all employees feel valued and included. This fosters a sense of ownership and engagement in CSJ initiatives.

Strategies:
- **Inclusive Leadership:** Promote leadership practices that value diversity and foster an inclusive environment.
- **Recognition and Support:** Recognize and support the contributions of ERGs and individual employees to CSJ initiatives.

6. **Implementing Well-Run Mentoring Programs**

   Well-run mentoring programs can provide personalized support and guidance, enhancing employee engagement in CSJ initiatives.

Strategies:
- **Alignment with CSJ Goals:** Ensure that mentoring programs align with the goals of CSJ initiatives, providing support and guidance in areas related to social change.
- **Diverse Mentorship:** Encourage diverse mentorship pairings that reflect the multifaceted nature of CSJ and identity, fostering a richer understanding and collaboration.

7. **Conclusion**

   Exploring the intersectionality of CSJ and identity is a vital aspect of engaging employees as agents of social change. By recognizing diverse perspectives, aligning CSJ initiatives with employee identities, and embracing the complexity of this intersection, organizations can create more inclusive, resonant, and effective approaches to social responsibility.

Step Five: Navigating Obstacles and Nuances

1. **Anticipate Challenges:**

   Recognizing potential obstacles early when engaging employees as agents of social change is essential for several interconnected reasons. It allows for proactive planning, where organizations can develop strategies to address challenges before they become significant barriers. This foresight can include allocating resources, engaging stakeholders, or modifying plans to mitigate potential issues.

   The importance of early recognition also extends to risk mitigation. By understanding potential obstacles, organizations can assess and mitigate risks associated with social change initiatives, leading to more resilient and sustainable efforts. This understanding fosters a more meaningful engagement with stakeholders, including employees, communities, and other interested parties, fostering collaboration and support for social change initiatives.

One common obstacle is resistance to change. Research, such as studies by Oreg, Vakola & Armenakis (2011), has shown that resistance is a prevalent issue in organizational change efforts. Strategies to overcome this resistance include building awareness, providing clear communication, and involving employees in decision-making.

Another challenge is conflicting priorities, which can undermine social change efforts as employees may be torn between different goals. Works like those by Cameron and Quinn (2006) highlight this conflict, and strategies to address it include aligning social change initiatives with organizational values and individual goals to create coherence and support.

Lack of resources is also a common challenge, particularly in resource-limited settings, as noted by experts like Kotter (1996). Leveraging partnerships, seeking external funding, and optimizing existing resources are strategies that can mitigate this challenge.

Strategies:

- **Resistance to Change:** Identify potential resistance from employees or stakeholders and develop strategies to address concerns and build buy-in.
- **Conflicting Priorities:** Recognize that employees may have conflicting priorities and work to align social change initiatives with individual and organizational goals.
- **Lack of Resources:** Plan for potential resource constraints and develop strategies to leverage existing resources or seek external support.

2. **Address Ethical Dilemmas:**

Ethical considerations are central to social change efforts and require careful navigation. The intersection of ethics and social change is complex and multifaceted, touching on various aspects of organizational behavior, decision-making, and stakeholder engagement.

Understanding ethical frameworks is crucial, as social change initiatives often involve diverse stakeholders with different ethical perspectives and values. Research by Crane and Matten (2007) emphasizes the importance of ethical theories in guiding organizational behavior and decision-making.

One of the significant ethical dilemmas in social change efforts is balancing profit motives with social goals. This balance requires a nuanced understanding of the organization's mission and values and how they align with social change objectives. Works like those by Porter and Kramer on shared value highlight strategies to align business success with social progress.

Transparency and accountability also extend to ethical considerations in social change initiatives. Being open about goals, strategies, and outcomes fosters trust and credibility with stakeholders. The Global Reporting Initiative (GRI) standards provide guidelines for transparent reporting on sustainability and social responsibility.

Social change efforts often intersect with diverse cultures and communities. Ethical considerations in this context include respecting cultural norms and values, engaging with local communities, and avoiding unintended negative impacts. Research by Leung et al. on cultural intelligence emphasizes the importance of cultural sensitivity in global initiatives.

Legal compliance is closely tied to ethical considerations. Ensuring that social change initiatives comply with relevant laws and regulations is essential for maintaining integrity and avoiding legal risks. Works by legal experts like Bagley (2008) provide insights into the legal aspects of CSR.

Engaging employees ethically in social change efforts includes respecting their autonomy, providing opportunities for meaningful participation, and recognizing their contributions. Research on ethical leadership, such as studies by Brown et al., highlights the role of leaders in fostering ethical engagement.

- **Balancing Profit and Social Goals:** Explore potential conflicts between profit motives and social goals, and develop strategies to align and balance these interests.
- **Transparency and Integrity:** Foster a culture of transparency and integrity, ensuring that social change efforts are conducted ethically and responsibly.
- **Stakeholder Engagement:** Engage diverse stakeholders, including employees, customers, and communities, to ensure that ethical considerations are explored and addressed.

3. **Adapt to Changing Contexts:**

Social change efforts are dynamic and require ongoing adaptation to remain effective. The landscape of social change is ever-evolving, influenced by technological advancements, political shifts, economic fluctuations, and societal trends. Organizations engaged in social change must be agile and responsive to these changes to maintain relevance and impact.

The dynamism of social change efforts is evident in the way organizations must continually reassess their strategies and tactics. For example, the rise of social media has transformed how organizations engage with communities, requiring new approaches to communication and advocacy. Research by Kaplan and Haenlein (2010) highlights the strategic use of social media in social change campaigns.

Economic factors also play a significant role in shaping social change efforts. Economic downturns or shifts in funding priorities can affect the availability of resources, necessitating adjustments in strategies and goals. Studies by Mook and Quarter (2006) on social enterprise financing provide insights into navigating economic challenges in social change work.

Political changes can have profound effects on social change initiatives. Changes in government policies, regulations, or leadership can either facilitate or hinder social change efforts. Research on policy advocacy, such as works by Andrews and Edwards (2004), explores the interplay between politics and social change.

The cultural context is another dynamic factor in social change efforts. Understanding and adapting to cultural norms, values, and expectations is essential for effective engagement with diverse communities. Hofstede's (2001) research on cultural dimensions offers a framework for understanding cultural differences in social change work.

Technological innovation continually shapes social change efforts, offering new tools and platforms for engagement, collaboration, and impact measurement. The work by Christensen (1997) on disruptive innovation provides insights into leveraging technology for social change.

Finally, the internal dynamics of an organization, including leadership, organizational culture, and employee engagement, contribute to the adaptability of social change efforts. Research on adaptive leadership, such as the work by Heifetz and Linsky (2002), emphasizes the importance of leadership in navigating change.

Strategies:
- **Continuous Learning:** Foster a culture of continuous learning and adaptation, ensuring that social change initiatives remain responsive to new information and societal shifts.

- **Agile Approach:** Adopt an agile approach to social change efforts, allowing for flexibility and responsiveness to organizational changes or external factors.
- **Monitoring and Evaluation:** Implement robust monitoring and evaluation mechanisms to assess the effectiveness of social change initiatives and make necessary adjustments.

4. **Conclusion**

Navigating the obstacles and nuances of engaging employees as agents of social change requires a thoughtful and strategic approach. By anticipating challenges, addressing ethical dilemmas, and adapting to changing contexts, organizations can create more resilient and effective social change initiatives. This section provides a roadmap for navigating these complex dynamics, offering practical strategies and insights for organizations seeking to leverage employee engagement for social change.

Step Six: Implementing and Monitoring Social Change Initiatives

1. **Importance of Implementation and Monitoring:**

Implementing and monitoring social change initiatives is essential for engaging employees as agents of social change. This process involves setting clear goals, establishing metrics, and celebrating successes, which contribute to maintaining momentum and enthusiasm.

2. **Setting Clear Goals and Metrics:**
   - **Research:** Defining specific social change objectives aligned with the organization's mission and values is vital for success (e.g., Doran, 1981 on SMART goals).
   - **Strategies:** Utilizing tools like Balanced Scorecards or Key Performance Indicators (KPIs) can help to track progress (e.g., Kaplan & Norton, 1996).

3. **Monitoring and Celebrating Success:**
   - **Research:** Regularly reviewing progress and celebrating achievements fosters a positive organizational culture (e.g., Brun & Dugas, 2008 on employee recognition).
   - **Strategies:** Recognizing and rewarding contributions through formal recognition programs, public acknowledgments, or informal celebrations builds a sense of community and shared purpose.

4. **Conclusion:**

Implementing and monitoring social change initiatives require a thoughtful approach that includes setting clear goals, establishing relevant metrics, and celebrating successes. Research supports these elements, highlighting effective strategies for creating a supportive environment that encourages employees to become active agents of social change. By fostering a culture of clarity, accountability, and celebration, organizations can drive meaningful social transformation.

Employee Engagement Process Flowchart

A flowchart that outlines the step-by-step process for engaging employees as agents of social change. This could include stages like identifying opportunities, aligning with organizational values, fostering a sense of purpose, and monitoring success (see Exhibit 5-1).

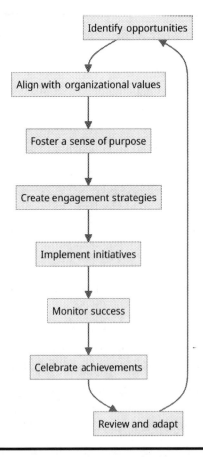

Exhibit 5-1 Employee Engagement Process Flowchart.

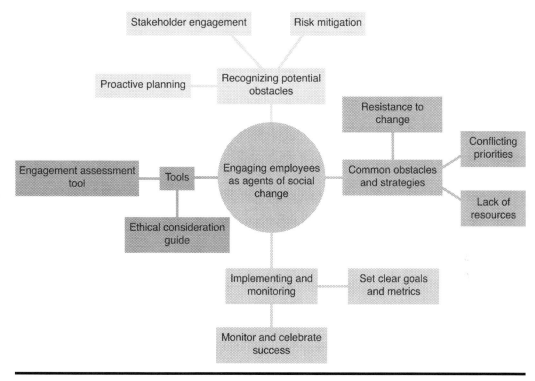

Exhibit 5-2   Obstacle Mitigation Mind Map.

Obstacle Mitigation Mind Map

A mind map that identifies common obstacles in engaging employees for social change and corresponding strategies to mitigate them. This can visually represent the interconnectedness of different challenges and solutions (see Exhibit 5-2).

Employee Engagement for Social Change Toolkit

Social Change Alignment Assessment

- **Purpose:** To identify how well the organization's social change initiatives align with its core values and mission.
- **Components:** A questionnaire or survey that assesses alignment, relevance, and employee perception of social change efforts.

Instructions:

1. **Distribute the Assessment:** Share this table with relevant stakeholders, including employees, management, and partners.

Section	Question	Rating (1–5)	Comments
Alignment with Core Values and Mission	How well do our social change initiatives align with our core values?		
	How do these initiatives reflect our organizational mission?		
	Are there any conflicts between our social change goals and other priorities?		
Employee Perception and Engagement	How aware are employees of our social change initiatives?		
	How engaged are employees in these initiatives?		
	What barriers prevent employees from participating in social change efforts?		
Impact and Effectiveness	What impact have our social change initiatives had so far?		
	How do we measure the success of these initiatives?		
	What improvements can be made to increase effectiveness?		
Ethical Considerations	How are ethical considerations integrated into our social change efforts?		
	Are there any ethical dilemmas or conflicts that need to be addressed?		
Future Directions and Adaptation	How adaptable are our social change initiatives to changing contexts and needs?		
	What future directions are planned for our social change efforts?		

Exhibit 5-3 Social change alignment assessment tool.

2. **Rate Each Question:** Respondents should rate their agreement or satisfaction with each statement on a scale of 1-5 (1 = Strongly Disagree, 5 = Strongly Agree).
3. **Provide Comments:** Encourage respondents to add comments or insights in the "Comments" column.
4. **Compile and Analyze Results:** Collect the completed assessments and analyze the results to identify trends, alignment, and potential challenges.
5. **Create and Share a Report:** Summarize the findings in a report, including recommendations for enhancing alignment and engagement.

This tool (see Exhibit 5-3) provides a structured and practical way to assess the alignment of social change initiatives within an organization. It can be printed or shared electronically and serves as a tangible resource for engaging employees as agents of social change.

Employee Social Change Agent Program

- **Purpose:** To empower employees to become active participants in social change initiatives.
- **Components:** A structured program that includes training, mentorship, volunteering opportunities, and recognition for employees actively involved in social change.

Employee Engagement and Social Responsibility Toolkit

Section	Activity/Initiative	Responsible Party	Timeline	Success Metrics	Notes
Fostering a Sense of Purpose	Identify and communicate how daily work connects to broader social goals.				
	Develop and share stories that illustrate the organization's impact on the community.				

(Continued)

Encouraging Volunteerism	Create opportunities for employees to volunteer in local communities.				
	Recognize and celebrate employee volunteer efforts.				
Building Inclusivity	Implement diversity and inclusion training.				
	Create Employee Resource Groups (ERGs) to support diverse perspectives.				
Promoting Ethical Behavior	Establish clear ethical guidelines related to social responsibility.				
	Conduct regular ethical audits to ensure compliance.				
Monitoring and Celebrating Success	Regularly review and celebrate achievements in social responsibility.				
	Share success stories internally and externally.				

Instructions:
1. **Identify Key Stakeholders:** Determine who will be responsible for each activity or initiative.
2. **Set Timelines:** Establish realistic timelines for implementation, monitoring, and review.
3. **Define Success Metrics:** Identify specific metrics or indicators that will measure success for each activity.
4. **Implement Initiatives:** Execute the planned activities and initiatives, ensuring alignment with organizational values and goals.

5. **Monitor Progress:** Regularly review progress against the defined success metrics and timelines.
6. **Celebrate and Communicate Success:** Recognize achievements and share success stories to maintain momentum and enthusiasm.

This toolkit provides a structured approach to fostering a culture of engagement and social responsibility within an organization. It can be customized to fit the unique needs and goals of the organization and serves as a practical guide for implementing and monitoring initiatives that connect employees with broader social goals.

Ethical Consideration Guide

- **Purpose:** To navigate ethical dilemmas and conflicts that may arise in social change initiatives.
- **Components:** A guide or checklist that outlines ethical considerations, potential conflicts, and best practices for ethical decision-making.

Ethical Consideration Guide

Ethical Principle	Description	Example Consideration	Action Steps	Responsible Party	Review Frequency
Transparency	Open and honest communication about goals, methods, and potential conflicts.	Are all stakeholders informed?	Communicate goals, methods, and any potential conflicts of interest.		
Integrity	Adherence to moral and ethical principles.	Are actions aligned with values?	Ensure alignment between organizational values and social change initiatives.		
Accountability	Responsibility for actions and decisions.	How are decisions made and evaluated?	Establish clear decision-making processes and hold individuals accountable.		

(*Continued*)

Respect for Diversity	Recognition and appreciation of diverse perspectives and needs.	Are diverse voices included?	Engage diverse stakeholders and ensure their perspectives are considered.		
Social Responsibility	Commitment to positive social impact.	What is the social impact?	Assess and monitor the social impact of initiatives, making adjustments as needed.		
Avoiding Harm	Minimizing potential harm to individuals and communities.	Could actions cause harm?	Identify potential risks and develop strategies to minimize harm.		

Instructions:

1. **Identify Ethical Principles:** Determine the key ethical principles that align with the organization's values and mission.
2. **Assess Ethical Considerations:** Evaluate each initiative or decision against the identified ethical principles, considering potential conflicts, impacts, and risks.
3. **Assign Responsibility:** Designate individuals or teams responsible for ensuring ethical compliance and decision-making.
4. **Establish Review Frequency:** Determine how often ethical considerations should be reviewed and assessed.
5. **Create Action Plans:** Develop specific action steps to address identified ethical considerations, ensuring alignment with organizational values.
6. **Monitor and Adjust:** Regularly review and adjust ethical considerations and action plans as needed, based on ongoing assessment and feedback.

This Ethical Consideration Guide provides a structured framework for navigating complex ethical dilemmas in social change initiatives. By following this guide, organizations can proactively address ethical considerations, align actions with values, and foster a culture of ethical responsibility. It serves as a valuable tool for organizations committed to ethical integrity in their efforts to engage employees as agents of social change.

Chapter Summary

When social change is not just a noble aspiration but a vital necessity, organizations are increasingly recognizing the role they can play in shaping a more just and equitable society. The journey toward engaging employees as agents of social change is multifaceted, complex, and filled with both opportunities and challenges.

This chapter has explored the intricate landscape of CSJ, delving into the strategies, tools, and ethical considerations that underpin successful social change initiatives. From fostering a culture of engagement and inclusivity to navigating the nuanced intersectionality of identity and social justice, the insights shared in this chapter provide a roadmap for organizations seeking to make a meaningful impact.

As we reflect on the key lessons and takeaways, note that the path toward social change is not linear or prescriptive. It requires continuous learning, adaptation, and a commitment to values that resonate with both the organization and its employees.

The following summary encapsulates the essential concepts and insights from the chapter, providing a concise overview and emphasizing the key takeaways for the reader. Whether you are a leader, a change agent, or an employee seeking to contribute to social transformation, these lessons offer valuable guidance and inspiration for your journey.

1. **Emphasizing Employee Engagement:** Recognizing employees as potential change agents is vital for driving social transformation. Engagement aligns with organizational values and fosters a sense of purpose, connecting daily work with broader social goals.
2. **Creating a Culture of Social Responsibility:** Organizations must foster inclusivity and create opportunities for open dialogue. This includes addressing microaggressions and biases to ensure psychological safety.
3. **Exploring Intersectionality of CSJ and Identity:** Understanding the complex relationship between social justice initiatives and diverse employee identities requires nuanced approaches and continuous learning.

4. **Navigating Obstacles and Ethical Considerations:** Anticipating challenges, addressing ethical dilemmas, and adapting to changing contexts are essential for resilient social change efforts.
5. **Implementing and Monitoring Initiatives:** Setting clear goals, monitoring progress, and celebrating success are key to maintaining momentum in social change initiatives.
6. **Utilizing Tools and Resources:** Practical tools such as the Ethical Consideration Matrix and engagement strategies can be helpful in putting these concepts into practice.
7. **Embracing CSJ:** Moving beyond traditional CSR to a focus on CSJ emphasizes systemic change, collaboration, transparency, and long-term commitment to addressing social inequalities.
8. **Recognizing the Dynamic Nature of Social Change:** Social change efforts are fluid and require ongoing adaptation, proactive planning, risk mitigation, and stakeholder engagement to remain effective.

References

Aguilera, R. V., & Cuervo-Cazurra, A. (2004). Codes of good governance worldwide: What is the trigger? *Organization Studies, 25*(3), 415–443.

Andrews, K. T., & Edwards, B. (2004). Advocacy organizations in the U.S. Political process. *Annual Review of Sociology, 30*, 479–506.

Bagley, C. E. (2008). *Winning legally: How managers can use the law to create value, marshal resources, and manage risk.* Harvard Business Press.

Benioff, M., & Southwick, K. (2009). *The business of changing the world: Twenty great leaders on strategic corporate philanthropy.* McGraw-Hill.

Brown, M. E., Treviño, L. K., & Harrison, D. A. (2005). Ethical leadership: A social learning perspective for construct development and testing. *Organizational Behavior and Human Decision Processes, 97*(2), 117–134.

Brun, J.-P., & Dugas, N. (2008). An analysis of employee recognition: Perspectives on human resources practices. *The International Journal of Human Resource Management, 19*(4), 716–730.

Cameron, K. S., & Quinn, R. E. (2006). *Diagnosing and changing organizational culture: Based on the competing values framework.* Jossey-Bass.

Carroll, A. B. (1991). The pyramid of corporate social responsibility: Toward the moral management of organizational stakeholders. *Business Horizons, 34*(4), 39–48.

Christensen, C. M. (1997). *The innovator's dilemma: When new technologies cause great firms to fail.* Harvard Business Review Press.

Cox, T. (1994). *Cultural diversity in organizations: Theory, research, and practice.* Berrett-Koehler.

Cox, T., & Blake, S. (1991). Managing cultural diversity: Implications for organizational competitiveness. *Academy of Management Executive, 5*(3), 45–56.

Crane, A., & Matten, D. (2007). *Business ethics: Managing corporate citizenship and sustainability in the age of globalization.* Oxford University Press.

Cummings, T. G., & Worley, C. G. (2014). *Organization development and change.* Cengage Learning.

Doran, G. T. (1981). There's a S.M.A.R.T. way to write management's goals and objectives. *Management Review, 70*(11), 35–36.

Elkington, J. (1997). *Cannibals with forks: The triple bottom line of 21st century business.* Capstone.

Freeman, R. E., Harrison J. S., Wicks A. C., Bidhan L., Parmar B. L., & de Colle S. (2010). *Stakeholder theory: The state of the art.* Cambridge University Press.

Garriga, E., & Melé, D. (2004). Corporate social responsibility theories: Mapping the territory. *Journal of Business Ethics, 53*(1–2), 51–71.

Global Reporting Initiative (GRI). (2020). *GRI standards.* https://www.globalreporting.org/standards/

Greenwald, A. G., & Krieger, L. H. (2006). Implicit bias: Scientific foundations. *California Law Review, 94*(4), 945–967.

Heifetz, R. A., & Linsky, M. (2002). *Leadership on the line: Staying alive through the dangers of leading.* Harvard Business Press.

Herring, C. (2009). Does diversity pay?: Race, gender, and the business case for diversity. *American Sociological Review, 74*(2), 208–224.

Hofstede, G. (2001). *Culture's consequences: Comparing values, behaviors, institutions, and organizations across nations.* Sage Publications.

Kaplan, A. M., & Haenlein, M. (2010). Users of the world, unite! The challenges and opportunities of social media. *Business Horizons, 53*(1), 59–68.

Kaplan, R. S., & Minton, B. (2012). *Understanding and managing organizational behavior.* Pearson.

Kaplan, R. S., & Norton, D. P. (1996). *The balanced scorecard: Translating strategy into action.* Harvard Business Press.

Kotter, J. P. (1996). *Leading change.* Harvard Business Review Press.

Lewin, K. (1947). Frontiers in group dynamics. *Human Relations, 1*(1), 5–41.

Mook, L., & Quarter, J. (2006). *Accounting for social value.* University of Toronto Press.

Nembhard, I. M., & Edmondson, A. C. (2006). Making it safe: The effects of leader inclusiveness and professional status on psychological safety and improvement efforts in health care teams. *Journal of Organizational Behavior, 27*(7), 941–966.

Oreg, S., Vakola, M., & Armenakis, A. (2011). Change recipients' reactions to organizational change: A 60-year review of quantitative studies. *The Journal of Applied Behavioral Science, 47*(4), 461–524.

Porter, M. E., & Kramer, M. R (2011). Creating shared value. *Harvard Business Review, 89*(1/2), 62–77.

Salesforce. (2021). Salesforce philanthropy cloud. https://www.salesforce.com/blog/what-is-philanthropy-cloud/

Senge, P. M., Laur, J., Schley, S., & Smith, B. (2006). *Learning for sustainability.* SoL.

Senge, P. M., Smith, B., Kruschwitz, N., Laur, J., & Schley, S. (2008). *The necessary revolution: How individuals and organizations are working together to create a sustainable world.* Doubleday.

Treviño, L. K., et al. (2003). Managerial leadership and ethical decision making: Influences on and consequences for long-term behavior. *Journal of Leadership & Organizational Studies, 10*(1), 24–36.

Unilever. (2021). Unilever sustainable living plan. https://www.unilever.com/planet-and-society/

Visser, W. (2008). Corporate social responsibility in developing countries. In Crane, A., et al. (Eds.), *The Oxford handbook of corporate social responsibility* (pp. 473–479). Oxford University Press.

Visser, W. (2011). *The age of responsibility: CSR 2.0 and the new DNA of business.* Wiley.

Werbach, A. (2009). *Strategy for sustainability: A business manifesto.* Harvard Business Press.

Chapter 6

Step 5: Building the Steps Toward Social Change

R. Adidi Etim-Hunting

Case Study: TOMS

Growing up in the United States in the 1990s, I often heard the phrase in the school cafeteria by teachers "Don't waste your food. There are people in 'Africa' that are hungry and could eat this." I never understood that phrase, as I could not see why anyone would want to eat what was passed as *spaghetti* cafeteria food. As a child, I lacked the words to articulate my feelings, but I recall feeling a mix of anger and discomfort whenever I heard such remarks. Many of my family members live on the continent of Africa, particularly Nigeria, and I could not help but feel that they were talking about them and me indirectly. The root of this mindset was based on a hyper-politicized, colonial, and racist belief that all people living on the continent of Africa lived in mud huts, wore grass skits, lived with lions, and were on the brink of starvation. I knew firsthand that this was not true, but a tiny fraction of doubt crept into my understanding, challenged by the conflicting tales I encountered in school and the media. The persistent chronicle that there are people, in a far distant place, who would be grateful for a fragment of my leftover cafeteria food, is a prevailing narrative that ensnares us all.

Organizations have used this tactic to pull on the heartstrings of their consumers, in the hopes that they will support an initiative that highlights the organization's prescribed corporate social responsibility. This can be

DOI: 10.4324/9781003439714-6

small, or large and built within the organization's very foundation like in the case of TOMS shoes. TOMS shoes use the business strategy known as a "double bottom line," meaning that their financial profit also benefits a social responsibility (Kozlowski, 2012). Their business model transcends mere footwear sales, as they ardently uphold their motto for every shoe sold, they donate a pair to children in developing countries.

For numerous U.S. consumers, particularly those who are not actively involved in global charities, TOMS shoes present a convenient route for them to experience a sense of altruism and contribute to the betterment of humanity. Despite the price of a pair of TOMS shoes often being significantly higher than the average footwear, many consumers willingly embraced the higher cost, fully aware that their purchase was for a noble cause (Kim, 2020). As a result, TOMS shoes became a highly sought-after and popular choice among consumers in the early 2000s (Kim, 2020).

While their strategy is rooted in altruism, it inadvertently reinforces the prejudiced belief that children in developing countries lack access to footwear. TOMS shoes double bottom line development intervention programs further supported that people, specifically children, were waiting for someone to "save" them from their current living situation. This can be observed in their early marketing techniques, often showcasing their philanthropic efforts. By prominently featuring seemingly joyful children dressed in slightly oversized and soiled garments, surrounded in an environment with dilapidated buildings you could see kids smiling and dancing around while wearing their TOMS shoes (Costello, 2012). This not only reinforced the deeply entrenched stereotype of extreme poverty, but it also subtly conveyed a message that merely providing TOMS shoes would magically solve all the challenges faced by these children.

In reality, researchers discovered that TOMS shoes had a detrimental impact on the local economies they were intended to benefit. One research team (Wydick, 2015) found evidence that in communities where TOMS shoes were donated, local shoemakers, frequently community members themselves, experienced a significant decline in sales, ultimately leading to the failure of their businesses. The local business economy proved unable to compete with a U.S.-based company that was distributing free products to their customers (Wydick, 2015). Their "buy-one, give one" model directly undermined the local economy's resilience and autonomy. In essence, TOMS shoes operated with an imperialistic mindset, presuming to know what communities needed and imposing an unnecessary and unwanted product on the people.

In addition to severely affecting the local economy, it fostered a concerning shift in the community's mentality toward charity, engendering a dangerous sense of reliance. A study revealed that 95% of the children in a town in El Salvador expressed satisfaction with TOMS shoes, and 77% utilized them at least three times a week (Wydick, 2015). However, a concerning trend emerged, as these children were more inclined to believe that their needs should be met by external sources rather than relying on their families to provide for them (Wydick, 2015). This resulted in a dependency on development intervention programs like TOMS shoes, perpetuating a cycle of reliance on external aid rather than fostering self-sufficiency within the community.

This case study does not suggest that organizations should forget or ignore the historical context and systemic practices that perpetuate health disparities, economic exploitation, educational decline, and other pressing social issues affecting our global community. Nor does it attempt to evade or deny the undeniable existence of people and regions in dire need of support. However, as organizations embark on building their path toward social change, they must adopt proactive and deliberate approaches, thoughtfully considering the implications of their actions and devising a well-structured plan to effect meaningful and sustainable transformation.

What Does the Research Say?

Social change can happen on multiple levels, which will be discussed later in the book (Chapters 8 and 11), however, this chapter will focus on building impetus for social change as an organization. As organizations are moving toward corporate social justice and activism, turning *moments* into *movements* is not an easy undertaking. Organizations have launched social change initiatives, only to encounter unintended consequences, such as the story for TOMS shoes in the case study above. Similar to any transformative process, the journey will encompass both moments of triumph and setbacks. For organizations to prioritize social responsibility, they must embrace adaptability and agility within their process toward building social change. Research affirms that organizations should be capable of adapting to evolving consumer preferences and shifting values, with such adaptations grounded in evidence-based research.

Some organizations engage in social change efforts merely to follow a megatrend, without going beyond superficial actions—a practice often referred to as "window dressing" or "box-ticking" (Stanley et al., 2019; Serafeim, 2020). While an organization's efforts appear commendable from an external perspective, eventually it will become evident that they were merely artificial gestures. In such scenarios, minimal progress was achieved, and the organization's operational approach remained stagnant. The research underscores the importance of social change and identifies factors that can propel organizations toward success or downfall in their change endeavors. Identifying these factors empowers organizations to navigate the implementation process with foresight and fortitude, fostering a higher likelihood of a positive lasting change.

Research has shown that corporations aligning their mission with social change initiatives can effectively enhance both the recruitment and retention of a diverse workforce, while simultaneously expanding their consumer base (Serafeim, 2020). Involving employees from diverse levels and positions of power within the organization, along with key stakeholders, in the mission development process, ensures the inclusion of varied perspectives and encourages collaboration across the organization (Rothwell, Ealy & Campbell, 2022; Serafeim, 2020). This holistic approach enhances the impact of social change initiatives, as it engenders active awareness among organization members. Utilizing it as a guiding force, organization members can direct their actions, initiatives, policies, talent management strategies, outreach, and various aspects of their work toward social change (Serafeim, 2020). For example, TOMS Shoes' mission of *buy-one-give-one* is synonymous with the organization's philanthropic and charitable design. The organization's mission resonates strongly with both employees and consumers, significantly shaping employees' decision-making process (Kim, 2020). The mission's pervasive influence fosters a sense of purpose-driven commitment among employees, contributing to a more aligned and impactful workforce experience (McPhail, 2020a). By aligning mission goals with social change initiatives, the organization's brand will become acknowledged within the community for its commitment to social change.

It is important to recognize that not all social change initiatives bring positive outcomes to the organization or the communities in which the organization operates. An organization should avoid assuming that it can unilaterally drive social change or dictate what the community perceives as its social change needs (Costello, 2012; Wydick, 2014; Kim, 2020). To foster genuine and impactful social change, research states that it is crucial to involve the community itself in the development and implementation of such initiatives (Wydick, 2015). Further, research (Rothwell et al., 2022) shows that when the community is removed from the development phases, there is a greater chance the efforts will fail as sufficient buy-in was not established. Additionally, the social change efforts should support a change the community needs and wants, rather than what an organization believes is needed (Frazer, 2008; Wydick, 2014, 2015). By engaging the community as active participants, the organization can build a collaborative and inclusive approach to drive meaningful social change.

The disconnect between the actual needs of the community and the organization's perceived understanding of those needs became a major headline for TOMS shoes, sparking widespread public attention (Kim, 2020). The organization faced scrutiny regarding the negative impact of its buy-one-give-one model on some local economies it aimed to support (Wydick, 2014; Kim, 2020). TOMS shoes received criticism for adversely impacting and, in certain instances, causing the collapse of local shoemaker businesses (Wydick, 2014, 2015). As families received free shoes from TOMS, they became less inclined to purchase shoes from their local small business owners (Wydick, 2014, 2015). This was devastating for those communities, as it took years for the economy to recover. As organizations begin their journey toward initiating social change, it is important to pose the question, "What is the wide-ranging impact on the community?". This inquiry extends not only to the local community but also encompasses the broader scope of influence the organization has on the public.

TOMS Shoes is one example of an organization that faced criticism for their efforts, but the same is true for other markets where organizations attempt to make a positive change in the community. One study showed that used clothing imports, similar to food aid, to developing nations had hurt the communities in which they were trying to support (Frazer, 2008). Throughout continental Africa, the impact was evident as this same study revealed a staggering 40% decrease in apparel production and a significant 50% decline in employment in the region between 1981 and 2000 (Frazer, 2008). These findings underscore the profound consequences of such practices on the region's economic landscape. Where food aid can harm local food producers, used-clothing imports can negatively impact the apparel industries in communities.

Corporations must prioritize the community and its needs, placing them at the forefront of their social change endeavors. Further, it is imperative to involve key community stakeholders in all stages, including the conception, planning, and implementation of these initiatives (McPhail, 2020b). By embracing a collaborative approach that actively engages the community, corporations can ensure that their social change efforts are both relevant and impactful to the community and its members.

As organizations contemplate their approach to making change with community members, they need to consider what is often referred to as the "rinse-and-repeat" method. This term refers to the phenomenon where organizations become entrenched in specific methods and ways of thinking, resulting in a culture where projects are consistently initiated using the same processes, often relying on past experiences or similarities to previous endeavors. As organizations face challenges and seek novel solutions, they often fall into the trap of applying the same past approaches, expecting different results.

While this approach can yield advantages in certain scenarios, it can prove detrimental to the social change process. This recurrent pattern hampers an organization's ability to truly address new problems and stifles opportunities for genuine growth and progress. Moreover, the repetitive nature of the "rinse-and-repeat" method may inadvertently lead organizations to impose their own perceived "best practices" onto communities without considering the perspectives of those communities. In contexts where individuals have long experienced marginalization, underrepresentation, and exploitation the "rinse-and-repeat" approach can be perceived as a form of imperialism and colonial oppression.

Therefore, research suggests the culture and the strategy toward social change must change from the current status quo. Organizations must understand that if they want change to occur there will be a new method of operation, through a DEIB lens. To cultivate a genuine drive toward social change, organizations must initiate a paradigm shift in both their mindset and actions, departing from their customary approach to the work (Emerson, 2022). The rhetoric "what we normally do" must be replaced with "this is where we are headed" and become the new cultural language of the organization. This strategy highlights the need for organizations to break away from the repetitiveness cycle toward a strategy that fosters innovation and adaptability.

In today's society, where individuals consider their phones and the internet essential for their existence, organizations find themselves under constant review. They are compelled to meet higher standards and expectations, as they are closely monitored by their consumers. Moreover, each new generation demands more from the organizations they choose to support, and they have no hesitation in publicly criticizing them through various communication channels and social media platforms.

Public opinion has further challenged organizations in their change efforts. It is no longer acceptable for organizations to engage in superficial efforts, reminiscent of past change efforts, to merely give the appearance of diversity, equity, and inclusion. Harvard Business Review (Serafeim, 2020) highlighted the COVID-19 pandemic and the Black Lives Matter movement in the United States as poignant examples when consumers demonstrated a heightened awareness of corporate responsibility. This point in time emphasized the importance of prioritizing societal needs over short-term profits. Actions such as announcing wage increases for employees while simultaneously cutting benefits, advocating for environmental causes while continuing practices that harm low-income areas through waste disposal, or establishing new offices in financially struggling cities without considering the consequences on residents, are no longer supported without public scrutiny.

Once the social change initiative is implemented, organizations can leverage evidence-based research to validate their efforts. There are various avenues through which organizations can obtain such research, and one common approach is through external evaluations conducted by reputable second or third-party entities. Studies indicate that organizations that undergo assessments and implement recommended changes are more likely to achieve their goals, make a meaningful impact on the community affected by the social change, and be perceived as authentic in their commitment to driving this change (McPhail, 2020b; Serafeim, 2020). By embracing evidence-based evaluations, organizations enhance their credibility and reinforce their genuine dedication to effecting positive social transformation.

In the case of TOMS Shoes, a study found that 95% of the kids in El Salvador liked the shoes, and 77% used them at least three times a week (Wydick, 2014, 2015). However, these kids were more likely to state that others outside their family should support their needs, rather than the family providing for their own needs, resulting in a more dependent relationship from development intervention programs like TOMS Shoes. Upon receiving this feedback, TOMS Shoes took decisive action and publicly shared the findings. Subsequently, they undertook a comprehensive overhaul of their model, placing greater emphasis on forging meaningful partnerships with local communities and distribution centers where their donated shoes were allocated (Wydick, 2014, 2015). This strategic shift enabled TOMS Shoes to align their efforts more closely with the specific needs and aspirations of the communities they sought to support.

Transforming an organization's mission and strategy demands a considerable amount of time and is a process that cannot be rushed.

Research findings indicate that organizational change is a gradual process, typically spanning a timeframe of 90 days or more to bring about impactful and enduring transformations within an organization (Kotter, 1995; McPhail, 2020c; Stanley et al., 2019). Some of this is due to systemic practices, procedures, and policies but much of it is due to resistance, internally and externally. This resistance can come from senior leaders, employees, shareholders, and more (McPhail, 2020c). Resistance to change is natural in organizations, as change can be perceived as different and brings about the fear of the unknown (Emerson, 2022). Research points out that establishing a strong connection between the mission and strategy with the business case is one of the most potent approaches to overcoming resistance (McPhail, 2020a; Serafeim, 2020).

Organizational leaders might pose questions such as "Is it feasible to effect positive social change within a community?" or "Are development programs effective and essential?" At times, leaders may even reach the conclusion that the effort required to mobilize stakeholders and managers toward the necessary transformative measures is strenuous, potentially discouraging an organization from pursuing the path of change. Experiencing doubt in the process is natural, and research highlights the importance of ongoing reflection (McPhail, 2020c). This reflective practice enables organizations to stay connected to their motivations and reinforce the alignment between their actions, strategy, and desired outcomes.

Creating a catalyst for change necessitates careful planning, a deep understanding of the ripple effects on both the organization and its communities, and a commitment to accountability for the outcomes, whether positive or negative. Strong leadership from the top is essential, empowering leaders at all levels to drive the change. Throughout this process, it is imperative to prioritize a nuanced understanding of the community's history, context, and diverse needs. The research underscores the importance of moving beyond superficial gestures toward genuine, impactful, and authentic change that benefits both the organization and the communities it serves.

Putting into Practice

One of the primary reasons behind the failure of social change efforts is the glaring absence of authentic preparation and thoughtful consideration of the change from the onset. This section will highlight key steps organizations should consider as they build their impetus toward social change.

Assessing Readiness

Before an organization can build its impetus for change, it must assess its readiness to embrace this transformation. It is crucial for organizations to do an introspective dive and determine if they are truly prepared to begin the journey toward social change. By conducting an assessment, the organization will be able to identify key indicators of their readiness for the change. Further, leaders will be able to determine if the ideal change efforts are achievable in the current internal environment of the organization (culture, employee satisfaction, workforce capability) and external environmental factors (global financial stability, societal pressure, political climate). There are several strategies to achieve this objective, but one effective approach is to conduct an initial assessment of the organization's readiness.

Exhibit 6-1 outlines a series of steps for organizations to thoughtfully contemplate as they embark on social change initiatives. As an organization navigate the change process, consider using the Assessment of Readiness Tool (Exhibit 6-2) to identify potential roadblocks and develop effective solutions.

Step One: Define Change

Prior to an organization's change effort, a crucial preliminary step is to establish a clear understanding of its present state and the desired destination. This initial stage is characterized by *defining change*, wherein organizations must comprehensively evaluate their current position and envision the desired future regarding social change efforts. It is imperative to involve not just senior leaders but also members throughout the organization in this process. This inclusive approach can involve activities such as conducting focus groups or distributing questionnaires. The fundamental objective of this step is to ensure that everyone within the organization is not only aware of the impending change but also has an opportunity

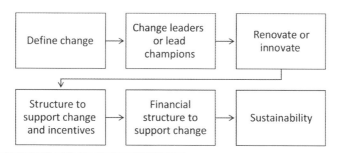

Exhibit 6-1   Assessment of the organization's readiness. (Created by Adidi Etim-Hunting.)

Assessment of Organization's Readiness Tool		
Directions: Use this tool to assess your organization's readiness to implement social change initiatives. Each step has prompts to help you think through where your organization currently sits.		
Step	*Prompt*	*Assessment*
Define Change	What is the desired state, what is the present state, and where are the gaps to achieve the desired state?	
Change Leaders/Lead Champions	Have you identified key individuals throughout the organization that can lead the change?	
Renovate or Innovate	Can you renovate current initiatives to meet your goals or will you have to innovate new initiatives?	
Evaluating the Organizational Structure	Does your organization currently have the structure and resources to support social change initiatives?	
Determining the Long-Term Sustainability	Will the organization be able to sustain the desired social change initiatives for a long duration (e.g., 10-20 years)? If not, what resources will be needed?	

Exhibit 6-2 Assessment of organization's readiness tool. (Source: Authors' original creation.)

to actively contribute to shaping a change they perceive as essential. Such inclusive engagement fosters greater stakeholder buy-in. Additionally, during this phase, leaders might discover that the organization is not yet primed for the anticipated change, necessitating potential interventions within the organizational culture as prerequisites for successful change implementation.

Step Two: Change Leaders or Lead Champions

After defining the desired change, the journey advances to a pivotal second stage: "Change Leaders" or "Leading Champions." This step underscores the importance of building change from within the organization, rather than depending solely on top leadership. The first task is to assess senior leaders' support for the social change initiative. Once confirmed, the focus shifts to identifying specific individuals to lead these efforts.

These change leaders should be individuals who have already garnered social and political influence within the organization but are not senior leaders. This approach ensures that change isn't imposed from the top-down but actively involves members from various organizational domains. Moreover, it is crucial to deliberate the inclusion of diverse voices in the change initiative at this stage. This encompasses a spectrum of potential stakeholders, ranging from external entities and employees across the organizational hierarchy to consumers. The organization must meticulously assess which additional stakeholders are relevant and to what extent their perspectives should inform the leadership and decision-making processes associated with change.

While senior leaders remain key supporters and champions of change, it is essential to have dedicated change leaders in place. The organization must evaluate the extent to which its leadership values the change and concurrently empowers individuals beyond senior leadership. If these conditions are not met, it may be advisable to postpone any change efforts until they can be properly determined and established.

Step Three: Renovate or Innovate

The third stage is "Renovate or Innovate." At this juncture, comprehensive knowledge of the organization's peer organizations in the realm of social change becomes indispensable. The organization must consciously choose between two approaches: whether to emulate the existing social change models adopted by their peers or venture into uncharted territory with fresh and innovative strategies for making a positive social impact.

While some may integrate this step into the actual change process, proponents argue that its significance is better realized during the readiness assessment. It is imperative for those spearheading the change initiative to gauge their organization's willingness to take calculated risks, which at times can be substantial, as opposed to seeking familiar and risk-averse paths. This decision profoundly influences the extent to which "Change Leadership" can push for new and, sometimes, financially intensive change efforts. This stage serves as an essential litmus test, revealing the organization's readiness and capacity to break away from past practices and the rinse-and-repeat model, ushering in a transformative and distinct trajectory to yield novel outcomes.

Step Four: Evaluating the Organizational Structure

The fourth step in assessing an organization's readiness for social change involves evaluating the organizational structure to ascertain its capacity to support the change endeavor. This goes beyond the mere presence of the *change leaders* and delves into the very fabric of the organization. The step seeks to determine whether the organization has the right individuals in positions to champion and facilitate the desired social change, or if there is a need to consider external consultants. Will current employees allocate a portion of their work hours to support this change effort, take leave from their regular responsibilities to participate, or volunteer their time? In the event that employees are called upon to commit their time or volunteer, what incentives are in place to encourage active and constructive engagement? Beyond the fundamental incentive of a salary, what motivators and attractors will inspire employees to contribute enthusiastically to the change effort?

This step also addresses the equity in selecting individuals to aid with the change effort and explores whether incentives are required. It is crucial to appraise whether the current organizational structure supports the selection and incentivization of employee contributions, ensuring an equitable approach. This step necessitates that organizations proceed with any form of change without evaluating their ability to establish a robust, structured foundation for creating, introducing, and guiding change initiatives.

Most change initiatives within an organization entail some form of financial backing. Even relatively modest social change endeavors carry associated costs, such as paying employees to allocate their time differently for leading the change. Organizations fully committed to their social change objectives must allocate resources to fund the change and provide operational budgets to empower these efforts. Depending on the chosen change and its scale, the budget can be substantial. Consequently, organizations should establish an initial budget with flexibility and sub-budgets for stakeholder engagement, community outreach, and other relevant aspects. Additionally, unforeseen external factors could influence the planned change, such as natural disasters affecting targeted communities. These budget discussions should involve the change leader, essential senior managers, and budget administrators. The objective is not to set a rigid budget but to establish a well-understood budget with adaptability to address specific circumstances defined by the change leader and support senior leadership. In cases where an organization lacks the required funds, it may need to modify or approach the change efforts differently. The key takeaway from this step is to facilitate open discussions regarding the financial requirements for supporting social change efforts and strategies to adapt the budget as needed.

Step 5: Determining the Long-Term Sustainability

The final stage of the assessment is a critical one, as it involves determining the long-term sustainability of the social change initiative. This step requires the organization to consider how they plan to sustain the change effort over time. While the organization may have assessed that everything is in place to initiate the social change effort, this step prompts them to think about what comes next once the change effort is underway and heading in a positive and stable direction.

Questions arise, such as: Does the organization intend to retain an external consultant indefinitely, or are they considering transitioning their existing staff to work permanently on this project? Alternatively, do they have a plan to hire full-time staff dedicated to overseeing this effort? The organization should also examine whether there will be allocated resources in future budgets to sustain the ongoing change efforts.

This step is of paramount importance because it involves contemplating the post-implementation phase. Organizations that have failed at this stage often do so due to a lack of planning for what happens after the change effort commences. The failure to prepare for this phase can lead to a reduction in the scope of the initial change effort. Consequently, the change effort is short-lived, creating the impression that it was executed without foresight and was merely a form of "window dressing" to enhance the organization's image with stakeholders.

Following a thorough assessment of an organization's readiness to embark on the change effort, they are poised to progress to the subsequent phases, encompassing planning and executing the change process. As the organization transitions into this critical phase, several pivotal factors warrant keen attention; Align with Mission and Goals, Define and Include the Community, Planning Ahead, Commitment to Transparency and Account for Flexibility, Resting and Organizational Doubt, and Keeping Momentum. These factors are not only vital considerations before initiating the change but also remain essential throughout the entire course of their social change initiatives.

Align with Mission and Goals

Evaluating the alignment between the organization's mission, values, and objectives before initiating a change effort is a critical consideration and marks the fourth step in this process. Extensive research, as demonstrated by Kim (2020), highlights that numerous initiatives falter because they lack a direct connection to the organization's core purpose and objectives. Often, this alignment corresponds closely with the values an organization holds and the role the change effort plays in enhancing its return on investment (ROI). Regrettably, in situations where corporations face financial challenges and are unable to meet their profit targets, they are often counseled to set aside their corporate social responsibility initiatives and prioritize profitability. This pressure typically stems from shareholders and business advisors who emphasize financial gains. The continuous alignment of the mission and goals with the social change effort is a shared responsibility held by senior leadership and the change leaders.

Define and Including the Community

As the organization deliberates on the nature of the change they wish to initiate, it is crucial to define the scale and reach of the community that will be impacted. The term "community" transcends the organization's immediate surroundings and encompasses the various locations where the organization operates, the neighboring town, county, state, or even the global community. The influence of the social change initiative may extend far beyond the initially intended community, making it paramount for the organization to address pivotal questions such as: How do we precisely delineate the community affected by the social change? How will our organization identify and actively engage with key stakeholders within this community?

It is imperative for the organization to have well-articulated answers to these questions, ensuring transparency in their choice of the target community. This approach minimizes the assumption that the organization is merely following a trend or engaging in superficial "window dressing" for social change. By addressing these inquiries comprehensively, organizations develop a profound understanding of the community they aim to serve and involve. Consequently, they lay the foundation for effective and inclusive social change. However, it is important to note that this consideration of the community should not transform into defining the change effort itself. Instead, the implementation of the change effort should involve and incorporate the community, ensuring that the change is co-created with them rather than being imposed upon them.

Planning Ahead

To foster progress toward social change, organizations must go beyond mere intentions and establish comprehensive plans that account for various scenarios. Collaborating closely with community stakeholders who are crucial to the change process, organizations should engage in ongoing inquiry, diligently seeking answers and solutions to pivotal questions such as: What could be the ramifications if the organization were to abstain from pursuing social change? And What course of action should be taken if the social change initiative encounters setbacks or, indeed, fails to yield the anticipated results?

This ongoing process of reflection will not only guide the organization toward its intended outcome for social change but also equip them with the necessary preparedness to navigate potential outcomes effectively. By embracing continuous reflection, organizations can cultivate the resilience and adaptability needed to address challenges, seize opportunities, and ultimately drive meaningful social change in their communities.

Commitment to Transparency and Account for Flexibility

Numerous organizations embark on social change initiatives with noble intentions, yet they often find themselves entangled in situations where the outcomes are not as positive as envisioned. Many philanthropic endeavors commence with the aim of aiding a specific community. However, when that community expresses discontent with the proposed changes, some organizations disregard these concerns and persist with their initial plans, seemingly asserting that they know what is best for the community better than the community itself. While acknowledging one's mistakes is never easy, the ability to exhibit transparency regarding one's shortcomings not only fortifies an organization but also magnifies the impact of its efforts.

Employing strategies such as allocating additional funding or commissioning an external assessment of the change initiatives, inclusive of community input, serves a dual purpose. It not only provides valuable insights into the impact of the organization's change efforts but also spotlights areas where enhancements are possible. Furthermore, incorporating flexibility within the change efforts is advantageous in this context, as it enables adaptations to align with the evolving needs of the community. When an organization pioneers an innovative social change effort, it should anticipate inadvertent missteps and be prepared to be accountable for them.

Resting and Organizational Doubt

To foster a robust impetus for social change, it is imperative for organizations to embrace the notion that change requires a different approach from the status quo. Change efforts inevitably face resistance and uncertainty, particularly when organizations are overhauling their conventional practices. Organizational leadership and change leaders must periodically realign the organization's understanding and purpose regarding social change initiatives. It's crucial to revisit the fundamental "why" behind the desire for social change. This core purpose not only links the change effort to the organization's mission but also serves as a guiding light when challenges arise. Reiterating this "why" to stakeholders reinforces the business case, increases stakeholder buy-in, and maintains a focus on overarching business priorities.

Keeping Momentum

It is essential to recognize that an organization cannot simultaneously address every aspect or change initiative identified. As an organization identifies areas for change, opportunities for transformation may emerge across various dimensions, both internally and externally. This can potentially overwhelm change leaders and others involved in the early stages of the effort. Implementing a system that allows change leaders to rotate and take breaks, especially when they are contributing to the initiative alongside their regular responsibilities or as volunteers, is crucial for sustaining momentum. This principle extends to community members, who may also experience compassion fatigue. Regardless of how the change process unfolds, patience is paramount, as change is an incremental journey that does not yield overnight results.

Chapter Summary

This chapter will come full circle, opening and closing with a contemporary case study featuring Bud Light and its parent company, Anheuser-Busch. In the spring of 2023, Bud Light encountered significant public backlash for retracting its support for diversity, equity, and inclusion initiatives. As is often the case with many organizations, financial constraints can lead them to prioritize profitability over their corporate social responsibility mission, succumbing to the pressures of shareholders, business advisors, and various stakeholders. This phenomenon was vividly illustrated in the recent incident involving Bud Light when their commitment to the transgender community in spring 2023 faced vehement challenges.

Bud Light and its parent company, Anheuser-Busch, have an extensive history of endorsing LGBTQ+ organizations and actively engaging in related events, earning them widespread acclaim not only within the LGBTQ+ community but also beyond (Romero, 2023). A notable instance of their commitment was in 2019 when Bud Light released a limited-edition rainbow aluminum bottle to express their unwavering support for World Pride (Romero, 2023). In recognition of their years of dedication, Anheuser-Busch achieved a perfect score of 100 on the Human Rights Campaign's Corporate Equality Index (Human Rights Campaign, 2022; Pride in Our Workplace, 2023). This index, established by the nation's largest LGBTQ advocacy group, evaluates companies based on four essential criteria: protection against workplace discrimination, comprehensive LGBTQ+ benefits, the fostering of an inclusive culture both inside and outside the workplace, and responsible corporate citizenship. Companies that attain a flawless score across these criteria, such as Anheuser-Busch, are bestowed with the prestigious "Best Places to Work for LGBTQ+ Equality" seal of approval by the Human Rights Campaign.

Nonetheless, when Bud Light opted to champion the transgender community by launching an ad campaign in support of the Bud Light March Madness contest, a campaign that encompassed the sponsorship of an Instagram post by transgender influencer Dylan Mulvaney, they encountered substantial resistance from conservative celebrities, politicians, and consumers. The slogan "Boycott Bud Light" gained traction within conservative circles, with several prominent figures leveraging their celebrity status to publicly chastise Bud Light for its support and rallying others to do the same (Dodgson, 2023). Videos emerged depicting consumers dramatically pouring Bud Light down sinks, crushing cans, and pressuring retailers and bars to withdraw the product from their shelves (Peters, 2023).

Bud Light initially stood firm on its position, even as a "buycott," a reverse boycott movement, began to gain traction, encouraging individuals to purchase Bud Light as an expression of support for the company's marketing campaign. Over a span of a few weeks in April, the negative publicity and growing public outcry reached a point where it raised concerns among Bud Light's investors about the potential damage to the brand. Eventually, company executives decided to terminate the marketing campaign and shift their focus to sports and music (Peters, 2023). Alongside altering their marketing strategy, they placed two executives involved in the campaign on leave. According to analysis (Holpuch & Creswell, 2023), Bud Light's sales saw a 17 percent decline by mid-April, constituting approximately 1 percent of the total global volume. In the same period, Anheuser-Busch's stock dropped to around $63. However, shortly after making the shift, Anheuser-Busch's shares rebounded, rising by 3 percent to $65.56 (Creswell, 2023). Bud Light representatives emphasized that their choice to conclude the campaign was not primarily driven by negative feedback. Rather, it was rooted in their desire to distance themselves from discussions that fueled division, as their initial aim was to foster unity through their business.

Bud Light's retreat from this pivotal campaign vividly exemplifies a pattern often seen in the corporate response to setbacks in their social change efforts. While Bud Light initially appeared receptive to the voices of both employees and customers, their final decision seemed to place a higher premium on their financial interests and the principles of capitalism. Consequently, the LGBTQ+ community and its allies view Bud Light's choice as a significant step backward, highlighting a stark disconnect between the company's professed commitment to diversity, equity, and inclusion, and their actual actions in the face of prevailing anti-trans sentiments (Pride in Our Workplace, 2023). By early May 2023, the Human Rights Campaign had notified Bud Light of the suspension and potential downgrading of their Corporate Equality Index score in response to the manner in which they managed the backlash stemming from Dylan Mulvaney's campaign.

This case study represents just one among a myriad of recent incidents over the past years where consumers have vehemently opposed organizations in pursuit of social change. Organizations are currently grappling with the intricate task of reconciling their consumer base, which has become distinctly polarized, with conflicting expectations and aspirations regarding social change. This chasm between these opposing perspectives is further exacerbated by the profound impact of the American political landscape.

While it might be unrealistic to eliminate all mistakes or potential public reactions, organizations can adopt vital measures to mitigate the negative consequences when they inevitably happen. Developing the drive for social change represents just one of the many steps organizations need to take as they advance their diversity, equity, and inclusion initiatives. Failure to take into account the research and their readiness could result in unsuccessful efforts. The following ten key takeaways presented in this chapter emphasize the strategies through which organizations can effectively and constructively foster their drive for social change.

Ten things to remember:

1. Go into it to make real change, not "window dressing"
2. Know the research and successful practices
3. Avoid "rise-and-repeat" and colonial oppression
4. Assess your readiness or preparedness to make change; Assessment of the Organization's Readiness
5. Align with Mission and Goals
6. Define and Including the Community
7. Planning Ahead
8. Commitment to transparency & Account for Flexibility
9. Resting and Organizational Doubt
10. Keeping Momentum

References

Costello, Amy. (2012). "TOMS Shoes: A Closer Look." Audio blog post. *Tiny Spark*. Tiny Spark, n.d. Web. https://nonprofitquarterly.org/toms-shoes/

Creswell, J. (2023). *Anheuser-Busch Changes Beer Marketing Focus After Transgender Promotion*. The New York Times. https://www.nytimes.com/2023/05/04/business/bud-light-transgender-promotion.html

Dodgson, L. (2023). *Conservatives called for a boycott of Bud Light after it partnered with trans influencer Dylan Mulvaney. The company stood by its choice*. Insider. https://www.insider.com/bud-light-stands-by-dylan-mulvaney-after-conservative-backlash-trans-2023-4?_gl=1*1smum70*_ga*MTk3Njg1MDU2OC4xNjgwNjUyMzE5*_ga_E21CV80ZCZ*MTY5ODEwOTQ2OS4xNC4wLjE2OTgxMDk0NzUuNTQuMC4w

Emerson, M. S. (2022, November 18). 7 Reasons Why Change Management Strategies Fail and How to Avoid Them. President and Fellows of Harvard College, *Harvard Division of Continuing Education.* https://professional.dce. harvard.edu/blog/7-reasons-why-change-management-strategies-fail-and-how-to-avoid-them/

Frazer, G. (2008). *Used-clothing donations and apparel production in Africa. The Economic Journal, 118(532),* 1764–1784. https://doi-org.ezaccess.libraries.psu. edu/10.1111/j.1468-0297.2008.02190.x

Hessekiel, D. (2021, April 28). *The Rise And Fall Of The Buy-One-Give-One Model At TOMS.* FORBES. https://www.forbes.com/sites/davidhessekiel/2021/04/28/ the-rise-and-fall-of-the-buy-one-give-one-model-at-toms/?sh=2204a4f71c45

Holpuch, A., & Creswell, J. (2023). *2 Executives Are on Leave After Bud Light Promotion With Transgender Influencer.* The New York Times. https://www. nytimes.com/2023/04/25/business/bud-light-dylan-mulvaney.html

Human Rights Campaign. (2022). *Corporate Equality Index 2022* [Annual report]. Human Rights Campaign. https://www.hrc.org/resources/ corporate-equality-index

Kim, I. A. (2020). How Toms went from a $625 million company to being taken over by its creditors. *Business Insider.* https://www.businessinsider.com/ rise-and-fall-of-toms-shoes-blake-mycoskie-bain-capital-2020-3

Kotter, J. P. (1995). Leading Change: Why Transformation Efforts Fail. *Harvard Business Review.* https://hbr.org/1995/05/leading-change-why-transformation-efforts-fail-2

Kozlowski, L. (2012). Impact Investing: The Power of Two Bottom Lines. *Forbes Magazine.* https://www.forbes.com/sites/lorikozlowski/2012/10/02/impact-investing-the-power-of-two-bottom-lines/?sh=6878eacf1edc

McPhail, N. [Nicole McPhail]. (2020a, December). How to develop a Corporate Social Responsibility Strategy: Solving Business Problems [Video]. YouTube. https://www.youtube.com/watch?v=QLKayMdqDMs

McPhail, N. [Nicole McPhail]. (2020b, December). How to develop a Corporate Social Responsibility Strategy: Solving Business Problems [Video]. YouTube. https://www.youtube.com/watch?v=S_sHQMrDjyI&list=PL-b_U5v6TQk3 x3sauaJ_gUGe2WIqb5KC9&index=1

McPhail, N. [Nicole McPhail]. (2020c, December). How to develop a Corporate Social Responsibility Strategy: Solving Business Problems [Video]. YouTube. https://www.youtube.com/watch?v=oXJ6L0Pl1EY&list=PL-b_U5v6TQk3x3 sauaJ_gUGe2WIqb5KC9&index=3

Peters, B. (2023). *Bud Light's anti-trans backlash has some weighing the potential 'chilling effect' on corporate LGBT+ support.* MarketWatch. https://www. marketwatch.com/story/bud-light-anti-trans-backlash-could-usher-in-a-cheap-beer-summer-unlike-any-since-2005-d73b1bbf

Pride in Our Workplace. (2023). What The Dylan Mulvaney X Bud Light Campaign Tells Us About Corporate Allyship and Integrity. Pride in Our Workplace. https://piow.org/2023/05/04/mulvaney-bud-light/

Romero, D. (2023). *Anheuser-Busch CEO says Bud Light partnership with trans influencer wasn't meant to divide.* NBC News. https://www.nbcnews.com/nbc-out/out-news/anheuser-busch-bud-light-dylan-mulvaney-trans-influencer-rcna79810

Rothwell, W. J., Ealy, P. L., & Campbell, J. (2022). *Rethinking organizational diversity, equity, and inclusion: A step-by-step guide for facilitating effective change.* Routledge. https://doi.org/10.4324/9781003184935

Serafeim, G. (2020). Social-Impact Efforts That Create Real Value. *Harvard Business Review.* https://hbr.org/2020/09/social-impact-efforts-that-create-real-value

Stanley, C. A., Watson, K. L., Reyes, J. M., & Varela, K. S. (2019). Organizational change and the chief diversity officer: A case study of institutionalizing a diversity plan. *Journal of Diversity in Higher Education, 12*(3), 255–265. http://dx.doi.org/10.1037/dhe0000099

TOMS Shoes. (2023, May 24). *Purpose.* TOMS Shoes Impact. https://www.toms.com/us/impact/purpose.html

Wydick, B. (2015). The Impact of TOMS Shoes. https://www.acrosstwoworlds.net/the-impact-of-toms-shoes-on-kids/

Wydick, B. (2014). Do in-kind transfers damage local markets? The case of TOMS shoe donations in el Salvador. *Journal of Development Effectiveness, 6*(3), 249–267. https://doi-org.ezaccess.libraries.psu.edu/10.1080/19439342.2014.919012

Chapter 7

"Marketing" the Organization as a Social Change Agent

Farhan Sadique

Case Study: Nike's Journey as a Social Change Agent

Nike, a renowned global sportswear brand, has emerged as one of the significant drivers of social change by going beyond superficial marketing claims and taking tangible steps to create positive impacts on society and the environment. Nike is a brand popular for their athletic quality products used by professional sports organizations and athletes around the world. Beyond being a retail organization, Nike described themselves as an organization committed to addressing systematic racism by raising awareness of controversial social problems (Urvater & Vandegrift, 2021).

One notable aspect of Nike's role as a social change agent is its strong commitment to sustainability. The company has set ambitious goals, aiming to achieve 100% renewable energy in its owned or operated facilities by 2025. Nike has also implemented sustainable practices throughout its supply chain, prioritizing the use of eco-friendly materials and adopting manufacturing processes that reduce waste. An example is Nike's innovative "Flyknit" shoe, which incorporates recycled polyester and minimizes production waste.

In addition to sustainability, Nike has become a leader in promoting diversity, equity, and inclusion. Through initiatives like the "Nike Equality Campaign," the company advocates for equal opportunities for athletes, regardless of their race, gender, or sexual orientation. Nike actively addresses social justice issues such as police brutality and systemic racism by

 DOI: 10.4324/9781003439714-7

partnering with organizations driving social change and making donations to support racial justice causes.

Beyond their sustainability and social justice efforts, Nike is deeply committed to promoting physical activity and sports participation, they have a strong presence and communication around social and political issues that impact athletes and communities around the country. They have launched programs and initiatives aimed at encouraging physical activity among young people and disadvantaged communities. Nike's sponsorship of athletes and sports teams provides a powerful platform for promoting the benefits of an active lifestyle and overall well-being. Often their integrity in branding comes into question, but their intentions are clear through the 29 targets focused on people, planet, and play including representation, inclusion, diversity, and sustainability (Nike Inc., 2021).

Nike's evolution as a social change agent can be attributed to its steadfast dedication to sustainability, diversity, equity, and inclusion, as well as its advocacy for physical activity. By translating its commitment into concrete actions and promoting positive social and environmental impacts, Nike has not only enhanced its reputation but has also attracted customers who align with its values and aspirations.

Case Study: Patagonia's Commitment to Environmental and Social Responsibility

Patagonia, a highly respected outdoor apparel company, has firmly established itself as a trailblazer in environmental and social responsibility. Through its unwavering commitment to critical issues such as climate change and its implementation of sustainable practices, Patagonia has emerged as a leading force in driving positive change.

At the core of Patagonia's mission is a steadfast dedication to sustainability throughout its supply chain. The company actively promotes environmental awareness and engages in meaningful actions to minimize its ecological footprint. Patagonia provides its employees with the opportunity to participate in nonviolent civil disobedience training, exemplifying its commitment to peaceful activism. The company has gone a step further by establishing a bail policy to support employees who engage in peaceful protests after completing civil disobedience training. By empowering their employees to stand up for their values, Patagonia demonstrates its commitment to fostering a culture of responsible citizenship.

In addition to its internal practices, Patagonia actively supports environmental causes through its 1% for the Planet program. This initiative involves donating 1% of the company's sales to nonprofit organizations dedicated to environmental conservation. The company's contributions have helped to fund projects that tackle pressing environmental issues and drive positive change.

Patagonia's commitment to reducing waste and promoting a circular economy is evident through initiatives like the "Worn Wear" program. This program encourages customers to repair and reuse their Patagonia clothing, reducing the need for new purchases and minimizing the impact of the fashion industry on the environment. By advocating for clothing repair and longevity, Patagonia sets an example for other companies and inspires them to adopt similar practices.

Patagonia's unwavering dedication to sustainability and social responsibility has garnered widespread recognition and admiration. The company's initiatives and practices not only contribute to their own positive environmental impact but also inspire others to take meaningful action. Patagonia's influential role as a socially responsible organization serves as a powerful reminder that businesses can be catalysts for change and advocates for a more sustainable and equitable future.

Case Study: Ben & Jerry's Advocacy for Social Causes

Ben & Jerry's, the renowned ice cream company famous for its unique flavors, has established itself as a powerful advocate for social causes. Through their impactful "Democracy is in Your Hands" campaign, they actively promote and support issues such as marriage equality, racial justice, and climate change. The campaign serves as a rallying cry, encouraging individuals to act based on their beliefs and engage in the democratic process to drive positive change.

Ben & Jerry's utilizes their brand and platform to raise awareness and generate support for social causes that align with their core values. Their commitment to social responsibility goes beyond mere messaging and extends to concrete actions. They contribute a portion of their profits to environmental causes, supporting initiatives aimed at preserving and protecting the planet. Additionally, Ben & Jerry's collaborates with various organizations dedicated to promoting social justice and sustainability, amplifying their impact through partnerships and collective efforts.

The company's efforts to advocate for social change have not gone unnoticed. Ben & Jerry's has received recognition and praise for their bold stance on critical issues. Their activism extends beyond their products, making them a beloved brand for those seeking to support businesses that prioritize social responsibility and progressive values.

Why Is It Important?

These case studies showcase how organizations like Nike, Patagonia, and Ben & Jerry's have become powerful agents of social change. Their actions and commitments to sustainability, diversity, equity, inclusion, and activism have not only enhanced their reputations but have also inspired others to follow in making a meaningful and lasting impact on society. Over the past thirty years, a growing number of organizations have been engaging in activities to promote positive social change (Bies et al., 2007). While this concept may not be novel, it has historical roots dating back to the late 1970s when Richard Hall proposed it. Subsequently, in 1984, R. M. D'Souza further developed this idea, suggesting three approaches for organizations to catalyze social change. These approaches involve organizations either striving to drive change directly by taking a proactive role and extending their influence, instigating incremental changes that can indirectly affect society, or harnessing the full spectrum of their organizational resources, including tangible assets and social influence, to instigate transformative change. Transformative change requires connecting idealized influence, intellectual simulation, inspirational motivation, and individual motivation, which can be done by a leader in judgment free zone (Sadique, 2023). This concept of influence aligns with Lenin's succinct rhetoric, wherein he posed the question, Can the strength of a hundred people be greater than that of one thousand people? It can and is when the one hundred are organized (D'Souza, 1984).

Traditionally, organizations were seen as business institutions that willingly contributed to socially responsible causes to enhance their brand name and value. The main goal of such investments was to improve brand image and provide added value to shareholders through marketing efforts. However, in today's competitive marketplace, brand activism has emerged as a marketing strategy for brands to differentiate themselves. This strategy involves publicly expressing positions on social and political issues, aiming to attract attention and stand out from competitors (Moorman, 2020; Sarkar and Kotler, 2018). Nevertheless, taking such a stance has become increasingly polarizing and comes with significant risks (Vredenburg et al., 2020).

Accommodation refers to an organization's adjustment of practices and policies in response to external pressure for social change, utilizing both internal and external resources. If we reflect on the case studies, Patagonia serves as a well-known example of accommodation, as the company has aligned its policies and practices with its values. They have implemented sustainable practices throughout their supply chain, supported fair labor practices, and donated significant money to environmental organizations, demonstrating their commitment to sustainability and social responsibility, which has helped build a loyal customer base. But there are always two sides to the coin, how organizations manage the people not in favor? They might have employees, customers, and business partners dissatisfied with their actions, and the decreased profit due to the incredible amount of investment in social issues, it's a new trend and hard to prove in pen and paper, even though Nike has been a different example in branding their action and campaigning activities.

As social change agents, organizations go beyond mere social responsibility and actively work towards creating positive social change in their communities. They often take a strong position in national and international debates, aligning their actions with their mission and values. However, from a marketing perspective, these actions undoubtedly bring risks, as they may make certain groups of people uncomfortable or unhappy with the organization's activities. To mitigate these risks, organizations must maintain clarity and consistency across all communication channels. This not only has a positive impact on the business but has also become an increasingly important factor in succeeding as an organization.

Organizations primarily invested money in social causes and collaborated with like-minded organizations. However, with the growing awareness among consumers regarding organizations' motives and missions, their perception now depends on the organization's efforts to create a diversified and inclusive culture both internally and externally in the broader community. The question arises: why is this emphasis on social responsibility so important now?

The 2019 Edelman Trust Barometer revealed that 75% of people trust their employers to do what's right, compared to only 47% who trust the media. People are increasingly concerned about fake news as a weapon (Edelman, 2019; Vredenburg et al.,2020). Additionally, consumers do not want to be disappointed by their preferred organizations' stance on critical issues such as sustainability, transparency, and employment practices. They are vocal about their support and wield significant influence in an era of radical visibility, technology, and media (Barton et al.,2018).

Having a higher purpose and affecting social change is not solely about economic exchange. The 2021 Edelman (2021) Trust Barometer Special Report based on 14,000 consumers in 14 countries concludes that brands have an unprecedented responsibility to improve society. It often reflects something more aspirational—how organizations or leaders are making a difference and providing a sense of meaning to their supporters. This concept may not always fit into the traditional economic understanding of a firm. Nevertheless, organizations are increasingly recognizing the importance of making a lasting and crucial impact on society, which ultimately benefits their businesses.

What Does the Research Say

During the industrial revolution and labor rights movements, business organizations played a pivotal role in shaping social changes. Some companies recognized the need for change and implemented reforms within their systems. In the early 20th century, businesses began acknowledging the importance of environmental issues and tried to address them, leading to the emergence of corporate environmental responsibility. Hall (1972) proposed three approaches through which organizations can act as social change agents: accommodation, alternative, and redefinition which are still valid for organizations in the new era.

The alternative approach involves developing new practices or policies as alternatives to existing ones, aiming to replace problematic or harmful situations. Tesla, for instance, has made a significant impact by developing electric vehicles as a more environmentally friendly alternative to traditional gas-powered cars. Their commitment to sustainability has garnered widespread popularity and support in a short period. Redefinition is an approach that involves reshaping an organization's mission to address social or environmental issues. The Body Shop is an exemplar advocating for animal rights, fair trade, and sustainability. They have redefined their mission to prioritize these goals and have successfully integrated them into their business practices.

Note that the role of businesses in social change has varied throughout history, with some driving progressive social changes, while others have resited or merely complied with legal requirements. Businesses are primarily proactive in influencing social changes in response to external pressures and internal values, albeit to varying degrees. However, recognize that influencing consumers' preferences for a product doesn't always hinge solely on organized social movements. A case in point occurred in the summer of 2020 when Starbucks opted not to permit its employees to wear attire associated with the "Black Lives Matter" social movement. Starbucks made this decision out of concern that it might alienate segments of its consumer base, a risk it would take due to its robust brand recognition. This move did not provoke significant objections, underscoring the resilience of the brand (Wagner, 2021). Considering the varied responses of organizations to external pressures, D'Souza outlined two pivotal factors that guide organizations in shaping their consistent objectives: 1. Level of Altruism: This factor reflects an organization's concern for its enduring role within a dynamic social system. It gauges an organization's commitment to long-term societal contributions. 2. Change Agentry: This factor measures the extent to which an organization is dedicated to participating in activities aimed at transforming its environment. It assesses the organization's proactive involvement in driving change within its surroundings (D'Souza, 1984).

However, in recent times, businesses leading social change have evolved and gained greater prominence. Consumers are fiercely responding to organizations taking stands on social issues, as seen in boycotts of products like Gillette razors, burning of Nike shoes, or canceling Costco memberships (Vredenburg et al., 2020). In response, businesses are increasingly committed to adopting more responsible practices, disclosing more information about their preferences, and engaging in activities that address societal issues. They strive to become leaders in social and environmental impact, even if it means alienating a certain group of consumers, especially the young people who look for brands with ethical alignment, which Edelman called "belief-driven" buyers consisting of 60% of the millennials, 53% of the Gen Z, and 51% of the Gen X (Edelman, 2019. As consumers become more socially responsible and prioritize ethical practices, organizations are stepping up their commitment to creating positive change by being at the forefront of collaborating with others. In facing monumental challenges like climate change, social injustice, and poverty, businesses recognize the need to play a crucial role, as highlighted by Gavin (2019). 57% of the total Gen Z believes brands are better partners in social change than government, and amazingly 73% of total Gen Z advocates for the brands based on their alignment with values and beliefs (Edelman, 2022).

Putting into Practice

Social change is a multilevel complex phenomenon, historical patterns demonstrate possibilities of more systems-level change if all participants of the group can utilize their full potential (Fisk et al., 2019). As a leader, it is important to adopt various approaches to effectively drive social change within the organization. Here are six key approaches you can take as a leader of the organization or unit.

Having a Vision and Identifying Values

A leader should have a clear vision of the desired social change and communicate it effectively to inspire and align employees. A compelling vision creates a sense of purpose and direction, motivating individuals to work toward the common goal. Chick-fil-A fast food restaurant has been criticized for its founder's opposition to same-sex marriage. While the company identifies its views by trying to be more inclusive, the consumers continue to doubt its core values and challenge the organization's credibility as a social change agent. Another example of a failed attempt was from Starbucks in 2015, where they launched the "Race Together" campaign. The campaign was launched to promote encouraging conversation but was criticized for its credibility to lead such conversation. It was perceived as an impression of opportunistic, solely marketing purpose, and the situation demonstrates the challenge and necessity to have the company's mission and vision aligned with the social and environmental goals.

It's evident that there is an impact from the consumer for playing a role on either side of the social issues, and brands might analyze within or about the alignment of their beliefs, and values, and the assessment should start from the core of the organization. Understand the leader's perspective and inclusive mindset of the whole organization, at some point, leaders become the spokesperson for an organization and conflicting roles will create doubts, and a negative consumer impression is damaging to the brand value.

Listening

Listening to employees is crucial in understanding their perspectives, concerns, and ideas regarding social change. By creating an open and inclusive environment where individuals feel heard, leaders can gain valuable insights and build trust and collaboration. When making positive changes, the goal is to attain a positive outcome, and often listening to what consumers have to say can generate the best result for the organization. One organization can't make the change as a single entity, but creating value and force through the customer base can have a positive impact on social change and business value.

Identify the Spokesperson

As an organizational leader, you possess the power of choice. You can choose strict control over your team or align your organization with an authentic higher purpose that encourages employees to act as self-interested agents, fostering experimentation, deep learning, risk-taking, and meaningful contributions to decision-making (Quinn & Thakor, 2018). Not everyone will agree on a single perspective, as a leader you can facilitate a conversation, which may go against the consumer's pressure. However, whether to allow employees to speak out on political issues is a legitimate concern.

According to Moorman (2020), a significant 52.8% of marketing leaders believe that employees should have the freedom to express their opinions, while 33.3% agree that executives should voice their stances on political matters. This issue encompasses various perspectives, including brand authenticity, corporate citizenship, cultural background, political mission, and employee engagement. Each perspective may have distinct implications for the organization and its brand.

Identifying Employees' Best Interests

Recognizing and addressing the best interests of employees in relation to social change is important. This involves considering their needs, aspirations, and potential impact on their well-being. By aligning social change efforts with employees' interests, leaders can foster engagement and commitment.

Being Aware and Influential

Leaders need to stay informed and aware of societal issues, trends, and evolving expectations. This awareness enables them to respond effectively to social change challenges and opportunities, keeping the organization relevant and responsive. Leaders play a vital role in influencing and mobilizing others towards social change. By effectively communicating the vision, building coalitions, and leveraging their influence, leaders can inspire and empower employees, stakeholders, and external partners to actively contribute to the change process.

Being Fearless But Consistent

Driving social change often requires boldness and the willingness to challenge the status quo. Leaders should take calculated risks, step out of their comfort zones, and embrace innovation. Being fearless encourages creativity and resilience in pursuing meaningful social change.

Being active as a social change agent can make a meaningful impact in society, but failing to maintain consistency might cause a community backlash for their efforts. Pepsi's Kendal Jenner ad in 2017 can be an example, where they released an ad featuring Kendall Jenner which was criticized for appropriating the Black Lives Matter movement and trivializing the issue of police brutality. Pretty Little Thing, a fashion brand released a picture that depicted a white hand and a black hand intertwined with the caption "stand together," the attempt was ruthlessly mocked as the Black hand was jet black, not a shade that resembles a skin tone (Wagner, 2021). The company removed its campaign and has not spoken in that matter since then.

Now the Fundamental Question for This Chapter Is: How Can You Market an Organization as a Social Change Agent?

Marketing an organization as a social change agent requires a thoughtful and strategic approach. Here are key considerations for effectively positioning and promoting the organization's role as a driver of social change, review Exhibit 7-1 for the steps to use.

Step One: Corporate Activism

Corporate activism is identified as a company's willingness to take a stand on social, political, economic, and environmental issues to create social change by influencing others in the environment (Eilert & Nappier Cherup, 2020; Wagner, 2021). Identify the values the companies care about and develop a clear mission statement that reflects the commitment. The first step to making social change is to redefine what you and your organization stand for (Mills, 2021). For example, Uber faced criticism for profiting while a taxi strike was protesting President Trump's travel ban in 2017. The company still offered rides and caused backlash led to calls for a boycott of Uber and the company's CEO had to apologize and step down from Trump's advisory council. Misalignment can cause serious trust and brand value, and the alignment must be reflected in the policies and practices. As you define the team values and explain productivity, profitability, and engagement at work, it's also an opportunity to reflect the change you and your organization want to see in the world and leverage the team's collective genius to encompass social change (Mills, 2021).

Step Two: Clarify Who Has the Authority to Lead Change

Networking and partnership can make a difference and gather more commitment, but it's also important to identify influential personnel in the organization, who will have the authority to speak on behalf of the organization supporting their position in the change process. CEO of Papa John's, John Schnatter was criticized for his controversial political views and opposition to NFL players kneeling during the national anthem, which conflicted with Papa John's efforts to position itself as a socially responsible company that values diversity and inclusion. In each case, there is an influential person as the face of the movement, and the organization should carefully recognize the lead. As the CEO or a top leader of an organization, your personal opinion often can be perceived as the organization's stance and might confuse the consumers. The incidents above highlight the necessity of clarifying the authority to lead changes and making sure it aligns with the organization's values and culture as a social change agent. A key consideration for defining organization's culture is understanding what the culture means to its employees and determining whether this culture is helping or hindering their success (Ealy, 2021).

Conflicting ideologies will create mistrust among consumers and are often attract criticism.

Step Three: Integrate Values into the Brand

Clarify the role of diversity, equity, and inclusion in shaping the organization's culture and align those together to define the company's standing. Organizations without being committed to a cause often take stands which are named "performative stands" to gain attention from the customers. One example of such performance activism happened on June 2, 2020 when corporations such as Spotify, Apple, HBO, and TikTok posted about BlackOutTuesday to support a popular trend but committed to no sustainable changes within their business or broader environment (Wagner, 2021).

Integrating value into a brand should start with the previous step, where the organization first identifies its position and willingness to contribute to social change. In the second step, the organization creates a clear communication strategy with the market. Several brands have failed to integrate their social and environmental values into their marketing as social change agents. For example, Pepsi's controversial advertisement with Kendall Jenner was criticized for trivializing political protest and using social justice issues as a marketing tool rather than acting as an agent of social change. H&M can be another example, criticized for 'greenwashing' as they continued to use unsustainable materials despite their claim as a sustainable company. The broken commitment to performance activism is not new, but social justice issues often confront their practices, which eventually damages the company's reputation and the cause (Abrams, 2019; Wagner, 2021).

Step Four: Navigating Emotions and Relational Dynamics

Leaders and employees need to develop emotional intelligence and come up as a team, crucial for leading a social change. Despite a high lack of faith in the system, one relationship remains strong: my employer. Fifty-eight percent of the general population of employees say they look to their employer to be a trustworthy source of information about contentious societal issues. An open and inclusive communication will foster a culture where individuals will feel safe expressing their thoughts, concerns, and emotions regarding social change. Derived from Brand Activism, organizations have four key characteristics which are purpose-driven and address controversial/political issues, progressive and conservative stances, or sociopolitical issues. The purpose and value must be identified, as it's the most important core for authentic activism of the organization. Some brands may disconnect their communication from brand purposes when engaging in socio-political movements, but authenticity is still a crucial factor for social acceptance. And if you don't earn the trust of consumers for the activism the strategies will have less effective social good outcomes.

Step Five: Developing a Group Mindset

The significant investments being made globally to drive changes in areas such as gender, race, ethnicity, social justice, and corporate responsibilities highlight the growing recognition of the need for equality and inclusion. As top management will ensure equal employment opportunities, it becomes crucial to assess the pipeline of talent within our organization and work on unlocking their potential. The group can work towards nurturing the potential of individuals from diverse backgrounds by focusing on their professional development. This can include organizing workshops, training programs, mentorship initiatives, and leadership development opportunities. By equipping these individuals with the necessary skills and support, we can enhance their upward mobility and contribute to creating a more inclusive talent. By forming a group dedicated to social change within our organization, we can leverage these investments and align with the broader global movement toward equity and justice.

Step Six: Evaluating Progress

To ensure effective progress evaluation, the group will implement robust mechanisms for monitoring and measuring our goals. We will prioritize regular reporting, thorough data analysis, and the establishment of feedback loops. By engaging in these practices, we will gain a comprehensive understanding of the impact our initiatives have and identify areas that require ongoing improvement. Demonstrating this commitment to accountability will showcase our dedication to effecting tangible change and foster continued engagement from all stakeholders involved (see Exhibit 7-1).

Marketing organization as social change agent		
Directions: Use this matrix to examine the organization's pulse. The matrix identifies key questions you should examine and the bases for the question. Enter your answer and compare and discuss with others to sharpen your leadership skills.		
Base	*Question*	*Answer*
Organization culture	What's our organization's core value?	
Integrate into the brand	What do people perceive as our organization's role in the social change attempt?	
Leadership Definition/Bases of Social Power	What is(are) the leader's base(s) of power? Where do they stand in the social change attempt? How does their view conflict with the organization's values?	
Navigating emotions and relational dynamics	How will people perceive the action? How many resources the organization will commit to making meaningful change? Is the statement inclusive?	
Developing mindset	What are ethical or value considerations? Where do organizations require improvement to align?	
Evaluating progress	As a social change agent, how the organization's activities are aligning? If not aligned, how we can create awareness or constructive programs to align the activities as a whole system?	

Exhibit 7-1   Steps for marketing an organization as a social change agent. (By Farhan Sadique © 2024.)

Chapter Summary

This chapter delves into the role of leaders in driving social change and its impact on the organization's image. It explores the reasons organizations should participate in social change efforts, focusing on the perspectives and experiences of leaders. The approaches taken by organizations align with those of individual social change agents and include identifying employees' best interests, listening, having a vision, being aware, being fearless, and influencing others. A distinction is made between Corporate Social Responsibility (CSR) and social change agents, highlighting the different approaches and motivations behind each. The chapter incorporates the work of Dr. William J. Rothwell, which offers insights into determining the level of organizational involvement in social change efforts (Rothwell & Sadique, 2022).

The chapter also discusses the importance of social representation for organizations, examining the role of resources, resource-employees, and resource-employees-leaders in driving social change and shaping the organization's image. Additionally, the chapter addresses the risks associated with marketing the organization as a social change agent, considering potential challenges and pitfalls. Throughout the chapter, case studies are shared to provide real-world examples and illustrate key points.

This chapter comprehensively explores the role of leaders in social change, the approaches organizations can take, the importance of social representation, and the potential risks associated with marketing the organization as a social change agent. It offers valuable insights and practical considerations for organizations seeking to make a meaningful impact on social issues while managing their reputation and brand image.

References

Abrams, K. (2019). Discourse and Debate: Is performative activism inherently bad? - Columbia Spectator. *Columbia Spectator*. Retrieved August 1, 2023, from https://www.columbiaspectator.com/opinion/2019/03/27/discourse-and-debate-is-performative-activism-inherently-bad/

Barton, R., Ishikawa, M., Quiring, K., & Theofilou, B. (2018). *To affinity and beyond: From me to we, the rise of the purpose-led brand*. Accenture Strategy.

Bies, R. J., Bartunek, J. M., Fort, T. L., & Zald, M. N. (2007). Introduction to special topic forum: Corporations as social change agents: Individual, interpersonal, institutional, and environmental dynamics. *The Academy of Management Review, 32*(3), 788–793. https://www.jstor.org/stable/20159335

D'Souza, K. C. (1984). Organizations as agents of social change. *The Journal for Decision Makers, 9*(3), 233–248. https://doi.org/10.1177/025609091984O306

Ealy, P. (2021). Defining your organization culture. In W. J. Rothwell, P. L. Ealy, & Campbell, J. (Eds.), *Rethinking organizational diversity, equity, and inclusion* (1st ed., pp. 29–34). Routledge.

Edelman. (2022). *2022 Edelman trust barometer: The cycle of distrust.* Global Report. https://www.edelman.com/sites/g/files/aatuss191/files/2021-03/2021%20 Edelman%20Trust%20Barometer.pdf

Edelman. (2021). *2021 Edelman trust barometer.* Global report. https://www. edelman.com/sites/g/files/aatuss191/files/2021-03/2021%20Edelman%20 Trust%20Barometer.pdf

Edelman. (2019). *2019 Edelman trust barometer.* Global Report. https://www. edelman.com/sites/g/files/aatuss191/files/2019-02/2019_Edelman_Trust_ Barometer_Global_Report.pdf

Eilert, M., & Nappier Cherup, A. (2020). The activist company: Examining a company's pursuit of societal change through corporate activism using an institutional theoretical Lens. *Journal of Public Policy & Marketing, 39*(4), 461–476. https://doi.org/10.1177/0743915620947408

Fisk, R., Fuessel, A., Laszlo, C., Struebi, P., Valera, A., & Weiss, C. (2019). Systemic social innovation: Co-creating a future where humans and all life thrive. *Humanistic Management Journal, 4*(2), 191–214. https://doi.org/10.1007/ s41463-019-00056-8

Gavin, M. (2019). How to Create Social Change: 4 Business Strategies. *Harvard Business Insight.* https://online.hbs.edu/blog/post/how-can-business-drive-social-change

Mills, R. (2021). 6 ways all organizations can influence social change. *Givebutter.* Retrieved July 14, 2023, from https://givebutter.com/blog/social-change

Moorman, C. (2020). Commentary: Brand activism in a political world. *Journal of Public Policy & Marketing, 39*(4), 388–392. https://doi.org/10.1177/ 0743915620945260

Nike Inc. (2021). *Nike—2025 Targets Summary—NIKE, Inc.* 2025 Targets Summary. https://about.nike.com/en/newsroom/resources/2025-targets-summary

Quinn, R. E., & Thakor, A. V. (2018). Creating a purpose-driven organization. *Harvard Business Review.* https://hbr.org/2018/07/creating-a-purpose- driven-organization

Rothwell, W., & Sadique, F. (2022, June 9). *Facilitating social and organizational change.* OD Network 2022 International Conference. https://doi.org/10.13140/ RG.2.2.31801.03686

Sadique, F. (2023). Transformational coaching methodologies: Implementing sustainable change through shifting paradigm. In B. Bakhshandeh, W. J. Rothwell, S. M. Imroz, & F. Sadique (Eds.), *Transformational coaching for effective leadership* (1st ed., pp. 183–196). Routledge.

Salpini, C. (2021). *Nike plans for $50B in revenue next year.* Retail Dive. https:// www.retaildive.com/news/nike-plans-for-50b-in-revenue-next-year/602456/

Sarkar, C., & Kotler, P. (2021). *Brand activism: From purpose to action.* Idea Bite Press.

Urvater, B., & Vandergrift, C. (2021, September 28). *Case study: Nike & Colin Kaepernick "Just do it" campaign.* Talkin' Baseball. Edublogs. https://sites.psu.edu/burv/case-study-nike-colin-kaepernick-just-do-it-campaign/

Vredenburg, J., Kapitan, S., Spry, A., & Kemper, J. A. (2020). brands taking a stand: Authentic brand activism or woke washing? *Journal of Public Policy & Marketing, 39*(4), 444–460. https://doi.org/10.1177/0743915620947359

Wagner, B. (2021). Black lives matter and communication technologies. *Duke University Press, 59* (2), 140–142. https://www.muse.jhu.edu/article/840312.

Chapter 8

Step 7: Facilitating the Development of an Organizational Strategic Plan

Wayne Gersie

A Tale of Two Case Studies

It's not enough simply to build a strategic plan for diversity, equity, inclusion and belonging (DEIB). (Note that DEIB is used to stand for an important social change effort, but the same principle would apply to other important social change efforts.) How the planning process is implemented, the leadership from the top of the organization, and the level of flexibility that units within an organization must take ownership of their process are also critical factors. These two case studies illustrate what can happen when the process is done well, and not so well.

University A

University A, a public university, created a detailed framework for DEIB strategic planning. The Chief Diversity Officer (CDO) office and the president worked together on this. The framework covers the whole institution and includes an overall planning framework, which spells out the rationale for the process. The framework was intended to guide colleges and major administrative units toward developing their own unit-based DEIB strategic plans.

DOI: 10.4324/9781003439714-8

It also specified domains for unit planning (for example, recruitment, retention, and curriculum) and outlined the process, including a timetable. The timetable had a "rolling due date" that spanned three semesters so units would have adequate time to plan and so the first plans could be shared with other units as proofs of concept. Additionally, a toolkit was provided to walk units through the process.

The toolkit was not mandatory. Colleges and units could draw from all of it, parts, or ignore it. The CDO office also offered to consult with units as requested. Finally, the planning structure was intended to be nimble. The overall planning framework document was a few pages long, and unit plans could focus on a few crucial items, perhaps holding other goals back until they had completed their most critical objectives. Unit plans were to focus on benchmarks, measurable outcomes with thresholds for success/KPIs, concrete actions intended to accomplish desired outcomes, and timelines. Long narratives were discouraged.

When the planning framework was released, one college dean relied heavily on its guidance and tasked their existing DEIB committee to develop the plan. The committee reviewed the materials, implemented the process, developed a first draft using the toolkit's planning template, and sent it to the CDO office for review. After several rounds of feedback and revisions, the plan was approved by all, passed legal and accessibility review, and was posted to the college website.

Several months later, the college had a new interim dean. This change in leadership might have stalled the progress in implementing the DEIB plan, but because the strategic plan was process-dependent, not person-dependent, a new dean did not hinder progress.

Company X

Company X, a large-scale public-sector corporation, also recognized the importance of implementing DEIB. However, the DEIB strategic planning processes at Company X differed from University A. Each planning cycle at Company X lasted approximately five years. Compared to the concise framework document used by University A, Company X's framework was much longer and more detailed.

While the president of Company X approved the process, they did not actively engage in the planning itself. Despite the comprehensive framework document, there were no toolkits or planning templates to assist the organization's units. Additionally, all units were given a fixed due date to submit their plans. The CDO's office offered to consult, but only a few units took advantage. Often the final plans were delivered to the CDO office with no prior review.

Subsequently, cross-functional teams were formed within the company to review and provide feedback on the plans. After the review process, formal feedback reports were issued, and the president and CDO met with each department head or unit leader to discuss the feedback. However, there was no communication about the outcome of these discussions. Although all the relevant documents were posted on the company's website, there was no legal review or verification of their accessibility.

At the middle and end of the planning cycle, each business division and unit prepared an implementation report. These were reviewed by an assessment team and feedback reports were provided. Finally, all these materials were posted on the company's website.

The entire process proved lengthy and complex.

Let's look at the results from one administrative unit as an example. This unit did not consult with the CDO office before submitting its plan for review. The plan itself was long and self-congratulatory. However, it lacked specific metrics and actionable items, as did the mid-term and final implementation reports. After the planning process ended a team member, who was considered a DEIB champion, expressed her frustration: "I have now been through three cycles of DEIB strategic planning (spanning over 15 years), and in my entire career, I have never experienced a greater waste of time." Many others shared her sentiments.

These case studies highlight valuable lessons.

First, leadership involvement is crucial. Although neither president played a significant role, University A's president was more engaged. The key leadership variable was the dean at University A, who engaged with all stakeholders. Additionally, the dean had established an active DEIB committee to support the planning.

Providing guidance was also critical. While Company X's planning framework may have been more elaborate and articulate, it failed to provide a practical toolkit. Even experienced academics and administrators may not be familiar with strategic planning. Without concrete guidance, the likelihood of creating a subpar plan increases. Similarly, when organizational units don't take advantage of the toolkit, its value diminishes.

An excessively detailed plan does not guarantee its effectiveness. A concise strategic plan can be as or more effective if it incorporates the essential components of excellent strategic planning, including establishing baseline measurements with success thresholds and defining concrete and actionable steps.

Crafting a successful DEIB strategic plan is indispensable for organizations seeking to realize their vision and aspirations for diversity, equity, inclusion, and belonging. Within this chapter, professionals will discover a comprehensive roadmap that guides them through the process, offering valuable insights on differentiating between desired outcomes and executable actions. This chapter provides expert advice on developing key performance indicators (KPIs) that effectively gauge the plan's most vital results. Most importantly, it underscores the pivotal difference between DEIB strategic plans that are merely performative or ineffective and those that generate a substantive and long-lasting impact, encouraging professionals to strive for the latter. An example of a properly executed strategic plan can be found in Exhibit 8-1 with a blank template for use is provided in Exhibit 8-2.

What Does the Research Say?

History and Evolution of DEIB Strategic Planning

DEIB strategic planning has evolved to address the increasing need for inclusive and equitable environments. Its original purpose was to ensure compliance, but it has since been recognized as a business benefit to be leveraged. Today, DEIB planning is typically integrated into an organization's core operations. However, the journey to this point has been long and challenging.

Initially, there was resistance and separation between DEIB planning and the rest of the organization. It has been mislabeled as quotas, seen as a drain on resources, and even labeled reverse discrimination. All of this took place while the United States strived to remain a leading economic power and leverage its significant advantage of demographic diversity.

As early as the 1990s, scholars including Roosevelt Thomas and Robin Ely recognized diversity's significance in organizational settings (Thomas & Ely, 1996). They emphasized diversity's value in fostering innovation, problem-solving, and overall organizational effectiveness. This early recognition marked the initial stage of DEIB planning.

Compliance-oriented Approaches

The origins of DEIB strategic planning were rooted in compliance and court decisions. With legal and regulatory changes such as 1964's Civil Rights Act and affirmative action, organizations began adopting compliance-oriented approaches to DEIB (Kossek & Lobel, 1996). This phase involved implementing policies and practices to ensure equal employment opportunities and mitigate discriminatory practices. Later, the landmark supreme court case Griggs v. Duke Power Co. (1971), solidified the importance of compliance-oriented approaches by establishing that employment practices that negatively affect protected groups are unlawful, even if the intent to discriminate is absent.

Business Case for Diversity

Eventually, the focus shifted from compliance to recognizing the strategic advantages of diversity in gaining a competitive edge and enhancing organizational performance. Scholars began making the business case for diversity, highlighting its positive impact on decision-making, innovation, and customer satisfaction (Cox & Blake, 1991, Smith, 2015). The business case for diversity was evident in a study by the Harvard Business Review, which found that companies with diverse teams are 45% more likely to report an increase in market share over the previous year (Jones, Bouquet & Snell, 2020).

This transition marked a new stage in DEIB strategic planning: emphasizing the business benefits associated with a diverse workforce. Companies that prioritize diversity are also more likely to attract and retain top talent since diverse work environments have been found to foster creativity and drive innovation (Smith, 2015). By embracing diversity, organizations can tap into a wider range of perspectives, ideas, and experiences, ultimately leading to better decision-making and customer satisfaction. Subsequent research amplified the business case. (Page, 2008).

Inclusion and Cultural Competence

In the early 2000s, organizations recognized that diversity alone was insufficient and began prioritizing inclusion and cultural competence. This shift emphasized the importance of creating a supportive environment where every employee feels valued empowered, and that they belong. Companies adopted strategies to address biases, foster cultural competence, and promote inclusivity (Thomas, 2004; Thomas & Ely, 1996). Additionally, they started relying on evidence-based approaches, such as Cox & Blake, 1991 study, which further confirmed the positive impact of cultural diversity on organizational performance and creativity. Strategies to tackle biases, foster cultural competence, and promote inclusivity became prevalent. (Harrison, Price & Bell, 1998).

The realization of the significance and strategic advantage of cultural competence sparked specific initiatives within organizations. These included training programs, inclusive policies and practices, and the creation of diversity and inclusion committees. Studies have demonstrated that organizations with diversity and inclusion committees have higher employee satisfaction, commitment, and financial performance (Nishii, Lepak & Schneider, 2008). By adopting inclusion and cultural competence, organizations not only harness the diverse perspectives and talents of their workforce but also cultivate an atmosphere of acceptance and collaboration. This fosters innovation, enhances employee engagement, and provides a competitive advantage in today's global marketplace (Jackson, Joshi, & Erhardt, 2003; Thomas, 2004).

Intersectionality and Multiple Dimensions of Diversity

Intersectionality and multiple dimensions of diversity also became part of the evolution of DEIB strategic planning. This concept recognizes that individuals hold multiple social identities—such as race, gender, and sexual orientation—and these identities intersect to shape their experiences (Crenshaw, 1989; Lituchy & Reavley, 2004). Organizations began considering these intersections in their diversity initiatives by developing more nuanced approaches to address the unique challenges people face at the intersections of various dimensions of diversity (Gutiérrez y Muhs et al., 2012). Specifically, the research found that intersectional approaches in organizations, in this case for higher education, helped create inclusive environments and promote social justice by acknowledging the interlocking systems of oppression that marginalized individuals face. This research confirms that including intersectionality in DEIB planning is important as it helps us understand and address the complex experiences and needs of diverse populations.

Current State and Future Directions

The history of DEIB strategic planning has evolved from early recognition to compliance-oriented approaches and to embrace the business case for diversity, inclusion, and intersectionality. Today, DEIB planning acknowledges our diverse and interconnected world and integrates diversity and inclusion into core operations.

As organizations gaze toward the 21st Century, they increasingly recognize the significance of diversity and the crucial role that strategic planning plays in achieving desired outcomes. Evidence-based practices, technology, and data-driven decision-making will be crucial here. This evolution becomes even more imperative as we consider the seismic demographic shifts workplaces are presently experiencing.

Research-based Approaches to DEIB Strategic Planning

Numerous studies have explored various aspects of DEIB planning, shedding light on its importance and providing insights into effective strategies. For instance, researchers analyzed DEIB planning in organizations and highlighted its positive impact on employee satisfaction, productivity, and innovation (Smith & Johnson, 2018). Their research demonstrated that organizations that incorporate DEIB planning into their operations create a more inclusive work environment and see enhanced business outcomes. In another study, researchers (Brown, Smith & Johnson, 2019) found that strong leadership commitment to diversity, coupled with the integration of diversity initiatives into the organization's overall strategic plan, is crucial for successful implementation. Their findings emphasized the need for leaders to actively champion diversity and ensure that any initiatives are aligned with the organization's broader goals and objectives.

Research conducted by Chen, Konrad, & Li, (2020) found a positive correlation between DEIB planning and organizational performance. They found that organizations that prioritize DEIB planning are more likely to have better financial and operational outcomes. The researchers also identified specific practices, such as establishing diversity goals, implementing training programs, and monitoring progress, as key drivers of successful DEIB planning.

These studies, among many others, have significantly contributed to the understanding and advancement of DEIB planning. By highlighting its benefits, identifying effective strategies, and emphasizing the role of leadership and organizational commitment, researchers have provided valuable insights for organizations seeking to foster diversity and inclusion in their workplaces.

Setting Clear Goals and Action Items

One prominent approach to DEIB strategic planning involves establishing clear goals and action items. Organizations must set specific and measurable outcomes that align with their diversity and inclusion vision (Thomas & Ely, 1996). These goals should be tailored to the organization's unique needs and challenges. For instance, an organization might have goals like increasing underrepresented groups in leadership, improving diversity in hiring, and boosting employee engagement and retention. These goals form a roadmap for organizations to track their progress and hold themselves accountable. Action items should be concrete and detailed enough to make it clear what behaviors and metrics will help meet those goals.

Conducting Thorough Assessments

To effectively implement DEIB strategic planning, organizations need to assess their current state of diversity and inclusion (Noe et al., 2020). The assessment in Chapter Two lays the groundwork for this approach, which involves collecting and analyzing data on workforce demographics, employee perceptions and experiences, and organizational practices. As also mentioned in Chapter 2, these assessments help organizations identify areas for improvement, make informed decisions, and monitor the impact of their diversity initiatives.

Engaging Stakeholders at All Levels

Engaging stakeholders at all levels is another crucial approach in DEIB strategic planning. Organizations should involve employees, leaders, and external partners in the planning process to ensure that diverse perspectives and expertise are considered. Employee resource groups, diversity committees, and other forms of employee involvement can foster inclusivity and create a sense of ownership in diversity initiatives. Collaboration with external stakeholders, such as community organizations, educational institutions, and industry networks, can also provide valuable insights and resources to support diversity goals (Shore et al., 2011).

Allocating Resources

Organizations should allocate dedicated resources, both financial and human, to support DEIB strategic planning. Committing resources demonstrates the organization's prioritization of diversity and inclusion and provides the infrastructure for implementation. Budgets that demonstrate a strong commitment to diversity might include sufficient funding for diversity training programs, recruitment efforts targeting underrepresented groups, and the creation of diversity and inclusion departments or roles within the organization (Noe et al., 2020). Human resources staff, diversity officers, and diversity task forces can play crucial roles in driving the strategic planning process and ensuring its successful execution.

Embracing Continuous Improvement

Evaluation and continuous improvement are essential components of DEIB planning.

Organizations should regularly assess the effectiveness of their strategic initiatives and adjust their strategies based on feedback and outcomes (Noe et al., 2020). This may involve tracking KPIs related to diversity, employee surveys, and soliciting feedback from stakeholders.

Folded into the Overall Plan or Self-Standing Plan

Ideally, DEIB strategic planning would not exist. A comprehensive general strategic plan would include DEIB as a distinct section within the plan and a crosscutting factor throughout the plan. For example, as a crosscutting factor, industry excellence must include inclusive excellence. Numerous studies have confirmed this point, perhaps most convincingly in Scott Page's book, The Difference: How the Power of Diversity Creates Better Groups, Firms, Schools, and Societies. Through mathematical models and an extensive review of the literature, Page concludes that cognitive diversity, which is well recognized as a plus factor to intellectual accomplishment, positively correlates with identity diversity when well managed (Page, 2008, pp. 314, 326, 335). This point is especially important for research teams in science, technology, engineering and mathematics (STEM) where complex problems are optimized by a multidisciplinary approach. Page compares diversity to a toolbox. You can build little with only a hammer or a saw, but with a hammer and a saw, many more possibilities open up (Page, 2008, pp. 105–06). So, wherever academic excellence exists in a strategic plan, if it does not include inclusive excellence, the plan gives both DEIB and academic excellence short shrift.

As critical as this is for higher education, Page's caveat, "well-managed," is important. When DEIB is not handled well, its benefits are mitigated or eliminated. Many general strategic plans show how poorly DEIB is implemented across higher education. DEIB is often mentioned marginally, usually as a distinct "add-on," separate from other domains. In institutions with this type of culture and approach, a separate process for DEIB strategic planning becomes necessary. It locates DEIB across all functional areas including curriculum, pedagogy, and research, and goes far beyond campus climate, advising, or student affairs. DEIB strategic planning promotes the point that we can't leave DEIB out in the cold.

The best model is perhaps not "either/or" but "both/and." Just because an institution engages in DEIB strategic planning does not mean DEIB should be left out of general strategic planning. That would keep DEIB marginalized. Instead, DEIB strategic plans should align with general strategic planning, running on parallel tracks, until an institution can take off the "training wheels" and allow general strategic planning to take over—this time with DEIB taking its rightful place as a central planning theme. It's hard to say when an institution reaches this point. Regression to the mean is always a threat so the true goal is to change the mean. The conversation about mainstreaming DEIB strategic planning into general strategic planning needs to occur at the highest levels of the institution with many voices, including students, in the mix. Also, institutions need to be ready to put the training wheels back on if necessary. But, with proper support and planning, integrating DEIB strategic planning into general strategic planning is a goal that can and should be met. (The same principle applies to other social change efforts.)

Putting It Into Practice

Step One: Your Role as the Facilitator Rather Than the Director

Effective DEIB strategic planning requires that leaders take a facilitative role instead of a directive one (see Exhibit 8-1). This approach has many benefits, including greater support and enthusiasm from stakeholders. Leaders can minimize resentment and enhance plan implementation by valuing input and involving others in decision-making. Facilitative leaders act as guides and enablers in the planning process, promoting active participation and collaboration. This empowers team members to contribute their ideas, perspectives, and expertise. Involving stakeholders at all levels encourages open dialogue, active listening, and consensus-building, generating diverse perspectives and identifying potential pitfalls and opportunities. When individuals actively participate in the planning, they also help drive its

Unit/Department Name: ABC Organization

Planning domain: Training and Coaching		Monitor/Team leader: Name	
Goal #1 (goal + vehicle to get there - be SPECIFIC): Enhance the Culturally Responsive Leadership Aptitude (CRLA) of Managers			
Benchmark/Best practices (link to resources where available): Leadership Development Tools, "Best Practices of Culturally Responsive Leaders"			
Projected outcomes from baseline:		**Timeline:**	**Actual outcomes** *(report at end of project):*
30% more managers responsible for DEIS in the organization will report that they employ at least two culturally responsive leadership practices when assessed post Culturally Responsive Coaching (CRC) Session		Fall 2021-Fall 2023	24.7% increase (from baseline 59/316, 18.7%, to 137/316, 43.4%)
Action items:		**Timeline:**	**Completed:**
1	A committee from the representatives of units across the organization and across all levels will be charged to assess training and coaching needs for managers	Fall 2021	√
2	Committee will develop in partnership with content experts at least one training module for CRC for managers in organization	Fall 2021	√
3	Committee will administer a pre organizational survey for managers to assess level of CRLA	Fall 2021	√
4	Organization will conduct all three developed CRC sessions for a fall and spring cohort of organization managers for a total of 30 managers to complete CRC session	Spring 2022	√
5	Committee will administer a post organizational survey for managers to assess level of CRLA	Spring 2022	√

Notes/Assessment plan:

☐ *Introduction (describe the current environment, why this initiative is important):*

☐ *Assessment plan (include pre-and post-program steps to measure the differences in diversifying practices between pre-program and post-program):*

☐ *Notes (include any observations, for example action items that may have fallen short or observations about outcomes)*

Exhibit 8-1   DEIS strategic planning and reporting template.

execution. This shared ownership strengthens commitment to achieving plan objectives and cultivates a collaborative and supportive work culture.

Additionally, a facilitative approach enables leaders to tap into the collective intelligence and creativity of the entire team. This collective process not only strengthens the strategic plan but also builds a sense of trust and camaraderie among team members, fostering a positive and productive working environment.

There are side benefits to this too: Stronger, more unified teams not only help the implementation of the strategic plan, but they also help the organization meet other workforce goals. Ultimately it is difficult to resist and or criticize a plan that you co-authored or are committed to.

Step Two: Preparing the Organization for Strategic Planning—Roll Out/Barnstorming the Concepts

Preparing an organization for the development and facilitation of a DEIB strategic plan requires careful planning and thoughtful execution. First, it is crucial to create awareness and a sense of need within the organization about the importance of diversity and inclusion. This urgency can be achieved by promoting workshops, training, awareness campaigns, one-on-one conversations with key influencers, and creating a knowledge base for stakeholders. The careful groundwork of building recognition, engaging leaders, and involving employees will foster confidence and set the stage for a successful implementation.

Once the organization is primed for strategic planning, it is essential to first advance the concepts by engaging leaders and key stakeholders in open discussions about diversity and its strategic relevance. These conversations early on help build understanding, alignment, and support for the upcoming initiatives. Leadership plays a vital role in spearheading diversity initiatives. They must lead from the front, championing diversity and inclusion as core values. Leaders should communicate the strategic plan, its goals, and the expected outcomes to the entire workforce, emphasizing the importance of individual and collective contributions to its success.

When leaders actively demonstrate their commitment to diversity, it encourages grassroots implementation of the strategic plan.

In addition, developing a knowledge base for stakeholders to learn more about the process is also crucial. For convenience, this knowledge base can be housed on a website or intranet portal with educational resources, such as articles, reports, case studies, and best practices on diversity, its benefits, and methodologies for implementing inclusive practices. By creating a robust knowledge base, organizations empower stakeholders to educate themselves, understand the importance of diversity and inclusion, and contribute actively to the strategic planning process. Creating an appetite for diversity planning requires establishing trust and confidence among employees that planning will not be an exercise in futility. To make this a reality, organizations should be transparent and communicative throughout the process.

Employees should be included in the planning stages. They should be allowed to provide input, share concerns, and help shape the diversity initiatives. This will give them a sense of ownership and build confidence that the strategic plan will lead to tangible changes and positive outcomes.

Step Three: Create a Knowledge Base or Learning Tool for Development

Reinventing the wheel has no merit in strategic planning. The goal is a simple process that is structured and well laid out. The best way to accomplish this task is with a planning framework and toolbox that guides the process step-by-step with detailed descriptions for each step. One such model is: 1) the leadership tasks a planning team to guide the process, representing all levels of the unit with ground rules and timelines; 2) the team conducts an overview of the process; 3) Strengths Weaknesses Opportunities and Threats (SWOT) analysis to gather stakeholder input on the most critical needs; 4) development and prioritization of planning goals from the SWOT analysis; 5) submission of proposed planning goals to stakeholders for further input and revision; 6) submission of planning goals to leadership for approval and revision; 7) first draft of plan with goals, benchmarks/best practices, projected outcome measures with thresholds for success/KPIs, a concrete and robust action plan, and timelines; 8) submission of draft to stakeholders and leadership for further input; and 9) finalize, submit, and publicize plan.

Along the way, other critical factors to consider are the difference between quantitative and qualitative metrics and how to best use them, the difference between outcomes and actions, approaches to SWOT analysis, optimal planning templates, responsible, accountable, consulted, and informed (RACI) charts, and definitions of strategic planning terms.

A reminder here: You are not competing with your benchmarks. Use them to understand best practices and try to exceed your own past performance. Don't go it alone. Reach out to those with planning expertise and lean on them heavily.

Once you reach the implementation phase, assign a team leader or planning monitor for each goal and have this person report frequently on progress. If you have an implementation team, it should consist of at least a few key members of the planning team. A best practice is to have some time, even five minutes, devoted at every staff meeting to implementation updates. Once one planning goal is completed, you can queue up another goal. Better to plan and accomplish one goal than plan for umpteen goals and accomplish none.

To mention planning templates again, see below for a useful approach. Many other templates exist, and teams should seek the one they think would work best for them. The goal is to put a lot of information into a compact space, minimizing narrative.

Step Four: Developing Internal and External Group Planning Groups

Similar to any strategic planning process, engaging both internal and external groups is essential. By involving internal stakeholders such as employees, managers, and executives, organizations can tap into their diverse perspectives, experiences, and expertise. Internally, organizations can create diverse task forces or committees with members from different departments, levels, and backgrounds. These groups can contribute by doing research and providing insights into the organization's DEIB landscape. They can also identify gaps, challenges, and opportunities for improvement, ensuring that the plan is rooted in a comprehensive understanding of the organization's internal dynamics.

At the same time, external groups such as community organizations, industry associations, and diversity consultants can bring fresh eyes and a broader range of experiences to the table. They can offer insights into industry trends, benchmarking data, and innovative approaches to diversity and inclusion. Engaging external groups also helps organizations build partnerships, establish credibility, and access resources that support plan implementation.

By leveraging the collective wisdom of both internal and external groups, organizations can create a robust and inclusive diversity strategic plan that aligns with their vision, engages employees, and drives meaningful change. This collaborative approach ensures that the organization embraces diversity and inclusion as core values.

Step Five: What Is the Current Environment Telling You?/Understanding the Need for Strategic Goals

Developing broad diversity strategic goals requires a deep understanding of the current organizational environment. By analyzing and understanding the existing diversity landscape organizations can effectively identify their strong points and areas for improvement. In Chapter 2, we discuss how to assess the current and existing environment for social change and employee attitude in a culturally responsive and equity-minded (CREM) manner. The CREM findings will make it possible to set strategic goals that address those specific needs and challenges. For example, if the analysis uncovers a lack of diversity in leadership positions, a strategic goal could be to increase the representation of underrepresented groups in managerial roles.

Further, understanding the organization's current culture, values, and practices is crucial for setting realistic and attainable goals that align with the organization's overarching vision and mission. For instance, if the organization values inclusivity and equity, the strategic goals may focus on fostering an inclusive work culture, promoting equal opportunities, and eliminating bias in recruitment and promotion.

Additionally, understanding the current organizational environment helps in assessing the internal and external factors influencing diversity initiatives. By examining factors such as workforce composition, community demographics, or regulatory requirements, strategic goals can be set that consider these influences. This enables organizations to proactively address diversity challenges and stay ahead of the curve. For example, if the organization operates in a highly diverse community, a strategic goal may be to enhance cultural competency among employees to better serve a diverse customer base.

Finally, understanding the organizational environment is crucial for developing broad DEIB goals. It enables organizations to identify specific areas of focus, align goals with the organization's values, and consider internal and external factors that impact DEIB initiatives. By setting informed and targeted goals, organizations can enhance their commitment to diversity and create a more inclusive and equitable work environment.

Step Six: Creating a Vision that Is Implementable (Length Does Not Equal Depth and Success)

Successful DEIB strategic planning is driven by an organization's vision. Ultimately, a well-crafted and realistic vision statement sets the stage for meaningful diversity and inclusion initiatives that can promote positive change.

Ambitious and aspirational vision must be successfully implemented to be meaningful. A lengthy vision statement may be comprehensive, but it does not automatically guarantee success. An excessively long statement can be overwhelming and challenging to translate into practical steps. Therefore, it is crucial to balance grand aspirations and practical realities.

Considering the organization's current capacity and readiness for change is critical. It also requires an understanding that it will be more of a marathon than a sprint, and the race will be won in the last few miles, not the first few. Sustaining momentum may be the biggest challenge. Leadership must assess whether the structures, policies, and systems are in place to support the vision. Additionally, understanding the organization's cultural dynamics and readiness for DEIB initiatives can help determine the pace and scale of implementation. By aligning the vision with the organization's current state, it becomes more feasible to build upon existing foundations and gradually introduce transformative changes.

Celebrating milestones along the way helps to motivate stakeholders to continue the work. Many employees may write off DEIB planning as just another management fad to be endured until the next flavor of the month comes along. However, when tangible progress and proofs of concept are reported, even skeptics can be recruited to the cause.

Step Seven: Differentiating Between Strategic Planning Terminology (Symbolic vs Performative)

Without training, especially when people are speaking informally about planning, some terms can be used in different ways, or two terms may mean the same thing. For example, actions and objectives may mean the same thing depending on the situation. We use actions here to avoid this ambiguity. When some individuals speak of goals, they actually mean what we call outcomes here. Some of these differences don't matter if terms are used consistently, and everyone understands their meaning. But without some training or at least clear definitions, planning can be hampered by miscommunication.

Planning Definitions

Goal—The desired result of successful planning. Goals need not be stated in terms of measurable outcomes, but goals must have measurable outcomes associated with them to determine if they have been met. A stated goal might be "To improve the climate and create a better sense of belonging among stakeholders." Such a goal communicates the desired accomplishment (improved climate) and a general outcome (better sense of belonging).

Benchmarking—The comparison of similar processes for desired goals across organizations and industries to determine which processes might be best to emulate to attain desired outcomes. Benchmarking can save time and effort because instead of reinventing the wheel, cues from proven performers can be used.

Best Practices—Plans and processes that demonstrate success with positive measurable outcomes.

Projected Outcome—The metric projected from the baseline(s) that is used to determine if actions taken to achieve the goal succeeded. Every goal should have at least one projected outcome with a specific measure to use as a threshold for success.

Actual Outcome—The outcome metric that results from actions for a goal.

Actions or Action Plan—Specific actions taken to attempt to accomplish projected outcome(s). Actions should be specific and concrete. A poor action item would be to "conduct workshops." A better action item would be to "conduct three academic success workshops each semester for first-year students on the topics of study skills, test preparation, and notetaking, with at least 25 students in attendance at each session. It is critical to distinguish actions from outcomes. An action is something you do to attain an outcome. Students don't study hard for tests for the sake of studying hard for tests. They study hard for tests to obtain a good grade. Confusing actions with outcomes is one of the most common mistakes in strategic planning.

Baseline—The metric that best determines progress toward an outcome and from which further progress will be measured with the actual outcome(s).

Assessment Method—The means chosen to gather outcomes to determine program success. The assessment will either be quantitative or qualitative, and the method chosen and actions taken to gather these metrics will determine the quality of the assessment.

Key Performance Indicator—Actual outcomes that measure the most important goals of an organization.

One facet of DEIB strategic planning to emphasize is the difference between symbolic/performative planning and an embrace of planning as a key tool for advancing DEIB goals. Too often planning, not just DEIB planning, is about completing an administrative duty. In this case, planning often becomes rushed and sloppy. Outcomes gravitate toward less precision without thresholds for success. Outcomes and actions get confused. Actions are generalized, lack useful specifics. Timelines are left unstated or show little logical connection to their actions or outcomes. If the leadership and/or stakeholders are not ready to engage the process seriously it would be better to not conduct planning. Poor planning begets cynicism about planning and process improvement. If organizations are not ready, planning can be harmful because it becomes a waste of time. Only engaged and thoughtful planning will benefit the organization and its goals.

Step Eight: Creating KPIs

KPIs are the most important outcomes for planning. In other words, all KPIs are outcomes, but not all outcomes are KPIs. KPIs are especially helpful when there are several intended outcomes. If retention is a key goal, then retention outcomes will be a KPI. Or, if several desired retention outcomes exist, KPIs will be the most important ones. Being especially mindful of constructing KPIs well is critical. Using retention again as an example, an outcome measure such as "improve retention" would be a poor choice because the threshold of success is ill-defined. However, using it as a KPI would be even worse. Such a KPI would be an indicator of sloppy planning. KPIs should be proportionate to the organization's size and the number of goals in the plan. Either way, there should always be fewer KPIs than projected outcomes.

Since KPIs are the gold standard for planning accomplishment, each should be a specific item on any DEIB strategic planning "scorecards" you may develop. Each should be monitored carefully, and when reached, it should be acknowledged and communicated throughout the organization. They are all "key" to your successful operation.

Step Nine: Considerations for Timelines to Achieving Goals

Timelines are crucial for achieving goals and tracking progress. A well-defined timeline starts with establishing clear milestones that outline the desired actions and outcomes. Key areas and initiatives are identified, and specific milestones are set to measure and monitor progress. For example, if the goal is to enhance diversity in leadership positions, milestones could include conducting a diversity audit, implementing targeted recruitment strategies, and providing diversity training for current leaders. Realistic timelines are assigned to each milestone to ensure alignment with the overall strategic plan.

The more visual the timeline, the better. Stakeholders should be able to easily see the various steps along the way and know the start and end dates for each, as well as any dependencies or interconnections between them. Visual timelines give stakeholders a comprehensive overview, enabling them to understand the sequence of activities and estimate the time required for each task. The timeline should be regularly updated as progress is made or adjustments become necessary.

Step Ten: Legal Concerns

Legal concerns emerge mainly regarding DEIB recruiting targets. It is well known that recruiting quotas are illegal. In some states, even targets may be problematic, such as setting a recruiting projected outcome of a 5% increase from baseline. A final step before posting a DEIB strategic plan is to have the institution's legal counsel review it; However, also be aware that lawyers are trained to hint at legal challenges. They may advise against something that is technically legal but could still attract a lawsuit.

Executive leadership is critical in determining how close to the edge plans can skate. Sometimes, presidents and trustees may retreat behind legal arguments to shield themselves from criticism over their lack of commitment to DEIB. This point again demonstrates the importance of leadership. Without strong leadership for DEIB, even with strong diversity champions elsewhere in the organization, DEIB endeavors across the institution, not just for DEIB planning, will be hindered.

Step Eleven: Check-ins

Successful implementation of the planning process is well served by open lines of communication and follow-up. One best practice is to schedule regular meetings among implementation teams as a place to discuss updates, address challenges, and provide guidance. This process enhances collaboration and keeps progress on track.

In addition to meeting regularly, continuous feedback and recognition are crucial for empowering teams to overcome challenges and excel in their efforts. By providing guidance and resources, we empower teams to overcome challenges and excel in their initiatives.

Unit/Department Name:_____

Planning domain:	Monitor/Team leader:	
Goal #1 (goal + vehicle to get there - be SPECIFIC):		
Benchmark/Best practices (link to resources where available):		

Projected outcomes from baseline:	Timeline:	Actual outcomes *(report at end of project):*

Action items:		Timeline:	Completed:
1			
2			
3			
4			
5			

Notes/Assessment plan:

☐ *Introduction (describe the current environment, why this initiative is important):*

☐ *Assessment plan (include pre- and post-program steps to measure the differences in diversifying practices between pre-program and post-program):*

☐ *Notes (include any observations, for example action items that may have fallen short or observations about outcomes)*

Exhibit 8-2   DEIS strategic planning and reporting template.

To gauge the effectiveness of diversity strategies, it is essential to establish metrics and measure the impact of initiatives. By regularly monitoring KPIs, we can assess progress and identify areas for improvement. This data-driven approach helps us make informed decisions and adjust our strategies if necessary. Sharing these metrics and engaging in discussions with teams promotes transparency and accountability, fostering a sense of collective responsibility in achieving our DEIB objectives.

By maintaining regular communication through meetings, providing feedback and recognition, and monitoring metrics, team dynamics can be optimized. This approach ensures that the momentum continues, challenges are addressed, and progress is tracked. DEIB strategic planning can be a big "win," for organizations, creating a sense of accomplishment and an inclusive and equitable workplace culture that benefits everyone (see Exhibit 8-2).

Chapter Summary

An effective DEIB strategy plan is required for businesses that want to accomplish their vision and ambitions for diversity, equity, inclusion, and belonging. This chapter has provided a comprehensive roadmap that takes professionals through the process, providing vital insights on differentiating between desired outcomes and actionable activities. This chapter offered expert guidance on creating KPIs that accurately measure the plan's most important outcomes. Most notably, it emphasized the critical distinction between DEIB strategic plans that are merely performative or ineffective and those that have a significant and long-term influence, pushing professionals to strive for the latter.

References

Brown, A. M., Smith, T. A., & Johnson, R. A. (2019). Leadership commitment, strategic planning, and diversity climate: Exploring a holistic model for diversity management. *Journal of Diversity Management*, *14*(1), 9–23.

Chen, Y., Konrad, A. M., & Li, Y. (2020). Strategic diversity management, board diversity, and organizational performance. *Journal of Management*, *46*(6), 957–985.

Cox, T. H., & Blake, S. (1991). Managing cultural diversity: Implications for organizational competitiveness. *The Executive*, *5*(3), 45–56.

Crenshaw, K. (1989). Demarginalizing the intersection of race and sex: A black feminist critique of antidiscrimination doctrine, feminist theory, and antiracist politics. *University of Chicago Legal Forum*, *1989*(1), 139–167.

Griggs v. Duke Power Co., 401 U.S. 424 (1971).

Gutiérrez y Muhs, G., Niemann, Y. F., González, C. G., & Harris, A. P. (Eds.). (2012). *Presumed incompetent: The intersections of race and class for women in academia*. University Press of Colorado.

Harrison, D. A., Price, K. H., & Bell, M. P. (1998). Beyond relational demography: Time and the effects of surface-and deep-level diversity on work group cohesion. *Academy of Management Journal, 41*(1), 96–107.

Jackson, S. E., Joshi, A., & Erhardt, N. L. (2003). Recent research on team and organizational diversity: SWOT analysis and implications. *Journal of Management, 29*(6), 801–830.

Jones, R., Bouquet, C., & Snell, R. (2020). Why diverse teams are smarter. *Harvard Business Review*.

Kossek, E. E., & Lobel, S. A. (1996). Human resource strategies to manage workforce diversity: Examining "the business case". In A. E. Brief & B. M. Staw (Eds.), *Research in organizational behavior* (Vol. 18, pp. 185–216). JAI Press.

Lituchy, T. R., & Reavley, M. A. (2004). Women entrepreneurs: A comparison of international small business owners in Poland and the Czech Republic. *Journal of International Entrepreneurship, 2*, 61–87.

Nishii, L. H., Lepak, D. P., & Schneider, B. (2008). Employee attributions of the "why" of HR practices: Their effects on employee attitudes and behaviors, and customer satisfaction. *Personnel Psychology, 61*(3), 503–545.

Noe, R. A., Hollenbeck, J. R., Gerhart, B., & Wright, P. M (2020). *Fundamentals of human resource management*. McGraw-Hill Education.

Page, S. (2008). The difference. The difference. Princeton University Press.

Shore, L. M., Randel, A. E., Chung, B. G., Dean, M. A., Ehrhart, K. H., & Singh, G. (2011). Inclusion and diversity in work groups: A review and model for future research. *Journal of Management, 37*(4), 1262–1289. https://doi.org/10.1177/0149206310385943

Smith, M. (2015). The business case for diversity management in the hospitality industry. *Journal of Human Resources in Hospitality & Tourism, 14*(1), 1–20.

Smith, J. D., & Johnson, L. T. (2018). Diversity strategic planning in organizations: A comprehensive review and proposal for advancement. *Journal of Applied Social Science, 12*(2), 89–103.

Thomas, R. R. (2004). Building on the business case for diversity. *Academy of Management Perspectives, 18*(4), 103–108.

Thomas, D. A., & Ely, R. J. (1996). Making differences matter: A new paradigm for managing diversity. *Harvard Business Review, 74*(5), 79–90.

Chapter 9

Step 8: Implementing a Social Change Plan: Strategies for Broadening Access and Developing Collective Consciousness

S. Ron Banerjee

Case Study: Microsoft Corporation

One real-life example of a company that has implemented effective strategies to address diversity and inclusion is Microsoft Corporation. Microsoft, a multinational technology company, recognized the need for social change and transformation to counter the injustice of underrepresentation and create a more inclusive and equitable workplace. Microsoft's leadership understood that implementing effective strategies was crucial to achieving its diversity and inclusion goals.

They embarked on a comprehensive social change initiative, starting with assessing the current state of diversity and inclusion within the company. This assessment included gathering data on employee demographics, representation in leadership positions, and employee experiences and perceptions of diversity and inclusion. Based on the assessment findings, Microsoft set clear goals and objectives for its social change plan. They aimed to increase diversity at all levels of the organization, create an inclusive and respectful work environment, and ensure equal opportunities for career advancement for all employees.

DOI: 10.4324/9781003439714-9

Microsoft engaged in extensive communication and dialogue to develop a change story that resonated with employees and stakeholders. They held town hall meetings, focus groups, and surveys to gather employee input and feedback. This collaborative approach helped create a shared vision and a collective consciousness among change champions and organizational stakeholders. Microsoft recognized the importance of implementing innovative strategies to counter injustice and promote diversity and inclusion. They invested in training programs and workshops to raise awareness and educate employees about unconscious bias, cultural competence, and inclusive leadership. They also established employee resource groups and affinity networks to support and foster a sense of belonging for underrepresented groups.

Microsoft partnered with external organizations and community groups specializing in diversity and inclusion initiatives to broaden access to and penetration into target communities. They collaborated on recruitment efforts, mentorship programs, and community outreach activities to attract diverse talent and engage with the broader community.

Throughout the implementation process, Microsoft continuously monitored and evaluated the progress of its social change plan. They collected data on key performance indicators, such as employee satisfaction, representation, and retention rates, to assess the impact of their strategies. This data-driven approach allowed them to make necessary adjustments and improvements to ensure the plan's effectiveness.

Microsoft also addressed potential challenges and missteps that may arise during the implementation process. They provided ongoing training and support to managers and leaders to ensure they had the skills and knowledge to foster an inclusive and equitable work environment. They established clear policies and procedures to address discrimination or bias and created channels for employees to report concerns or seek assistance (Sehgal et al., 2020).

By implementing these strategies, Microsoft successfully transformed its organizational culture and created a more diverse and inclusive workplace.

Problem statement: Microsoft wished to counter social injustice inside its company and to show internal and external stakeholders they were committed to making transformational large-scale changes to build employee and consumer trust and loyalty.

Why is it important to understand social change plan integration? The social change plan acted as a catalyst for countering injustice and championing social and civic change within the organization and its communities (Sehgal et al., 2020). More so, future organizations will continue developing their stakeholders through adaptive planning strategies such as implementing a social change plan.

Future organizations will continue to strive for innovative ways to make sense of new social injustice challenges. They will need to build and effectively deliver "strong narratives that work on reassembling the past, the present, and the future .... and guide new courses of action" (Gordon et al., 2020, p. 26) Sarpong, Eyres & Batsakis, 2019).

Social change and transformation often grow organically from a need for social and civic change. Fueled by the desire to counter injustice, social transformative change requires organizations and change leaders to develop and implement effective, innovative, creative, and collaborative change strategies to counter injustice. In this chapter, we will explore strategies for broadening access to target communities, ensuring message and intention clarity, developing collective consciousness, and utilizing the power of the social change story to drive the successful implementation of a Social Change Plan.

What Does the Research Say?

Research on implementing social change plans has shown that organizations and change leaders must effectively develop innovative, creative, and collaborative strategies to counter injustice (Choi, Oh & Colbert, 2015). These strategies should focus on broadening access to and penetration into target communities while ensuring message and intention clarity. Developing a collective consciousness between change champions and other organizational and community stakeholders is essential for successful implementation.

According to recent research, elaborating a social change action plan or strategy mandates that the organization maintains continuity in messaging to key stakeholders. One study assessing almost 30 United Nations-affiliated companies and organizations suggests that securing continuity in action plan messaging assists in conveying priorities and critical immediate needs. Additional importance is placed on giving those who receive the social change action plan communication "a sense of ownership and accountability" (Achamkulangare, 2014, p. iii). The result is the penetration of target communities as partners, affiliates, advocates, and participants in social change.

This clarity of action also increases employee engagement in the future steps the organization is planning. By having a strong, planned communication effort, in the case of 28 United Nations affiliates, implementing a robust delivery system for the organization's social change plan would increase organizational chances of receiving up-front pipeline resources, which could be directed to the highest priority needs for immediate impact. By delivering and implementing a social change plan using an established mechanism, the ultimate result is that anyone doing so creates a transformative avenue for growing organic social change while "enabling atmosphere for successful resource mobilization" (iii).

Strategies for Broadening Access to Target Communities

Reaching diverse communities is crucial for the success of a social change plan. Developing strategies that can effectively engage and involve individuals from different backgrounds and communities is essential. This can be achieved through various means such as community partnerships, targeted outreach programs, and utilizing technology and social media platforms (Durlak et al., 2011; Van Zomeren, Postmes & Spears, 2008).

In addition to innovative and creative strategies, collaboration is vital in broadening access to target communities. Organizations can gain valuable insights and build trust by partnering with community organizations, stakeholders, and individuals who influence and know the target communities (Zomeren, Postmes & Spears, 2008). Collaborative approaches have succeeded in school-based universal interventions, where school teaching staff successfully conducted social and emotional learning programs (Zomeren, Postmes & Spears, 2008).

To effectively broaden access to target communities, it is essential to consider the role of social identity in collective action. Research has shown that social identity plays a significant role in predicting collective action and engagement in social change initiatives (Zomeren, Postmes & Spears, 2008). When individuals perceive injustice and identify strongly with a politicized social group, they are more likely to engage in collective action to address the perceived injustice (Zomeren, Postmes & Spears, 2008). Therefore, organizations implementing a social change plan should consider strategies that foster a sense of social identity and mobilize individuals to act (Zomeren, Postmes & Spears, 2008).

It is essential to recognize the impact of perceived discrimination on collective action and social change. Perceived discrimination can harm psychological well-being. However, it can motivate individuals to unite, advocate for social change, and hope for the future (Kim, 2008). By addressing and challenging discrimination, organizations can create an environment that fosters collective action and promotes social justice (Kim, 2008).

To effectively broaden access to target communities, it is crucial to consider the unique experiences and perspectives of different groups. This includes understanding the specific challenges and barriers faced by marginalized communities and tailoring strategies to address their needs (Zomeren, Postmes & Spears, 2008). By involving and empowering these communities in the social change process, organizations can ensure their voices are heard, and their needs are met (Schreiber, 2016; Zomeren, Postmes & Spears, 2008).

Strategies for broadening access to target communities in implementing a social change plan include developing partnerships, utilizing technology and social media, fostering social identity, addressing perceived discrimination, and tailoring strategies to the specific needs of marginalized communities. Organizations can effectively engage diverse communities and promote meaningful social change by employing these strategies.

Ensuring Message and Intention Clarity

Clear communication is essential in implementing a social change plan. Organizations must develop effective messaging strategies that convey the plan's purpose, goals, and intended outcomes. It is essential to address potential barriers to understanding, such as language or cultural differences, and tailor the messaging to resonate with the target communities (Durlak et al., 2011). Communication strategies used in school-based interventions have positively "improved social and emotional skills, attitudes, behavior, and academic performance" (Aidman & Price, 2018, p. 26, Durlak et al., 2011).

Ensuring message and intention clarity is crucial in implementing a social change plan. Organizations must develop effective messaging strategies that convey the plan's purpose, goals, and intended outcomes. It is essential to address potential barriers to understanding, such as language or cultural differences, and tailor the messaging to resonate with the target communities (Bostrom, Böhm & O'Connor, 2013). By doing so, organizations can ensure that their message is effectively communicated and understood by the intended audience.

Research has shown that communication strategies used in school-based interventions positively improve social and emotional skills, attitudes, behavior, and academic performance (Bostrom, Böhm, & O'Connor, 2013). Effective communication is vital in engaging individuals and motivating them to participate in social change initiatives. By clearly articulating the purpose and goals of the social change plan, organizations can inspire individuals to act and contribute to the desired social transformation (Bostrom, Böhm, & O'Connor, 2013).

Effective communication is essential in addressing potential misconceptions or resistance to change. By providing clear and accurate information, organizations can dispel misunderstandings and build trust with the target communities (Cherry & Borshuk, 1998). This can help overcome barriers and resistance to change, fostering a supportive environment for implementing the social change plan.

Tailoring the messaging to resonate with the target communities is also crucial. Different communities may have unique cultural, linguistic, or social contexts that influence their understanding and perception of social change initiatives. By considering these factors and adapting the messaging, organizations can ensure their message is relatable and meaningful to the target communities (Cherry & Borshuk, 1998). This can enhance communication effectiveness and increase the likelihood of engagement and participation.

Ensuring message and intention clarity is essential in implementing a social change plan. Organizations can effectively communicate the plan's purpose, goals, and intended outcomes by developing effective messaging strategies, addressing potential barriers to understanding, and tailoring the messaging to resonate with the target communities. This can inspire individuals to act, overcome resistance to change, and foster a supportive environment for implementing the social change plan.

Developing Collective Consciousness

Developing collective consciousness between change champions and other organizational and community stakeholders is crucial for successfully implementing a social change plan. This involves building relationships and partnerships, engaging stakeholders in the change process, and fostering a sense of shared purpose and responsibility (Cohen, 2013; Durlak et al., 2011). Creating collective consciousness among change champions and stakeholders effectively drives social change initiatives (Cohen, 2013; Durlak et al., 2011).

Building relationships and partnerships are essential in implementing a social change plan. Organizations can gain valuable insights, support, and resources by connecting with key stakeholders, such as community leaders (Cohen, 2013). Collaborative efforts can lead to a more comprehensive understanding of social issues and generate innovative solutions (Cohen, 2013). Partnerships can help mobilize collective action and create a united front in advocating for change (Cohen, 2013).

Engaging stakeholders in the change process is crucial for their buy-in and commitment to the social change plan. By involving stakeholders from the early stages of planning and decision-making, organizations can ensure that their perspectives and needs are considered (Siminoff & Step, 2005). This participatory approach fosters a sense of ownership and empowerment among stakeholders, increasing their motivation to actively contribute to implementing the plan (Siminoff & Step, 2005). Additionally, engaging stakeholders can help identify potential barriers and challenges, allowing for proactive problem-solving and adaptation of strategies (Siminoff & Step, 2005).

Fostering a sense of shared purpose and responsibility is vital in creating collective consciousness. By clearly articulating the mission, vision, and values of the social change plan, organizations can align stakeholders around a common goal (Siminoff & Step, 2005). This shared purpose creates a sense of unity and collective identity, motivating individuals to work together toward the desired social transformation (Siminoff & Step, 2005). Fostering a sense of responsibility among stakeholders encourages them to take ownership of their roles and actively contribute to the plan's success (Siminoff & Step, 2005).

Research has shown that collective consciousness and stakeholder collaboration can produce positive outcomes in various domains. In the workplace, studies have found that employee satisfaction and engagement at the business-unit level are associated with improved business outcomes, including customer satisfaction, productivity, profit, employee turnover, and safety (Nahrgang, Morgeson & Hofmann, 2011). In healthcare settings, collective consciousness and collaboration among healthcare professionals have been linked to improved patient safety and quality of care (Nahrgang, Morgeson & Hofmann, 2011). These findings highlight the importance of developing collective consciousness in driving positive change.

Developing collective consciousness between change champions and stakeholders is crucial for successfully implementing a social change plan. Building relationships and partnerships, engaging stakeholders in the change process, and fostering a sense of shared purpose and responsibility are key strategies to promote collective consciousness. By involving stakeholders and creating a collaborative environment, organizations can harness individuals' collective power and expertise to drive meaningful social change (Crowther et al., 2016).

The Role of the Social Change Story

The social change story lies at the center of successfully implementing a Social Change Plan and is the mechanism for transformation. Crafting a compelling change story that reflects the mission and vision of the Social Change Plan is essential in engaging and inspiring individuals to support and participate in the change process (Crowther et al., 2016).

Storytelling uniquely captures people's attention, evokes emotions, and connects the audience and the message. By crafting a compelling change story, organizations can effectively communicate the social change plan's purpose, goals, and desired outcomes (Flory & Iglasias, 2010). This narrative can inspire individuals to actively participate in the change process, fostering a sense of ownership and commitment to the cause (Prasetyo, 2017).

Storytelling is effective in changing attitudes and behaviors. By presenting real-life examples and personal narratives, organizations can illustrate the impact of the social change plan on individuals and communities (Heckelman, Unger & Garofano, 2013). This can help individuals relate to the cause and understand the importance of their involvement in driving the desired change (Heckelman Unger & Garofano, 2013).

Additionally, storytelling can help break down complex concepts and make them more accessible to a broader audience. By using narratives and relatable characters, organizations can simplify complex social issues and engage individuals who may not have prior knowledge or understanding of the topic (Cohen, 2013). This can promote inclusivity and ensure that diverse perspectives are considered in the social change process (Cohen, 2013).

The social change story is a powerful tool for successfully implementing a Social Change Plan. By crafting a compelling narrative that reflects the mission and vision of the plan, organizations can engage and inspire individuals to support and participate in the change process. The power of storytelling has been recognized in various fields, including healthcare, where it has been used to reduce unnecessary antibiotics and improve patient-oriented interventions. By harnessing the power of storytelling, organizations can effectively communicate their message, change attitudes and behaviors, and drive meaningful social change.

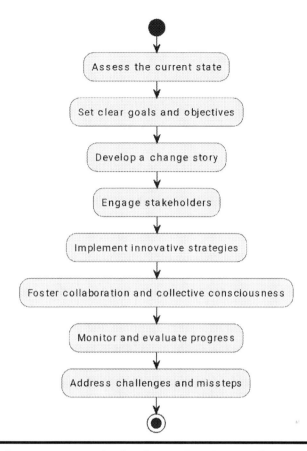

Exhibit 9-1   Step-by-step process for implementing the social change plan.

Putting It Into Practice

Step One: **Assess the Current State:** Conduct a thorough assessment of the organization's culture, practices, and policies to identify areas requiring change and improvement. This assessment should include gathering data on diversity and inclusion metrics, employee experiences, and perceptions (see Exhibit 9-1).

Step Two: **Set Clear Goals and Objectives:** Define clear and measurable goals and objectives for the social change plan. These goals should align with the organization's mission and vision and reflect the desired outcomes of the plan.

Step Three: **Develop a Change Story:** Create a compelling narrative that communicates the need for change, the vision for a more inclusive and equitable organization, and the benefits of the social change plan. This change story should resonate with employees, stakeholders, and the broader community.

Step Four: **Engage Stakeholders:** Involve key stakeholders, including employees, leaders, customers, and community members, in the development and implementation of the social change plan. Seek their input, feedback, and support to ensure a sense of ownership and commitment to the plan.

Step Five: **Implement Innovative Strategies:** Utilize innovative strategies to broaden access to and penetration into target communities. This can include leveraging technology, social media, and community partnerships to reach a wider audience and engage them in social change efforts.

Step Six: **Foster Collaboration and Collective Consciousness:** Create collaboration and collective consciousness opportunities among change champions and stakeholders. This can be achieved through regular communication, training programs, workshops, and forums that promote dialogue, understanding, and shared commitment to the social change plan.

Step Seven: **Monitor and Evaluate Progress:** Continuously monitor and evaluate the progress of the social change plan. Collect data, measure key performance indicators, and assess the impact of the implemented strategies. Use this information to make necessary adjustments and improvements to ensure the plan's effectiveness.

Step Eight: **Address Challenges and Missteps:** Anticipate potential challenges and missteps during implementation. Develop contingency plans and strategies to address these challenges proactively. Regularly communicate with stakeholders, provide support, and address concerns to maintain momentum and engagement.

Chapter Summary

1. Implementing a social change plan requires organizations and change leaders to employ strategies that broaden access to target communities, ensure message and intention clarity, develop collective consciousness, and utilize the power of the social change story.
2. Organizations can champion social and civic change in their communities by following a step-by-step process and countering injustice.

3. It is essential to learn from successful case studies and leverage evidence-based practices to improve any chances for not only the success of the social change plan but also the cultural change acceptance that follows.

References

Achamkulangare, G. (2014). An analysis of the resource mobilization function within the United Nations system. A joint inspection unit report in Geneva, Switzerland.

Aidman, B., & Price, P. (2018). Social and emotional learning at the middle level: One school's journey. *Middle School Journal, 49*(3), 26.

Bostrom, A., Böhm, G., & O'Connor, R. E. (2013). Targeting and tailoring climate change communications: Targeting and tailoring climate change communications. *Wiley Interdisciplinary Reviews: Climate Change, 4*(5), 447–455.

Cherry, F., & Borshuk, C. (1998). Social action research and the commission on community interrelations. *Journal of Social Issues, 54*(1), 119–142.

Choi, D., Oh, I., & Colbert, A. E. (2015). Understanding organizational commitment: A meta-analytic examination of the roles of the five-factor model of personality and culture. *Journal of Applied Psychology, 100*(5), 1542–1567. https://doi.org/10.1037/apl0000014

Cohen, A. P. (2013). Symbolic construction of community. https://doi.org/10.4324/9780203131688

Crowther, S., Ironside, P., Spence, D., & Smythe, E. (2016). Crafting stories in hermeneutic phenomenology research: A methodological device. *Qual Health Res, 27*(6), 826–835. https://doi.org/10.1177/1049732316656161

Durlak, J. A., Weissberg, R. P., Dymnicki, A. B., Taylor, R., & Schellinger, K. B. (2011). The impact of enhancing Students' social and emotional learning: A meta-analysis of school-based universal interventions. *Child Development, 82*(1), 405–432. https://doi.org/10.1111/j.1467-8624.2010.01564.x

Flory, M. J., & Iglasias, O. (2010). Once upon a time: The role of rhetoric and narratives in management research and practice. *Journal of Organizational Change Management, 23*, 113–119.

Gordon, A. V., Ramic, M., Rohrbeck, R., & Spaniol, M. J. (2020). 50 years of corporate and organizational foresight: Looking back and going forward, *Technological Forecasting and Social Change, 154*, 119966, https://doi.org/10.1016/j.techfore.2020.119966

Heckelman, W. L., Unger, S., & Garofano, C. (2013). Driving culture transformation during large-scale change. *OD Practitioner, 45*(3), 25–30.

Kim, J. (2008). Perception of social change and psychological well-being: A study focusing on social change in Korea between 1997 and 2000. *Journal of Applied Social Psychology, 38*(11), 2821–2858. https://doi.org/10.1111/j.1559-1816.2008.00415.x

Nahrgang, J. D., Morgeson, F. P., & Hofmann, D. A. (2011). Safety at work: A meta-analytic investigation of the link between job demands, job resources, burnout, engagement, and safety outcomes. *Journal of Applied Psychology, 1*(96), 71–94. https://doi.org/10.1037/a0021484

Prasetyo, Y. (2017). From storytelling to social change: the power of story in the community building. *SSRN Electronic Journal.* https://doi.org/10.2139/ssrn.3094947

Sarpong, D., Eyres, E., & Batsakis, G. (2019). Narrating the future: A distentive capability approach to strategic foresight, *Technological Forecasting and Social Change, 140*, 105–114, https://doi.org/10.1016/j.techfore.2018.06.034

Schreiber, R. (2016). Community-based prototypes play an integral role in effecting lasting healthcare change. *Generations Today, 37*(5), 1.

Sehgal, G., Kee, D. M. H., Low, A. R., Chin, Y. S., Woo, E. M. Y., Lee, P. F., & Almutairi, F. (2020). Corporate social responsibility: A case study of microsoft corporation. *Asia Pacific Journal of Management and Education, 3*(1), 63–71.

Siminoff, L., & Step, M. (2005). A communication model of shared decision-making: Accounting for cancer treatment decisions. *Health Psychology, 4*(24), S99–S105. https://doi.org/10.1037/0278-6133.24.4.s99

Zomeren, M. v., Postmes, T., & Spears, R. (2008). Toward an integrative social identity model of collective action: A quantitative research synthesis of three socio-psychological perspectives. *Psychological Bulletin, 134*(4), 504–535. https://doi.org/10.1037/0033-2909.134.4.504

Chapter 10

Step 9: Managing Opposition Inside and Outside the Organization

Jamie Campbell

Case Study: The Story

An old story goes like this:

> On an early freezing morning, a little bird fell out of its nest and
> onto the wet freezing ground below, as luck would have it the
> bird's wings froze, and they appeared trapped in the grass. In their
> despair came a large brown cow and did what cows do in the
> mornings *right on top* of the partially frozen bird. The bird thought
> to itself, *what else can happen?* As the warmth of the cow's passing
> began to melt the ice the bird then thought, *well this is better, but
> I am such a mess, won't anyone help me?* At that moment, the bird
> felt something brushing it off and setting it upright. At last, the bird
> thought *I am free! My luck is changing!* As the bird turned to thank
> its benefactor, it realized its savior was…. *a cat.*

The moral of the story is *everyone who dumps something on you is not
always your enemy and everyone who elevates you is not your friend.*

If you are wondering how this story and its moral relate to dealing with
opposition in advancing social change in society through the corporate
world, let us take the story apart.

DOI: 10.4324/9781003439714-10

First, there is the *environment*. The *bird* goes from starting in a comfortable position to one of distress and despair. There is also a point of confusion about the environment, essentially what to do next because the situation seems so overwhelming. The *cow* is adding to the problem due to the bird's perspective. Last, there is the savior, the *cat*. A seemingly helpful individual, but whose self-involved motives can harm, or create a perilous situation for the bird.

In this chapter, we will look at how the environment, the bird, the cat, and the cow can affect the efforts of social change in the corporate environment. After reading this chapter you should be able to

- ■ Understand who is opposing the change.
- ■ Define ways to bring individuals to your cause.
- ■ How to engage upper, middle, and lower management
- ■ Confront naysayers.
- ■ Build alliances.

Let us continue to review our story and apply it to implement social change in the workplace while dealing with opposition to not only the social change taking place but also the prospect of your organization engaging in it.

Understanding the Why

After reading that story, if you are mad at the cat, you do not understand the cat's why. The cat is a hunter, and the bird, for the cat—is prey. In the natural order of things can you be mad at the cat being itself? Of course not! And in your thought process, you may have rationalized it as, *well the cat is just being itself and that is too bad for the bird, but a cat is a cat.*

Some individuals you work with will be "engaged" in the work for many reasons. These reasons can be varied and many. First, they may be part of the *true believers'* group. Merriam-Webster defines a true believer as either a person who possesses total faith in something or someone, or a zealot. This group can be opposed to your idea from everything from the idea is not their idea, to progression with this space idea impedes a project they are championing.

Either way, the people in this group can be hard to deal with, and almost impossible to move. This is because they believe strongly in their positions based on their individual life experience. Once a cause or social movement is added, it can be complicated, multifaceted, and just plain hard to engage with (Crawford, 2000).

What Does the Research Say?

First, to understand something, you must first be able to define it. *Opposition,* if you looked it up across various places (when researching this chapter, I reviewed six sites: Merriam-Webster.com, dictionary.com, dictionary.cambridge.org, thefreedicitionary.com, Britannica.com, and vocabulary.com). They all have three words in common: 1. Against, 2. Resisting, and 3. Combating. In considering these words, it can be understood that each word has a different positioning when dealing with persons in the workplace. Let us review the three types of opposition in the workplace:

■ *Against,* in the workplace does not mean total disagreement. Against can mean there are other concerns as to *why* people can be counter to your current idea. Against can mean an individual wants to agree with you, but things such as fear of failure, funding, timelines, and views of the political climate. You may hear questions like:
  • Can we do this?
  • Is this the most effective/efficient use of resources?
  • How does this help?
■ *Resisting* is usually an elevation of against, in that the individual stands opposed to your thoughts because of their bias (both conscious and unconscious), beliefs, or culturally defined positions. Resisting can sound like but is not limited to statements such as:
  • This is not how we have done ____ in the past.
  • Our business is not structured for this.
  • Do you think our board will support this?
■ *Combating* is the most complicated to deal with of the stages. The reason is that the individual does not care about the validity of your idea, the strength of agreement for the idea, or even their relationship with you. They are positioned to argue with you because they are (possibly) looking to enhance their status in the organization, society, or political affiliations. These people are sometimes opposed just because they find it the easiest thing to do. Of the types combative is the most challenging because the individual often *refuses to actively listen* to you. Active listening here means not letting you have space to present your idea. The combative push can sound like (but is not limited to)
  • This is a dumb/stupid idea/plan.
  • You cannot be serious about trying to implement this!
  • Who gave *you* the authority to do this?

In dealing with opposition, you may also find it is almost like dealing with a change management situation (Norton, 2008). Karl Lewin, a noted researcher, and author on change management simply took change management apart to mean having a three-step process 1. unfreezing, 2. moving, and then finally 3. freezing (Wirth, 2004). Think of it this way, when you first encounter your "opposition" they may be entranced in their position. This position can be so locked in, that it could be seen as trying to pick up an iceberg. Looks like an easy task when you are only looking at the top of the iceberg because it's small at the top, trying to get a grip on things gets larger as you go deeper dealing in this frozen space. Hence, you have to thaw the individuals out of their "blocked" position, all the time remembering you might not melt the whole situation down. However, as the situation begins to melt—there is movement! Remember this movement will be disruptive and *onion-like*. By using the term onion-like, this speaks to the layers of dealing with opposition. Engaging opposition means tackling layers that opposition brings: the presenting issue, the underlying issue, the resolution, and implementing an agreed solution (Rothwell, Imroz & Bakhshandeh 2021). Instead of using a strengths, weaknesses, opportunities, and threats analysis. This process is better known as a strengths, opportunities, weakness, and threats (SWOT) analysis. Most people would use this method to gather information for persons who may oppose their ideas. However, a possibly better tool can be used for this exercise. Built on a four-square model that looks like a SWOT analysis, the Johari Window focuses on *how* and *why* individuals behave in certain ways (Luft & Ingham, 1961). Exhibit 10-1 details what a Johari Window (with some mediation) would look like to assess intergroup relationships (Rothwell, Ealy & Campbell 2022). The breakdown of the

What everyone else knows	Q1: Known issues	Q2: Blindsides
The unexpected	Q3: Unforced errors	Q4: The grey
	What you do know	What you do not know

Exhibit 10-1   Johari opposition window.

quadrants (Q) would be represented like this, note the quadrants have been slightly modified for this text (Luft & Ingham, 1961).

- The top left (Q1) would be the Known Issues.
  - The presenting issues—the things you know are coming.
- The top right (Q2) would be Blindsides.
  - The things you do not know about, but everyone else seems to.
- The bottom left (Q3) the Unforced Errors.
  - These are errors you can see, but others are running headfirst into them.
- The bottom right (Q4) can be considered the Grey Area.
  - These are the people/issues that come out of nowhere! They surprise all with their concerns. These individuals are usually there *after* everything has been negotiated or "settled" which can cause a complete restart if not dealt with effectively.

Another way to look at dealing with opposition can be to look at it from a *restorative justice Exhibit 10-2* lens (Costello, Wachtel & Wachtel, 2019). As this is a text focused on helping the organization bring its social justice efforts, it would stand that a review of an organizational change window to go along with the Johari window would be appropriate.

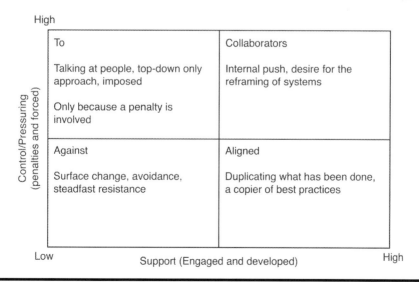

Exhibit 10-2   Oppositional organizational change window.

Adapted from Wachtel and McCold 1969

Putting It into Practice

The newly created position of DEIBA Director has been occupied by **Aki Smith** for the past year. They have begun to make significant headway. They have done a job that everyone has recognized has been beneficial to Atlas Organization, but they have been charged by the CEO **Allison King** to move the organization into the social justice realm of diversity. King has tasked them with creating a program that highlights the efforts that Atlas was making in the social justice arena. Aki recognized that they needed to assemble a team of high-level managers and entry-level team members. They chose people with power, but more importantly, they had *influence* as well. They gathered; **Naomi Wes**, senior financial officer, **Antonio Villi**, senior marketing officer, **Jacob Sims**, deputy director of staff, **Mark Ironshoe**, assistant DEIBA director, **Michelle Baque**, leader of people engagement, **Harriet "Harri" Mans**, vice president of Atlas' employee resource group—AtBlk. They also invited two relatively recent (**Mike Jenkins** and **Mary Briggs**) hires that have been fast-tracked for future leadership in the organization. Aki is not sure how to engage the community in this endeavor, but they hope that the head of the Atlas Foundation, **Stacey Woods**, can assist.

Step One: Checking In

Before pulling everyone together at the first meeting, Aki wanted to do a *climate check* first with the people they would have on the committee. In a meeting with their assistant director, they found that Mark did not want to be involved, but felt he had to as his boss, Aki, was involved. He also expressed his desire to lead a change effort in the office. They also ran into Naomi at another meeting but had a hallway meeting with her. Naomi said at this point she could not see how this effort would work because Atlas has tried this before and it has not worked before but *doing something is better than doing nothing*. Her parting question to Aki was *"How much is this going to cost?"* Jacob came by their office to express his support and gave Aki information from a blog he read that discussed the need for business to just" be business. Having coffee with Mike and Mary, they heard that Mike was engaged because he saw how this could help his career and personal development. Mary would work because she felt called to be in a social justice engagement both within and outside the organization. They also found that Michelle and Harri were both excited to be working on the project but seemed overwhelmed with *the task* of integrating social justice into an already complex organizational structure and pushing it out to external stakeholders. Antonio communicated directly to her that he should lead this effort because it is not a diversity effort but an effort around a simple message. He felt that though they were qualified they did not have the best expertise to lead this endeavor. He also wanted to know: *how long will this take?* Last, they met with Stacey, and he explained that movements such as Atlas' efforts often hinder or hurt the community. He would be on the committee *to ensure the people were heard.*

Aki felt that all persons were engaged and had a reasonable idea of every person's concern and possible points of contention. They began to produce a plan of operation to deal with the opposition that they were facing.

Step Two: First Concerns

Aki recognized that to begin to deal with general opposition they needed to prevent *mission creep* or *overreaching* the project. Opposition to ideas or planned programs can come about because individuals cannot understand what the goal is or what the desired outcome should be. Aki also heard that money and time were also concerns of the assembled group. This recognition helped them to define an agile budget and a comprehensive timeline. Creation of these two items, with the recognition that for this idea to work they would need to receive input from the table at large on specific ties to the budget and timeline could alleviate some of the group's fears with illustrated efforts of what is coming next, while they did not intend this to be a complete road map, they intended for these documents to provide direction and intent while not just demonstrating activity for activity's sake.

Initially, Aki thought to create a SWOT analysis of the situation but realized because they were dealing with more than just facts, the personalities involved called for something more. They used a Johari window (Exhibit 10-1) to give themselves a sense of transparency with the current situation and everyone's concerns. They then took that knowledge and applied it to their oppositional change assessment (Exhibit 10-2).

After putting these two squares together, they began to review how they would approach each individual member of the committee to move the whole group forward successfully in accomplishing the goal that they were assigned.

Step Three: Dealing with Underlying Problems

They began working to meet with Antonio to understand what his additional concerns were, before having the larger meeting with the whole team. In conversation with him, she found that he was genuinely interested in the project but had been overlooked for leadership because he had been seen as too "combative" when dealing with groups that did not report to him. They also found that he felt he was not being heard inside the organization as this "new initiative" was something he proposed last year. Aki also found that they had positive ideas but felt they were a part of the "corporate machine," and they would not hear him. They thought the best way to engage him was to; first ensure ways he could be heard at the table, second observe him to see where they could be supportive to him in working with members outside his immediate circles, last they wanted to help him to see that his engagement with the project was not about marginalization but how his idea is coming to fruition.

Next, they moved ahead with speaking again to Michelle and Harri and though they had met with them, Aki wanted to follow up to be sure they had all the issues lined up appropriately. In reviewing the conversation, they found that the issue was not just the scope, but the seriousness that Atlas was going to engage in the work that needed to be done for this effort to be a success. Both Harri and Michelle had been involved in other Atlas efforts where things have been offered to the public as new initiatives and change efforts but had no actual support, budget, or accountability. Aki felt that to alleviate these concerns they needed to present the budget at the charge meeting, have the CEO as an ex-officio member—attending the first meeting, and have her strongly suggest other unit heads be engaged. They also thought it would be important to show this group will not be a "placeholder" or change management exercise of nothingness, but that metrics will identify success and failures to ensure overall positive outcomes.

Last, they engaged Stacey. Aki felt that by engaging the foundation last, they would have a better idea of where and what the external opposition is and be able to clearly collaborate with the external stakeholders to present a positive viewpoint after engaging the internal conflicts. In engaging Stacey, they found that he was happy to help but he did not want to engage the effort with the community. He felt three things about this project:
1. The organization had stranded him once before in trying to engage the community. It took time and effort to regain the trust of the community

leaders and elders who saw promises unfulfilled. 2. He saw no actual engagement of the people and thought Atlas was being too "parental" about the current situation. 3. He did not believe there would be a budget for the program to be a success.

Aki first had to convince Stacey he would not be deserted in the difficult points of the project to get his support. As with other members of the team, they recognized the need to demonstrate that Atlas had the financial backing for the efforts. They also accepted the idea that the social change movement would need members of the community at the table once everyone was finally at the table.

Step Four: Pulling Things Together

After having these conversations, Aki then began to envision the first meeting. In thinking of all things, they heard and observed both presenting and underlying concerns, they needed to map out the organizational structure and profiles for the newly forming team. When reviewing their notes, they created a form to help them keep track of the issues and concerns that could become potential problems at a later time (the tool they created can be seen in the tool section of this chapter).

Aki created a chart that could show them where the team was and set the project up for success. The headers for their chart were;

1. Who are the people that could be/are the opposition?
   a. What position do they hold?
   b. Use their preferred name.
2. The individuals' presenting and underlying concerns.
   a. Determine what is more important to deal with first the presenting or the underlying, but both must be addressed in the early part of the project.
3. Who could influence them, or who they could influence?
   a. Recognizing spheres of influence in any project is necessary for successful outcomes. Know the streams of influence members of the team have or how they can be influenced.
4. Help or Hindrance
   a. If they are a help, thoughts on how to keep them there.
   b. If they are a hindrance—how to deal with their contention to push them into becoming some help?

Step Five: Moving Forward

Aki felt they had enough information to work through the genuine issues of the project. They found that the project would still have opposition and conflict, but they now had a better handle on both internal and external opposition to the project.

In going past the traditional SWOT analysis, they felt they had solutions for traditional and non-traditional problems. In creating an Opposition Profile Tool they could create a plan for dealing with gripes and complaints that could occur by dealing with the problems head-on in a positive manner. Aki also recognized that even with all the preliminary work they had done, they still might not have everyone as engaged as they would have liked, but they now had a constructive path for that situation.

Four B's

As individuals create opposition make sure that you recognize where your positions stand. In dealing with these persons, it is also important to remember fourthings:

1. Be gracious in victory.

   It was thought (by some people) that rubbing a pet's nose in its mistakes was a great teaching tool. But this was one of the worst possible things to do (Pevny, n.d.)! The same can be said with people. There is a way to be right without *"rubbing their noses in it"* Like it or not you may have to work with these individuals on another project. Creating a space where individuals can present opposing viewpoints without fear of denigration or retaliation will go further in creating a stronger team for difficult challenges that may be ahead.

2. Be quick to acknowledge when/if you are in error.

   Sometimes, those who oppose your plan or idea might be...*right*. Despite how many times they have been wrong, they got it right this time. Do not wait for others to bring it to your attention, deal with it—upfront (Wachtel & McCold, 2001). Admit where the error(s) were and present possible solutions to the situation. Acknowledge the individual's idea, or statement that was correct. Engage them in a solution(s) to the problem. This is not an easy thing to do, but it will position your leadership in a better position. It should demonstrate the ability to hear disagreement and listen to it earnestly and justly to the rest of the team.

3. Be secure in your mission.

    The approach may need to change as information and data come into focus. The goal of the group must kept at the forefront of the team. Engage people in various areas to provide different viewpoints that allow you to hear and understand different perspectives. This will help you to understand the different points without feeling attacked or persecuted when opposing ideas are presented.

4. Be wise about the well-meaning

    Last, it was mentioned that in dealing with opposition there may be those who seem to support an idea or an effort but cast negative opinions for various reasons, saying things like *that's not the way I would do it, but if you think it's right.* Sometimes those who are well-meaning in their intent do not recognize the barriers that they are creating. Being aware of their "why" will determine if they are helping and how to work around them, or through them, for successful project completion.

Chapter Summary

Opposition to innovative ideas and efforts is not only natural but necessary for projects to succeed. For there not to a be constant level of *groupthink,* opposition can be a key form of course correction and project alignment.

As members team just "go along to get along" they contribute to the possible failure of the project. Opposition becomes a problem when the true concerns of individuals on the team are hidden. Total agreement in a project does not mean moving to success; rather, it could mean *everyone* is thinking in the same wrong way! Many people get stuck or cemented in what or how the opposition is doing to counter their efforts. By stripping away the bluster and seeing the argument for what it is truly, individuals can see what direction they need to take to ensure a positive outcome (Somer, McCoy & Luke, 2021).

Opposition is a tool, and when used positively it can be a tool that creates effective change and remains true to OD and change management principles.

Directions: Use this tool to help you deal with your organization's internal opposition. There are no right or wrong answers in any absolute sense, but to the extent, you can recognize the individuals in your organization's culture/working space that have opposition the more successful you are likely to be in dealing with it. Be appropriate to you and your leaders. But at least this gives you a flexible action plan as a place to start. Add rows as needed. Review the examples given and modify as you need to.

	Who are the people who have problems? What is their title?	What is their outward concern? What are their "cards on the table" concern	Do they have power, influence, neither, or both?	Help or hindrance
1.	Naomi, Senior Financial Officer	Wants demonstrated stewardship of funds. Does not believe in the efforts because they do not see the return on investment.	Both: have the ear of the CEO, go to church with the CIO, and control the section budget	Help: will help keep the budget on the positive side
2.	Antonio, Senior Marketing Office	Timeline of project rollout. Feels they should be in charge, wants additional power	Great deal of influence, is well-liked by all, and has no decision-making power	Small hindrance: – until his voice is heard to his liking, he will voice his displeasure with the project
3.				
4.				
5.				

Exhibit 10-3   Tool for dealing with opposition.

Key Points

1. Do not look at the opposition as a negative proposition. Think of it as a preventive measure to ensure success.
2. You may not win your opposition over by restating your points. Sometimes you have to take their agreements away from them.
   - Let the opposition speak about their position.
   - Consider the rational points.
   - Work those points into your argument.

3. Be willing to engage in uncomfortable situations.
    • The opposition rarely thinks that individuals will engage openly. Hence those against your idea will often create uncomfortable situations, so they can silence your points. Embrace the discomfort and make your voice heard.
4. Remember the opposition may just want to be heard (Norton, 2008) (see Exhibit 10-3)

References

Costello, B., Wachtel, J., & Wachtel, T. (2019). *The restorative practices handbook: For teachers, disciplinarians, and administrators.* International Institute for Restorative Practices.

Cox, T. H., & Blake, S. (1991). Managing cultural diversity: Implications for organizational competitiveness. *Academy of Management Perspectives, 5*(3), 45–56.

Crawford, J. (2000). *At war with diversity: US language policy in an age of anxiety.*

Luft, J., & Ingham, H. (1961). The Johari window. *Human Relations Training News, 5*(1), 6–7.

Meares, M. M., Oetzel, J. G., Torres, A., Derkacs, D., & Ginossar, T. (2004). Employee mistreatment and muted voices in the culturally diverse workplace. *Journal of Applied Communication Research, 32*(1), 4–27.

Norton, P. (2008). Making sense of opposition. *The Journal of Legislative Studies, 14*(1–2), 236–250.

Pevny, L. (n.d.). https://littledogtips.com/does-rubbing-your-dogs-nose-in-their-own-poop-or-pee-really-work/. Little Dogs Tips. https://littledogtips.com/does-rubbing-your-dogs-nose-in-their-own-poop-or-pee-really-work/

Rothwell, W. J., Ealy, P. L., & Campbell, J. (Eds.). (2022). *Rethinking organizational diversity, equity, and inclusion: A step-by-step guide for facilitating effective change.* Routledge. https://doi.org/10.4324/9781003184935

Rothwell, W. J., Imroz, S. M., & Bakhshandeh, B. (Eds.). (2021). *Organization development interventions: Executing effective organizational change.* CRC Press.

Somer, M., McCoy, J. L., & Luke, R. E. (2021). Pernicious polarization, autocratization, and opposition strategies. *Democratization, 28*(5), 929–948.

Wachtel, T., & McCold, P. (2001). Restorative justice in everyday life. *Restorative justice and civil society,* Cambridge University Press, 114–129.

Wirth, R. A. (2004). Lewin/Schein's change theory.

Chapter 11

Step 10: Showcasing Your Organization's Talent: Beyond Organizational Borders

Phillip L. Ealy

Case Study: Patagonia

Patagonia is a company immersed in innovation and a commitment to live with the environment according to the history listed on its website. Yvon Chouinard, Patagonia founder, started a climbing equipment company where they innovated climbing gear to be more environmentally friendly moving away from steel pitons. Going from steel pitons that damaged the wall face to aluminum chocks (Patagonia, 2023b). Chouinard expanded into clothing and showed the same innovation there. As Patagonia grew, the innovation and commitment to the environment continued as they developed their 1% for the planet philosophy. Sonsev (2019) stated that "Patagonia donates 1% of their sales to grassroots environmental organizations (approximately $20MM annually) and spends more time advocating for environmental causes than they do marketing their own products. And their business continues to thrive as a result" (last paragraph). Patagonia's website states:

> Since 1985, Patagonia has pledged 1% of sales to the preservation and restoration of the natural environment. We've awarded over $140 million in cash and in-kind donations to domestic and international grassroots environmental groups making a difference in their local communities. In 2002, founder of Patagonia, Yvon

                                        DOI: 10.4324/9781003439714-11

Chouinard, and Craig Mathews, owner of Blue Ribbon Flies, created a non-profit corporation to encourage other businesses to do the same.

(Patagonia, 2023a, 1% for the Planet)

While Patagonia devotes resources to fighting climate change (for example, money, website), they also reaffirm their commitment by allowing their employees to volunteer on company time. Perrone (2021) outlines some of the volunteer initiatives from Patagonia. They highlight how Patagonia provides employees the opportunity to volunteer in various ways, including helping to create a national park in Chile. Patagonia has a Vice President of Environmental Activism (VPEA). The VPEA oversees the company's international environmental grants program. Patagonia has developed a dedicated website, Patagonia Action Works, which helps link volunteers with organizations based on the skillsets needed. The VPEA also oversees this project as well. By embracing volunteerism, Patagonia is fighting climate change and other social justice issues.

What Does the Research Say?

There are multiple ways organizations can showcase the talent they have. One way is to develop a corporate volunteer program. Establishing a volunteer program will have benefits for the organization. Harvard Business Review outlines the benefits of volunteer programs including boosting productivity, attracting new talent, retaining current talent, and increasing employment engagement (Rodell, 2021). Haski-Leventhal, Kach & Pournader (2019) studied the effects of corporate volunteerism and found that volunteering directly affects commitment and job satisfaction. Having a volunteer program also has a positive impact on the organization's reputation (Ford, 2021; Rodell, Sabey & Rogers, 2020; Sonsev, 2019). Developing a volunteer program has decided benefits for the organization.

There are benefits for the employee as well. Allowing employees to volunteer also provides opportunities for them to gain new skills or practice skills underused at the workplace. Volunteering also creates a sense of purpose, connects volunteers with the community, expands volunteers' networks, builds self-esteem, and reduces stress (Perrone, 2021).

A key finding in a study by CIVICUS: World Alliance for Citizen Participation, the International Association for Volunteer Effort, & United

Benefits of Volunteering

Organization	Individual	Social Justice
Boost in productivity	Gain new skills	Shines a light on causes
New talent	Practice skills	Influences others to participate in SJ issues
Reduced turnover	Sense of purpose	
Increased employment engagement	Increased network	Provides support where other resources may be lacking
Positive organization reputation	Builds self-esteem	
Increased job commitment	Increased mental well-being	

Exhibit 11-1   Benefits of volunteering.

Nations Volunteers (2008) was that "[b]oth volunteering and social activism are important strategies for fostering people's participation in social change and human development" (p. 1). Volunteering can also inspire others to participate in social justice causes (Jiranek et al., 2013). Exhibit 11-1 outlines organizational, individual, and social justice benefits of volunteering.

Putting into Practice

Developing a volunteer program need not be a complex endeavor, however, there should be some thought that goes into setting up a program. Organizations should think about the resources they want to apply to the process, where people within the organization volunteer, the overall volunteer process, how the organization evaluates the program, how the organization incorporates feedback, and the organization shares the results of the program. Below are steps organizations can take to develop a volunteer program. You can use the tool on the next page (Exhibit 11-2) which incorporates these steps to capture proposed actions for developing your volunteer program.

Step One: Level of Involvement

The first step in developing a volunteer program is to determine what resources the organization wants to apply, or can apply, to the volunteer program. The National Football League may have complex volunteer programs based on their

Volunteer Program Development Tool		
Directions: Use this tool to develop a volunteer program. For each step shown in the left column below, identify actions you will take in the right column.		
Step	*Example*	*Action*
Level of involvement	Provide 3 paid hours per month for volunteering	
Determine where to volunteer	Develop an approved list of places or causes to volunteer with	
Volunteer process	First-line supervisor approves volunteer time	
Program evaluation	Evaluate total hours donated, employee feedback	
Incorporating evaluation results	Update volunteer list based on employee feedback	
Sharing evaluation results	Share with the local community how much money saved the community through volunteer hours served	

Exhibit 11-2   Volunteer program development tool.

Source: Authors' Original Creation.

resources whereas a small startup with only four employees may not be able to devote the same level of resources. Organizations should determine how many hours of work time employees will be allowed to use for volunteering. This may depend on whether volunteer hours are paid hours or just hours protected (e.g., employees are not penalized vacation time to volunteer) to allow employees to volunteer. This will also correspond with the person's status at work. Meaning, that are they hourly wage, salaried, or some other category.

Another area to consider is an organization's sphere of influence. The more influence an organization has, the more they should consider not only volunteering but the level of resources applied to their volunteering program.

When those with influence volunteer, it will encourage others to participate in those causes as outlined by the research stated previously. Seeing prominent members or organizations volunteer can galvanize communities to get involved. Thus, providing more action for social justice causes.

As organizations and volunteer programs change, the level of involvement will also need to change. That small startup may grow into a regional power. They may change their volunteer program as they hire new employees, and their sphere of influence and resources grow.

Step Two: Determining Where to Volunteer

There are a lot of options when determining where to volunteer. One way to break down the options is to look at it as an open volunteer plan, semi-open volunteer plan, directed volunteer plan, or a combination of the three. An open volunteer plan would allow people to volunteer wherever they want. This allows those in the organization to volunteer for whatever causes or organizations they feel passionate about. However, where they volunteer may not be aligned with the organization's mission, vision, or values and could even be in direct contrast.

A semi-open volunteer plan would allow those in the organization to volunteer with projects that align with the organization's mission, vision, or values. Employees would submit to the organization where they wish to volunteer for approval. This ensures they would only volunteer with causes that align with the organization's mission, vision, and values. This plan would require more involvement and resources (e.g., someone reviewing the volunteer requests).

A directed volunteer plan would incorporate a pre-determined list of organizations and causes that employees may volunteer with using company time. This would also ensure employees would only volunteer with causes that align with the organization's mission, vision, and values. It also does not require as many resources as the approval is already pre-planned. The final option is choosing a combination of these that fits with your organization's needs and resources.

Step Three: Volunteer Process

Once the level of involvement and how/where people may volunteer have been decided, establishing the volunteer process can be completed. One thing to think about is what the approval process will be within the organization. Even if people are allowed to volunteer wherever they want, there still should be a process to approve their volunteer time. Who approves the volunteer time? How is volunteer time counted? What aspects of the volunteer time need to be captured for organizational records (e.g., hours, place, and effects of volunteer time)? These are some questions that should be answered when outlining the volunteer process. Having a written process will also protect against unconscious bias against allowing some to volunteer as opposed to others. You may need to revisit the level of involvement and how/where people may volunteer as you develop the volunteer process.

Step Four: Evaluating of the Program

Evaluating your volunteer program will provide valuable feedback as discussed in the next two steps. First, establish who are the stakeholders. Stakeholders could be organizational leadership, the board of directors, consumers, employees, or others you identify. Then determine what will be important to each group of stakeholders. For instance, will the leadership be interested in seeing more employee engagement? Will consumers be interested in the impact you are having on the community? Now you can determine what metrics you want to use to capture each area. How will you measure employee engagement? How will you measure the impact on the community? Finally, you will need to determine the vehicle for capturing these metrics. For example, will you use a survey to capture data or use data you capture from your volunteer process (e.g., hours of volunteer service performed)? Do not forget to get feedback from the volunteers themselves.

Step Five: Incorporating Evaluation Results

You can use the evaluation results to strengthen your volunteering program. Organizations should periodically review evaluation results to determine what changes can be made to strengthen the program. Changes to the program should also consider changes to the organization such as changes in size, influence, and resources.

Step Six: Sharing the Results of the Volunteer Program

A key step is sharing the results of the volunteer program. Share the results with your stakeholders. Whether it is showing higher levels of employee engagement to the board or influencing others to volunteer for a specific cause, sharing the results will increase support for the volunteer program.

Chapter Summary

1. Establishing a corporate volunteer program is a great way to showcase your talent and promote social justice causes.
2. Corporate volunteer programs need to be tailored to the organization based on mission, values, and resources.
3. Corporate volunteer programs should not be stagnant, however, continue to evolve based on feedback and changes to the organization.

References

CIVICUS: World Alliance for Citizen Participation, the International Association for Volunteer Effort (IAVE), & United Nations Volunteers (UNV). (2008). *Volunteering and social activism: Pathways for participation in human development.* Retrieved from https://www.unv.org/sites/default/files/ Volunteering%20and%20social%20Activism%20-%20Pathways%20for% 20participation%20in%20human%20development.pdf

Ford, S. (2021). The business case for employee volunteer & skills giving programs. America's Charities. https://www.charities.org/news/business-case-employee-volunteer-skills-giving-programs?gad=1&gclid=CjwKCAjw8symBhAqEiwAaTA__ BlDkONYXcexKkgBpHlnmavIwdyhoU5N5syree64vB6SD9F33 wgvChoC0OAQAvD_BwE

Haski-Leventhal, D., Kach, A., & Pournader, M. (2019). Employee need satisfaction and positive workplace outcomes: The role of corporate volunteering. *Nonprofit and Voluntary Sector Quarterly, 48*(3), 593–615. https://doi.org/ 10.1177/0899764019829829

Jiranek, P., Kals, E., Humm, J. S., Strubel, I. S., & Wehner, T. (2013). Volunteering as a means to an equal end? The impact of a social justice function on intention to volunteer. *The Journal of Social Psychology, 153*(5), 520–541. https://doi.org/10.1080/00224545.2013.768594

Patagonia. (2023a) *1% for the planet.* https://www.patagonia.com/one-percent-for-the-planet.html

Patagonia. (2023b). Company history. https://www.patagonia.com/company-history/

Perrone, G. (2021). *30+ companies with significant volunteer programs.* Twentynow. https://www.twentynow.com/sustainability-initiatives/social/30-companies-with-significant-volunteer-programs/

Rodell, J. (2021). *Volunteer programs that employees can get excited about.* Harvard Business Review. https://hbr.org/2021/01/volunteer-programs-that-employees-can-get-excited-about

Rodell, J. B., Sabey, T. B., & Rogers, K. M. (2020). "Tapping" into goodwill: Enhancing corporate reputation through customer volunteering. *Academy of Management Journal*, *63*(6), 1714–1738. https://doi.org/10.5465/amj.2018.0354

Sonsev, V. (2019). Patagonia's focus on its brand purpose is great for business. *Forbes*. https://www.forbes.com/sites/veronikasonsev/2019/11/27/patagonias-focus-on-its-brand-purpose-is-great-for-business/?sh=6421c95b54cb

Chapter 12

Step 11: Communicating Your Organization's Social Change Efforts

Barbara Hopkins

Case Study: University of Michigan

In 2020, a convergence of events was happening at the University of Michigan's Taubman College of Architecture and Urban Planning. As told by Joana Dos Santos (2022), who was the Chief Diversity, Equity, and Inclusion officer at the time, it was a time of increased calls across the United States for equity concerning people of color. Scores of people across the country were demanding that organizations focus on social justice and the students of Taubman were no different. They charged the administration with creating a culture where diversity, equity, and inclusion values would be integrated into the work of the college. Incidentally, just before this request, the administrators had received professional development on preventing sexual harassment and misconduct and were considering how to develop a set of behavior expectations to ensure safety and respect. It was decided that these two efforts should be merged together into one cohesive project, which would eventually become an official statement of values called the Campus Contract.

Although this undertaking was admirable, just getting started required some careful planning. There was focused intention in the selection of the team members who would lead this endeavor in order to make sure there was representation from those who are often left out of decision-making

                                      DOI: 10.4324/9781003439714-12

processes. With this in mind, there were voices from multiple races, identities, experiences, and organizational roles. Because this initiative was a collaboration with faculty, staff, and students, the group led a series of conversations within the college community using a process called appreciative inquiry. This method uses positive psychology to help individuals and organizations build outcomes based on existing strengths (The Center for Appreciative Inquiry, 2023). The process involved significant reflection on and affirmation of the environment within the community and what it could become in the future. More than 800 stakeholders were engaged and the inclusion of all of these participants was critical to ensuring ownership of the values produced and the commitment by the community to uphold them.

More than one year after beginning this project, a combined set of value statements and an accountability framework called the Campus Contract was launched (Dos Santos, 2022). This framework aimed to promote respect and appreciation for all community members. The next step was to produce a marketing campaign to embed the values and framework into the college culture. To accomplish this task, leaders of the initiative used several tactics over two semesters. First, a series of emails and social media were created to explain each component of the Campus Contract. The series included simple tools to help the community understand how to use the framework and employ the values. A second tactic was to create a kind of mascot, which was introduced in the tools from the email campaign. These gender- and racial-neutral robots were portrayed in comic-style guides demonstrating how to practice the accountability framework with one another. A third tactic was to create a webpage outlining the resulting work of the initiative so the community would have a referential resource once the initial campaign was completed (University of Michigan, n.d.). This website serves as a reminder of the Contract, its purpose, and its meaning to the college community. These are some of the foundational pieces of communication that assisted in indoctrinating the campus to a new and positive culture change. However, note that the communication of this important project took careful planning and had a multi-layered approach.

As organizations become more involved in equity and inclusion initiatives and projects that serve the greater community, this story reminds us that a key step to incorporating these initiatives is the communication effort that will introduce and sustain the project. This type of messaging must be a strategic function so the result will be increased support for the cause and a positive relationship with important organizational stakeholders (Jakob et al., 2022). In order to have an initiative that is more than a one-time contribution to society, there has to be a structured effort both inside and outside of the organization. The workforce must be engaged so that a culture change is created within the organization and the external environment must be engaged so their perception of the organization becomes aligned with the social responsibility project. This two-pronged communication approach requires an intentional plan as part of the initiative. Let's see how to put that plan together so all stakeholders of the organization can support the community effort.

What Does the Research Say?

Once a social responsibility initiative has been established, there must be communication of the initiative, its purpose, and its benefits to the community at large. This includes not only the employees of the organization, but also the external stakeholders such as customers and the overall public. Effective marketing allows an institution to broadly inform stakeholders, increase the visibility of the initiative, and provide opportunities for increased stakeholder involvement (Yang & Basile, 2022).

The first place to begin is within the company. It is no secret that employees are a vital part of any organization. Their continued engagement in the workplace not only completes projects and delivers products, but also creates life in the organization and its mission. Despite the fact that a company needs employees to operate, keeping employees active in office activities is sometimes difficult. There are times when personnel become frustrated about low pay, long hours, too much work, lack of trust in leadership, or not enough job satisfaction. If an organization is managing these typical concerns, how can it contemplate asking employees to consider extra efforts toward a charitable or social justice initiative?

Literature has established a positive relationship between employee engagement and the employee perception of their employer's corporate social responsibility (Rupp et al., 2018; Opoku-Dakwa, Chen & Rupp, 2018; Yang & Basile, 2022). In other words, the employee is more likely to find organizational social change initiatives meaningful and credible if they are more engaged in workplace responsibilities. With this in mind, the first thought must be to reflect on what motivates employees to become engaged at work and then consider how employers can tap into and support that motivation for objectives beyond the typical job responsibilities. After all, creating involvement in cultural or community activism is outside of the specific job roles of the organization and, therefore, what many employees may deem as 'extra work'. So, what messages would make this work so compelling that employees would be willing to take part without extra pay?

The Oxford Handbook of Work Engagement, Motivation, and Self-Determination Theory (Gagné, 2014) shares that one of the common concepts in motivation is the idea of psychological needs. That is, the notion that employees are motivated if their basic, evolved psychological needs are met. These universal needs include competence, autonomy, and relatedness. Competence refers to the employee feeling capable of completing the required task and having opportunities to grow. Professional development, support of higher education, or appropriate on-the-job training are examples of how an employer can make sure this need is met. Autonomy refers to the employee's need to have some independence and flexibility in the workplace. Allowing options in how tasks are accomplished and self-sufficiency to make some decisions are ways an employer can help meet this need. In the context of this book, this psychological need is supported by a meaning-making approach, which suggests employees as social change agents should participate in determining what social problems are actually 'issues' (Sonenshein, 2016). Key to this concept is avoiding the tendency to mandate participation in social good initiatives or pitting employees against one another by publicly showing who is participating and who is not (Rupp et al., 2018). These practices are against the idea of autonomy and tend to generate undue pressure that reduces the perceived value of the initiative. Finally, relatedness refers to the employee's connection with the organization and its people. Creating opportunities for employees to collaborate and develop relationships will assist with meeting this need. When these basic needs are satisfied, employees typically have higher job satisfaction in the workplace and corporate engagement also increases.

Continuing to explore the power of human psychology, the literature also discusses the concept of psychological contracts when studying employee engagement. This concept alludes to the mental agreement that is often subconsciously made between an employee and employer during the work career (Aggarwal, 2007). Some research states that psychological contracts can be transactional and relational. The transactional contract refers to concrete items such as performance outcomes and material rewards during the employment period. The relational contract, however, is broader and more focused on intangibles such as level of commitment. This type of contract can be influenced by a number of factors such as prior work experiences and early life experiences. However, current organizational culture will also have an impact on an employee's relational psychological contract. This would cover everything from human resources practices to organizational social norms, to relationships with supervisors and co-workers. As an example, the worldwide package delivery company United Parcel Service (UPS) supports its workforce in both large and small charitable endeavors (United Parcel Service, 2023). In one of its staff stories about delivering over 13,000 stuffed backpacks to area schools, an employee shares about the rewarding experience. They expressed pride in the fact that the company supports volunteer work of this kind and interpreted this gesture as a corporate statement that employees matter. This further supports the psychological need for relatedness in the workplace.

Putting these ideas into the context of corporate social responsibility, communication efforts for internal employees should focus on building an affinity for the endeavor and garnering employee support for the cause because they feel it is the right thing to do. Messaging should also focus on connecting the good of the cause to the organization and its mission. Communication of this nature will help employees to feel as though they are making positive contributions to the community as they reap the volunteerism benefits mentioned in the previous chapter. Outside of emails and updates, this messaging can be modeled through the influence of an organization's leaders on employee participation in charitable activities. The idea of social justice leadership has been around for decades (Bozkurt, 2022). While there are varying definitions of this term, the basic thought is that there are characteristics of leaders who are supportive of social justice. They tend to focus on improving the achievements of those who are typically left out or underrepresented, approach their role with committed passion, and humbly serve others rather than themselves. These managers and influencers model social justice behavior and inspire others to not only join the cause but also see the benefits for the organization and its members.

Once the internal employees are aware of the social responsibility activities, the organization needs to consider how to inform and educate external stakeholders of the cause. Advisory board members, foundation donors, customers, and even regulatory agencies may be impacted by the chosen advocacy activities. Sharing the strategy and benefits may improve or strengthen relationships with these groups. Customers and investors increasingly favor organizations that are giving back to society so the right messaging can improve the organization's image (Du & Yu, 2021). Social activism can influence consumer behavior and help develop strong connections between organizations and those they serve (Udomphoch & Pormsila, 2023). However, a case must be made for why stakeholders should be involved and how they can benefit from these efforts. Building relationships in this way promotes sustainability of the advocacy initiative. Additionally, this external community can help increase awareness of and support for your cause.

There are multiple ways to communicate with those outside of the company. Social media, corporate advertising, community sponsorship activities, annual reports, and web pages are just a few (Harrison & Huang, 2022). And while it may be tempting to simply copy the same message in every form of communication, special attention must be paid to the content of the message and the context in which the various stakeholders will hear it (Pompper, 2021). A group of school children will think about a social cause differently than a group of industry partners. Additionally, community members of different cultural backgrounds may interpret certain words or phrases in various ways. These and other differences highlight the need to consider the target of your messaging and contemplate how the words, format, and social cause will be received by your audience.

Putting It into Practice

Now that there is an understanding of how stakeholders become motivated and engaged, let's consider some practical ways to incorporate this knowledge into a plan for social justice communication.

Step One: Identify and Involve All Stakeholders

Consider all of the stakeholder groups that are aligned with your organization. Internally, there are employees who will need to understand the initiative in order to support the efforts. When possible, make sure employees are involved from the beginning, including determining the initiative. Employees desire to feel like they are part of something with a positive impact (Kuligowski, 2023) and are more likely to participate in activities where they have been involved in the decision-making since this supports the psychological need for autonomy (Reckmann, 2023). This involvement serves as a foundational way to communicate the larger purpose of the initiative and prepare for the sustaining messages to follow. Emails, newsletters, social media, and posts to the company intranet are ways to communicate town hall meetings about the initiative, progress on

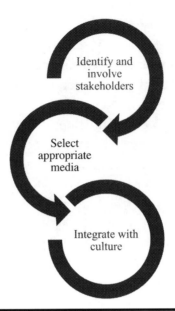

Exhibit 12-1   Steps for communicating corporate social responsibility. (Created by Barbara Hopkins.)

developing a strategy to carry out the initiative, and ways employees can be involved. Ensure that the communication emphasizes how the activity aligns with the institutional strategic objectives. A social justice initiative that appears to be an extension of the structural mission is easier to integrate and reduces potential tension caused by conflicting employee interests. As the social responsibility activity is established, messaging on how the initiative connects with the corporate mission and values will be critical to employee adoption (Opoku-Dakwa, Chen & Rupp, 2018) (see Exhibit 12-1).

Don't forget that external stakeholders such as customers, investors, and regulatory agencies may also be impacted by the organization's activities. For these external partners, introduce the activity, the connection with the corporate mission, and the beneficial purpose for undertaking the initiative (Harrison & Huang, 2022). This will garner credibility and backing for the activity. If there are activities the community can support, make sure those events are widely shared and external involvement is explicitly described. Also, remember to consider what populations are in these groups of external stakeholders. Race, gender, socio-economic status, and age should all be contemplated when developing the wording and tone of the messaging (Pompper, 2021). It is most helpful to find ways to dialogue and build relationships with the outside community in order to make the public relations work more impactful and relevant.

Step Two: Select the Appropriate Media

Social media is certainly becoming an important part of the communication effort for institutions (Wang & Huang, 2018). This form of interaction can increase visibility to those with similar interests and the organization can have more control over the message compared to more traditional forms of media. It is also an easy way to build involvement from the surrounding community and provide real-time updates of social justice efforts. However, make sure leaders' social media wording matches the official organization's social media accounts so there are no conflicting messages (Jakob et al., 2022).

Issuing formalized corporate reports on advocacy activities is another way to communicate with outside stakeholders. When using this option, keep in mind the tone and wording of the reports. Making the reports easy to digest and breaking down complicated topics not only helps consumers understand the material, but may also lead to increased market value and brand loyalty (Du & Yu, 2021). This kind of reporting requires strategic consideration of the data to present and the development of a set of quantified social justice goals. The progress on these goals should be reported at regular intervals.

Additionally, encouragement from managers should be directed at all employees equally, not just those who may appear to have the most interest. For example, if an organization is working to increase the number of Native Americans in science, technology, engineering, and math fields, a supervisor should not just be asking Native American employees to participate. All employees should be approached so they all understand the significance and purpose of the initiative and so they can see how the activity can be beneficial to them.

Step Three: Integrate with Organizational Culture

In order to be effective in the initiative, there has to be more than just an announcement of the activity followed by the expectation of participation. As an organizational enterprise, the tenets of the activity must be incorporated into the institutional culture (Kuligowski, 2023). This culture must be intentional and not just by accident. Furthermore, employees must be provided with the resources to participate in the social justice endeavor and have an impactful effect on the cause. This may mean mentioning events and activities of the initiative in company newsletters and announcements or offering assistance with employee giving to the cause through payroll deduction. In addition to providing resources, careful attention must be paid to removing obstacles to participation. Conversations regarding the initiative should be focused on institutional values and not on politics, which tends to make people uncomfortable. Also, promoting these activities during an organization's busiest time of the year will only create negative pressure for personnel. Instead, be mindful of the company productivity cycle and schedule events and communications accordingly. Furthermore, it could be helpful to identify a day or event where the organization comes together to support the cause. Or, better yet, one or two days of employee paid time off could be dedicated to volunteer time working with the community activity. This would allow employees to determine what time works best for them and provide a way to meet the psychological need for autonomy.

Professional services giant Deloitte, which has received numerous awards for its caring and supportive work environment, provides significant flexibility in its social justice opportunities for employees (Deloitte, n.d.). Not only does the firm impact a large range of social issues such as equity and sustainability, it also provides options in how employees may contribute to the causes. From a workplace giving program, to mentorship opportunities, to pro bono work, Deloitte ensures all team members have an outlet that suits their personal purpose.

The focus on culture should also be considered in hiring practices. If the values of social justice are important to the organization, that should be communicated in the hiring process and the expectations should be shared with potential employees. Once employees are hired, there should be an organized onboarding process that includes professional development on the company's commitment to social justice.

Finally, remember that the organization's leaders also need to exhibit behaviors that show support for the social justice initiative and positively impact employee perceptions of the employer's stance on the issue (Bozkurt, 2022). If an employee has a strong connection with their supervisor, they tend to feel more psychologically safe and be more open to involvement in workplace activities (Finnegan, 2017). As an example, if the organization is focused on saving trees to preserve the natural environment, a manager should not be requesting paper copies of a 50-page report for a 10-person committee at the office. Similarly, a supervisor who does not participate in any of the community service activities may be perceived as disingenuous and lead workers to believe that the initiative is only for appearances. This negative perception could directly impact the motivation of employees to participate and is, in itself, an impactful form of communication. Keeping this in mind, professional development should be created for all supervisors so they will understand the expectations of their behavior. This type of training would also standardize how supervisors discuss the goals of the chosen social activities with their subordinates and external partners. If all managers share the same message with the organizational community regarding the initiatives and how they benefit the organization, it will be easier to incorporate these themes into the organizational culture.

Just remember that the idea is to encourage participation, not demand it. If employees feel pressured to participate, it becomes an additional stress to them. However, communication that shares the benefits to the organization, its external partners, and the employees will help generate feelings of positivity and meaningfulness. A great way to support this effort is to have key employees on board who can help promote the social justice or community initiative. Involving employees who are influencers and well-respected will increase the likelihood that employees will consider being engaged and help the message spread more broadly throughout the community.

Chapter Summary

Participating in corporate social responsibility is an admirable endeavor for any organization, particularly when there are so many societal concerns to be addressed. And while the effort can build positive perceptions and relationships with corporate stakeholders, the right messaging is critical to garnering energy and enthusiasm for the cause. By understanding the basic psychological needs of team members, organizations can tailor communications such that they are likely to become more engaged. This concept is also true with external stakeholders, who tend to vary greatly in demographics, ideology, and organizational perceptions.

There have been several examples of how to incorporate the steps mentioned in this chapter. However, every company is different and has to evaluate its internal and external stakeholders to develop the best communication plan. The checklist at the end of this chapter should help with that evaluation so you can create the messaging that works for your situation. Remember to consider the various target audiences, the culture of the organization, the sensitivity of the corporate social responsibility initiative, and the various channels of communication available to you. In the end, the most important message is one of sincerity and support for your contribution to the society that is supporting you (see Exhibit 12-2).

Step	Questions to Ask	Answers
1. Identify and involve stakeholders	Who are your groups of stakeholders?	
	What information is pertinent to them?	
	How can these groups be involved in the advocacy activities?	
	What is the best way to communicate with these groups?	
2. Select the appropriate media	Identify the appropriate media for the various intended audiences.	
	Ensure all media messages are aligned with all other organizational communications.	
	Ensure tone and wording of messaging is appropriate for the intended audiences.	
	Consider routine reporting of activities as a communication tool and align the reporting with the organizational mission.	
3. Integrate with culture	What are the best ways to share with all stakeholders?	
	How can initiative activities be integrated into regular processes?	
	What types of communication are best for sustaining the initiative effort internally and externally?	

Exhibit 12-2   Checklist tool for corporate social responsibility communication.

References

Aggarwal, U. (2007). The relationship between HR practices, psychological contract and employee engagement. *IIMB Management Review, 19*(3), 313–325.

Bozkurt, B. (2022). The relationship between social justice leadership and organizational citizenship behaviours. *Participatory Educational Research, 9*(2), 88–102.

Center for Appreciative Inquiry, The. (n.d.). *What is appreciative inquiry (AI)?* Retrieved August 2, 2023, from https://www.centerforappreciativeinquiry.net/resources/what-is-appreciative-inquiry-ai/

Deloitte. (n.d.). *Life at Deloitte: Awards and recognition.* https://www2.deloitte.com/us/en/pages/careers/articles/awards-and-recognition.html

Dos Santos, J. (2022). Using appreciative inquiry to develop organizational values rooted in social justice and diversity, equity and inclusion. *AI Practitioner, 24*(4), 12–17.

Du, S., & Yu, K. (2021). Do corporate social responsibility reports convey value relevant information? Evidence from report readability and tone. *Journal of Business Ethics, 172*, 253–274.

Finnegan, R. P. (2017). *Raise your Team's employee engagement score: A Manager's guide.* American Management Association.

Gagné, M., (Ed.). (2014). *The Oxford handbook of work engagement, motivation, and self-determination theory.* Oxford University Press.

Harrison, K., & Huang, L. (2022). Not all corporate social responsibility (CSR) is created equal: A study of consumer perceptions of CSR on firms post fraud. *Journal of Marketing Theory and Practice, 30*(4), 494–511.

Jakob, E.A., Steinmetz, H., Wehner, M.C., Engelhardtm, C., & Kabst, R. (2022). Like it or not: When corporate social responsibility does not attract potential applicants, *Journal of Business Ethics, 178*, 105–127, https://doi.org/10.1007/s10551-021-04960-8

Kuligowski, K. (2023). 20 employee engagement ideas that work. *Business News Daily.* https://www.businessnewsdaily.com/15969-employee-engagement-ideas.html

Opoku-Dakwa, A., Chen, C. C., & Rupp, D. E. (2018). CSR initiative characteristics and employee engagement: An impact-based perspective. *Journal of Organizational Behavior, 39*, 580–593.

Pompper, D. (Ed.). (2021). *Public relations for social responsibility: Affirming DEI commitment with action.* Emerald Publishing.

Reckmann, N. (2023). What is Corporate Social Responsibility? *Business News Daily.* https://www.businessnewsdaily.com/4679-corporate-social-responsibility.html

Rupp, D. E., Shao, R., Skarlicki, D. P., Paddock, E. L., Kim, T., & Nadisic, T. (2018). Corporate social responsibility and employee engagement: The moderating role of CSR-specific relative autonomy and individualism. *Journal of Organizational Behavior, 39*, 559–579.

Sonenshein, S. (2016). How corporations overcome issue illegitimacy and issue equivocality to address social welfare: The role of the social change agent. *Academy of Management Review, 41*(2), 349–366.

University of Michigan Taubman college of architecture and urban planning. (n.d.). *Taubman college contract.* https://taubmancollege.umich.edu/about/taubman-college-compact/

United Parcel Service. (2023). *Big brown stuffs big yellow buses for charity.* https://about.ups.com/us/en/our-impact/values/inclusion-belonging/big-brown-stuffs-big-yellow-buses-for-charity.html

Udomphoch, P., & Pormsila, W. (2023). Communicating corporate social responsibility through green packaging: A case study in Thailand. *TEM Journal, 12*(1), 241–252.

Wang, R., & Huang, Y. (2018). Communicating corporate social responsibility (CSR) on social media: How do message source and types of CSR messages influence stakeholders' perceptions. *Corporate Communications: An International Journal, 23*(3), 326–341. https://doi-org.ezproxy.umgc.edu/10.1108/CCIJ-07-2017-0067

Yang, J., & Basile, K. (2022). Communicating corporate social responsibility: External stakeholder involvement, productivity and firm performance. *Journal of Business Ethics, 178,* 501–517.

Chapter 13

Reflecting on the Future Role of Business Social Activism

Jamie Campbell and Phillip L. Ealy

No Answer Is an Answer

When we knock on a door, we are looking for someone to answer. If nobody answers the knock, we in essence receive an answer: no one is home, wants to entertain whoever knocked on the door, or they are indisposed and cannot come to the door. We received our answer.

If you are still on the fence about whether your organization should get involved with social change, guess what you already are. With the current political climate around the world, any action an organization takes or doesn't take can be considered as taking a stand (Lin, 2018). Organizations must consider where they want to stand in times of social crisis (Mirzaei, Wilkie & Siuki, 2022). When the US Supreme Court overturned the *Roe v. Wade* decision, organizations had a choice. If employees lived in a state where abortions are now illegal, you could either provide resources (for example, paid time off or subsidized travel to a state where abortion is legal) to assist or do nothing. Both actions send statements to the employees. If we look at the current DE&I climate in the US State of Florida, an organization's decision to either implement diversity programs or not makes a loud statement (Spicer, 2022; Thornhill, 2023). International organizations that chose to continue to operate within Russia when Russia invaded Ukraine made a statement. Inaction is action. Every day our organizations make social change statements, whether intentional or not. It is up to the organization to decide whether to purposefully direct the social change messaging that is sent.

DOI: 10.4324/9781003439714-13

Using the analogy from Chapter 1, we can allow any picture frame (society) to shape our picture (organization), or we can be involved in what that picture frame looks like. We can choose a frame that better highlights our picture. This book highlights how organizations can be involved in choosing that picture frame.

The Tortoise vs the Hare

Organizations that choose how they will participate in social change must understand the road is long and constant. Opponents to the 1973 *Roe v. Wade* case law in the United States have been working to overturn the decision ever since. It took almost 50 years of constant protest, lobbying, and work to reverse federal law (Greenhouse & Siegel, 2010). The fight for civil rights in the United States has been going on since slavery was abolished, and arguably since the first European settlers landed in North America. It was not until 1964 that the Civil Rights Act became law (Zietlow, 2004). However, there are still many more miles to go in the United States, as evident with the rise of Black Lives Matter and the constant reminders of bias and discrimination that still exist.

The choice to engage in social change should not be taken lightly. It should come with the knowledge that it is a long-term strategic plan. However, it is important for corporations to intentionally engage in social change. In 1926, Henry Ford led the charge in the United States to go to a five-day work week (Reiderer, 2022). The organization's social change involvement helped to build the middle class. One could argue that Ford's actions were as much, if not more, based on business models. However, the actions helped speed the transition from a standard six-day workweek to a five-day workweek. Corporations involvement in social change can help speed up the social change clock.

As stated previously, organizations are involved in social change, whether they believe so or not. It is critical for organizations to leverage their standing in society to conscientiously direct the direction of social change. This text was designed to assist organizations to move past performative diversity, equity, and inclusion and consider their role in social change. The mission is for organizations to engage their employees in productive, meaningful, and active social engagement. Earlier in this text, it was discussed that this generation of millennials and younger cohorts want to believe and firmly understand that the companies that they are working to generate profit for are going to have a commitment to make the world that they live in a better place. The organizations that will succeed will not only have an eye toward innovation but will also engage in keeping a watchful eye on the concerns of their clients and employees.

Moving Beyond Corporate Social Responsibility (CSR) to Social Activism (SA)

Businesses and organizations' roles in today's ever-changing socioeconomic context go far beyond profit generation. While corporate social responsibility (CSR) has been an important step in acknowledging the importance of societal welfare, there is an increasing desire for corporations to adopt a social activist role in solving prominent social concerns and difficulties. Going beyond CSR to become a social activist can have far-reaching consequences for both an organization and society.

To begin with, actively engaging in social concerns can improve an organization's reputation and brand value. A proactive response to social issues can build a favorable brand image and foster customer loyalty at a time when consumers are increasingly conscious of the moral position of the firms they support. Companies that show genuine care and take concrete steps to address relevant social concerns—from those in the local community to those of national and even international scope—are more likely to acquire the trust and respect of their consumer base, ensuring long-term sustainability.

Taking a social activist attitude allows organizations to make a significant contribution to the welfare of society. Companies may achieve major change and have a demonstrable impact on the communities in which they operate by using their resources, influence, and experience. Businesses have the potential to be significant catalysts for constructive social reform, whether it is campaigning for environmental sustainability, embracing diversity and inclusion, or promoting equitable practices. Organizations can amplify their efforts and execute sustainable solutions that address systemic challenges at their root through strategic collaborations with non-profits, government agencies, and local communities.

Furthermore, adopting social causes can help employees develop a feeling of purpose and dedication. Individuals are more likely to be motivated, engaged, and devoted to an organization when they believe their job is aligned with a wider mission to create a more just and equal society.

According to a 2022 CNBC/Momentive poll, 40% of workers indicated they would likely quit their jobs if their company made a statement on a political topic with which they disagreed. According to another survey, more than half of respondents would not even contemplate working for an organization that did not share their beliefs. Encouraging employee involvement, supporting social causes, and allowing employees to actively participate in activities that reflect the organization's values can boost employee morale and satisfaction, contributing to a better workplace culture and higher productivity.

Finally, taking a proactive approach to social concerns might result in legislative and policy reforms with far-reaching consequences. Organizations can impact public debate and convince decision-makers to implement laws that promote fairness, equality, and sustainability by leveraging their influence and lobbying for reforms. Businesses may play a critical role in building a conducive regulatory climate that supports responsible and ethical activities across industries by effectively lobbying and actively participating in public forums.

In conclusion, while CSR is an important step toward recognizing corporations' societal responsibilities, embracing social activism (SA) reflects a proactive commitment to promote significant change and address serious social concerns. Beyond the constraints of typical CSR, businesses can not only improve their brand reputation and employee engagement but also significantly contribute to the creation of a more socially just, equitable, and sustainable world for future generations.

The Role of Diversity, Equity, Inclusion, and Belonging in Facilitating Social Change

The value of diversity, equity, inclusion, and belonging (DEIB) in organizations cannot be emphasized. These values are essential for fostering an environment in which all employees, regardless of background, feel valued, respected, and empowered. However, corporations must go beyond DEIB efforts to address social concerns beyond their immediate borders, and diversity practitioners are well positioned to take the lead to facilitate social change efforts.

DEIB is a crucial basis for developing justice and equality inside organizations, but it should not exist in isolation. Organizations must extend their influence and resources to address bigger social concerns to make a difference and engineer societal change. This is why:

1. *Issue Interconnectedness*: Social issues, such as racism, gender inequity, environmental concerns, and economic imbalances, are inextricably linked. Organizations that demonstrate a narrow understanding of diversity and inclusion may unintentionally perpetuate, or even be complicit in, larger systemic injustices. Organizations can help to dismantle the underlying mechanisms that perpetuate discrimination and unfairness by tackling these larger issues.

2. *Reputation and Stakeholder Expectations*: Firms are increasingly held accountable for their behavior outside of the workplace. Customers, investors, and employees expect companies to connect with their values and actively contribute toward a more equitable and sustainable society. Organizations that take the initiative to solve social concerns display their dedication to making the world a better place, improving their reputation and appeal.

3. *Resources*: Organizations have a wealth of resources, including financial capital, talent, and technology. They can have a substantial impact on sectors such as education, healthcare, poverty reduction, and environmental conservation if these resources are directed toward social causes. These initiatives benefit society while also increasing an organization's social significance and contribution.

4. *Diversity practitioners are frequently at the forefront of DEIB activities within enterprises.* Their abilities to create diversity, manage complicated interpersonal relationships, and facilitate uncomfortable conversations position them as change agents in addressing larger social concerns. Using their knowledge, they can assist groups in becoming larger-scale advocates for social justice and equality.

5. *Employee Engagement and Attraction: Millennials and Generation Z, who account for a sizable proportion of the workforce, are increasingly drawn to firms that are well-known for being socially responsible and actively involved in addressing social concerns.* Organizations that take a stand on larger social issues not only attract top talent but also enhance employee engagement by purveying a feeling of purpose beyond their everyday job tasks.

Finally, while DEIB activities are critical for fostering inclusive workplaces, businesses must acknowledge that they are part of a larger societal ecosystem. Organizations should embrace their responsibility in tackling social concerns outside their doors to be responsible corporate citizens. Diversity practitioners are well-positioned to lead this transformation as Organization Development (OD) practitioners because their skills and expertise in encouraging inclusivity and managing diversity may be leveraged to address larger social issues. Organizations may help to make the world a more just, equitable, and sustainable place while simultaneously reaping the advantages of a more engaged and socially conscious workforce.

A bottom-up approach to OD comprises empowering employees at all levels to promote change. This method is especially suitable for taking the lead in tackling social change both inside and outside an employer since it generates a sense of ownership, collaboration, and inclusivity, leading to more sustainable and impactful outcomes. A bottom-up strategy is acceptable in this setting for several convincing reasons:

1. *Diverse Points of View and Insights*: Employees at different levels of an organization bring diverse ideas and experiences to the table. A bottom-up strategy allows for a more thorough knowledge of social issues by promoting an environment in which every voice is heard and valued. This inclusiveness means that projects tackling social change are well-rounded, take into account many viewpoints, and are more likely to resonate with the larger community.
2. *Organizational Agility and Adaptability*: A bottom-up strategy fosters an experimentation and innovation culture. When people are given the authority to suggest and implement ideas, the organization develops a culture of agility and adaptability. This allows the organization to respond more effectively to society's changing requirements, ensuring that its efforts to address social change stay relevant and effective over time.
3. *Increased Employee Engagement and Commitment*: Involving employees in decision-making and allowing them to contribute to social change efforts promotes a sense of ownership and commitment. Employees who have a strong sense of purpose and belonging are more likely to be engaged and motivated to devote their best efforts to the organization's social change goals.
4. *Leadership Development (LD) at All Levels*: Encouraging employees to take the lead in tackling social change fosters leadership development at all levels of the firm. Employees who are given the opportunity to drive change learn crucial abilities such as communication, cooperation, and

problem-solving, all of effective leadership requires. LD not only improves the workforce's general capabilities, but it also produces a pipeline of future leaders who understand the need to act on social concerns.

5. *Community Participation and Trust-Building*: Organizations that take a bottom-up strategy to social change efforts are more likely to engage with local communities and stakeholders. Organizations can create trust and strong relationships among the communities they serve by incorporating these external partners in decision-making. As a result, the organization's efforts gain credibility and efficacy, ensuring that the initiatives are well-received and accepted by the community.

6. *Long-Term and Sustainable Impact*: Bottom-up initiatives frequently result in more durable and long-term solutions. Organizations can ensure that solutions are based on the specific needs and difficulties of the community by incorporating employees in the creation and implementation of social change programs. This method increases the possibility that the efforts will be adopted and sustained by the community over time, resulting in long-term positive change.

Finally, addressing social change requires a bottom-up approach to organizational reform that is not just suitable but also necessary. Organizations can create durable and impactful projects that lead to significant and enduring social transformation by empowering employees, creating inclusion, and forging strong partnerships with communities.

Organization Development, Transorganization Development, and Social Change Efforts

OD and Transorganization Development (TOD) are ways to facilitate change, although their focus and scope align. Understanding the distinctions between these two notions is critical for firms wanting to implement effective internal and external transformational change initiatives.

The primary goal of OD is to facilitate participative change within companies. It is a systematic process that entails putting in place planned actions to improve organizational effectiveness and employee well-being. Organizational structure, culture, processes, and human resources are common targets for OD interventions. The primary focus of OD is on improving communication, teamwork, employee growth, and overall organizational performance. OD practitioners collaborate closely with internal stakeholders to identify areas for improvement, devise change strategies, and foster an organizational culture of continual learning and development.

TOD, on the other hand, focuses on creating changes outside of the bounds of a particular organization. TOD broadens the scope of OD principles to encompass collaboration with external entities such as partner organizations, communities, and other stakeholders. TOD's major purpose is to encourage collective action and collaboration across various groups to address complex societal concerns that cannot be solved by individual entities alone. To address concerns such as environmental sustainability, social fairness, and community development, TOD activities frequently involve the formation of partnerships, alliances, and networks. To promote meaningful and durable change at a larger systemic level, TOD practitioners attempt to build trust, facilitate communication, and create a common vision across diverse stakeholders.

In conclusion, the primary distinction between OD and TOD is found in their respective scopes and target areas. While OD focuses on implementing participatory change within a single business, TOD extends this approach to create collaborative efforts for tackling social concerns that extend beyond organizational borders. Both OD and TOD play important and complementary roles in driving organizational and societal change, but they do so at various levels and with varying levels of collaboration and influence.

What's Next

Many of the companies that currently operate within the confines of the United States are multinational organizations. This means that they must think beyond the traditional United States-defined norms of diversity. These institutions must determine what type of country they are working in.

References

Greenhouse, L., & Siegel, R. B. (2010). Before (and after) Roe v. Wade: New questions about backlash. *Yale LJ, 120*, 2028.

Lin, T. C. (2018). Incorporating social activism. *BUL Rev, 98*, 1535.

Mirzaei, A., Wilkie, D. C., & Siuki, H. (2022). Woke brand activism authenticity or the lack of it. *Journal of Business Research, 139*, 1–12.

Reiderer, R. (2022). A brief history of the five-day workweek. *Sidekick.* https://www.morningbrew.com/sidekick/stories/history-five-day-work-week

Spicer, R. (2022). The marketplace of ideas, cancel culture, and misunderstanding the first amendment. *Communication and Democracy, 56*(2), 192–197.

Thornhill, T. (2023). Goodbye Florida, I'm Out! For Good. *Sociology of Race and Ethnicity, 9*(4), 440–443. https://doi.org/10.1177/23326492231201500

Zietlow, R. E. (2004). To secure these rights: Congress, courts and the 1964 civil rights act. *Rutgers Law Review, 57,* 945.

Appendix A

Selected Social Impact and Social Change Resources

Books

Centola, D. (2021). *Change: How to make big things happen*. Little, Brown Spark.

Crutchfield, L. (2018). *How change happens: Why some social movements succeed while others don't*. Wiley.

Ebrahim, A. (2019). *Measuring social change: Performance and accountability in a complex world*. Stanford Business Books.

Nilsen, E. (2022). *Understanding social justice: To see the end of bias and oppression we need social change and true equity for everyone*. No publisher.

Articles

Bartunek, J., & Moch, M. K. (1987). First-order, second-order, and third-order change and organization development interventions: A cognitive approach. *Journal of Applied Behavioral Science, 23*. 483–500.

Barth, F. (1967). On the study of social change. *American Anthropologist, 69*(6), 661–669.

Websites

Best websites for social change. See: https://www.intechnic.com/blog/best-websites-for-social-change/

25 best social change blogs and websites. See: https://blog.feedspot.com/social_change_blogs/

Videos

Social change definitions and characteristics. 5 minutes and 9 seconds.
See: https://www.youtube.com/watch?v=W2Pw0hrVkMk
Theories of social change. 13 minutes and 6 seconds.
See: https://www.youtube.com/watch?v=Q0j23nDx4sk&t=81s
Theories of social change. 12 minutes and 13 seconds.
See: https://www.youtube.com/watch?v=ejjl9VgR2nM
Theories of social change: Cyclical, indological, pendulum theory. 8 minutes and
    3 seconds.
See: https://www.youtube.com/watch?v=y1KRoxdPs0M

Appendix B

Frequently Asked Questions

Question 1: What Is Social Change?

The alteration of a society's social order—which may include changes in social institutions, social behaviors, or social interactions—is called *social change*. If sustained on a broader scale, it may result in social or societal transformation.

Question 2: What Is Social Impact?

Any major or positive changes that solve or at least address social inequality and issues are called *having a social impact*. Businesses and organizations attain these objectives by deliberate efforts in their operations.

Question 3: What Is Social Justice?

Social justice is usually understood to mean the equitable distribution of resources, opportunities, and privileges in society. Originally a theological idea, it is loosely defined as social institutions that provide access to economic benefits. Social justice is a wide concept with numerous differences in how advocates apply it. However, social determinants such as the racial income gap or unequal access to health care play a significant role in social justice studies. Some social justice applications, such as critical race theory, have become battlegrounds in the United States.

Question 4: How Do Diversity, Equity, and Inclusion Relate to Social Change?

People are the lifeblood of any organization. A workgroup can collectively produce something larger than any one individual by bringing varied experiences, talents, and capabilities to bear on issues—and that is *group synergy*. To apply the talents best of all team members, the members of the group must be integrated. Only when this occurs will the group be able to realize their full potential in propelling an organization's vision forward.

Strong teams are built on the foundations of diversity and inclusion. Often, an environment with gender balance and representation from multiple nationalities, races, genders, ages, and cultures may be called diverse because it looks to be so. It is long past time to embrace a broader notion of diversity that goes beyond race and gender which includes socioeconomic position, work methods, ability and education levels, age, values and beliefs, sexual orientation, and other factors. We are likely to exclude people and miss the benefits of nurturing true diversity if we do not consider these distinctions while constructing our companies.

Equally important, we must acknowledge that the sheer presence of varied individuals in an organization is insufficient to stimulate innovation. Understanding, accepting, and respecting individual differences so everyone feels valued is essential. Employees do their best work and play to their strengths when they are meaningfully included, according to research. This means that rigid processes should be replaced with flexible ones that enable people to select how to execute their work most efficiently and support their choices to achieve satisfactory or exemplary results. Individual differences should also be respected and celebrated since they create chances to increase teamwork, learn from one another, and improve processes, which can boost organizational growth and attract additional strong people. Everyone is unique, and when given the opportunity to be themselves at work, they may achieve amazing things.

Social change comes about when diverse people are brought together—and particularly when focused on making the world a better place.

Question 5: What Is Meant by the Term *Corporate Social Responsibility* (CSR), and How Does that Term Relate to Social Change and Social Impact?

Corporate social responsibility (CSR) is a self-regulatory business model that assists a corporation in becoming socially accountable to itself, its stakeholders, and the public. Organizations practicing CSR, also known as *corporate citizenship*, can know the impact they have on all parts of society– including the economic, social, and environmental. CSR implies that the organization operates in ways that benefit society and the environment.

CSR can be passive or active. A *passive CSR strategy* means that the organization merely donates money or other resources to worthy causes but does not actively involve itself in taking direct action to improve conditions outside the organization's boundaries. An *active CSR strategy* means that the organization actively involves itself in social causes by lending financial, human, and other resources to make the change happen.

Question 6: Who Should Lead Social Change Initiatives in an Organization?

A good corporate citizen—and that can refer to any organization (including governmental and charitable institutions as well as businesses)—will involve all managers and employees of their organizations in social change efforts. Each person in the organization will have a clear role in bringing about the social change sought by the organization.

But maybe Diversity, Equity, and Inclusion (DE&I) practitioners/leaders may take the role of facilitator in bringing about external social change. DE&I practitioners typically focus on a social change effort inside their organizations, and it therefore can make sense for them to be facilitators of externally directed social change efforts.

It is also possible that Organization Development OOD) practitioners can have a role in bringing about social change. OD is often focused on internal organization,nal change. However, a related field, known as *Transorganization Development* (TD), can focus on bringing about change across two or more organizations.

Question 7: Should an Organization Focus on Only One Social Change Effort (a So-called Laser Focus) or on Many Social Change Efforts (a So-called Shotgun Focus)?

Most organizations that adopt a focus on improving social conditions will often use a laser focus. That has the advantage of concentrating resources and making communication about that sought-for change effort easier with internal and external stakeholder groups. A shotgun strategy—where the organization broadly tries to do everything to make the world a better place—will often lead to confusion and a dilution of the resources to have the greatest impact.

Question 8: What Is Meant by the Term ECG Strategy, and How Does It Relate to Social Change Initiatives?

An *ECG strategy* is a company-wide approach to improving its environmental, social, and governance (ECG) policies to increase customer loyalty, reduce expenses, and increase commercial value. It is one of many ways to bring about social change.

Question 9: What Are the United Nations' Goals, and How Do They Relate to Social Change Initiatives?

The *Sustainable Development Goals* (SDGs) are a global call to action to achieve a more just, equitable, and fair world. The 2030 Agenda for Sustainable Development was accepted by all United Nations member states in 2015. This agenda comprises of 17 Sustainable Development Goals (SDGs) that give a shared blueprint for a more peaceful, prosperous, and sustainable future. All the SDGs are interconnected.

The SDGs can be a focal point for organizational leaders to consider when establishing social change goals and strategies for action.

The 17 UN SDGs are (2015; see https://sdgs.un.org/2030agenda):

- *Goal 1*: End poverty in all its forms everywhere
- *Goal 2*: End hunger, achieve food security and improved nutrition, and promote sustainable agriculture
- *Goal 3*: Ensure healthy lives and promote well-being for all at all ages

- *Goal 4*: Ensure inclusive and equitable quality education and promote lifelong learning opportunities for all
- *Goal 5*: Achieve gender equality and empower all women and girls
- *Goal 6*: Ensure availability and sustainable management of water and sanitation for all
- *Goal 7*: Ensure access to affordable, reliable, sustainable, and modern energy for all
- *Goal 8*: Promote sustained, inclusive, and sustainable economic growth, full and productive employment, and decent work for all
- *Goal 9*: Build resilient infrastructure, promote inclusive and sustainable industrialization, and foster innovation
- *Goal 10*: Reduce inequality within and among countries
- *Goal 11*: Make cities and human settlements inclusive, safe, resilient, and sustainable
- *Goal 12*: Ensure sustainable consumption and production patterns
- *Goal 13*: Take urgent action to combat climate change and its impacts*
- *Goal 14*: Conserve and sustainably use the oceans, seas, and marine resources for sustainable development
- *Goal 15*: Protect, restore, and promote sustainable use of terrestrial ecosystems, sustainably manage forests, combat desertification, and halt and reverse land degradation and halt biodiversity loss
- *Goal 16*: Promote peaceful and inclusive societies for sustainable development, provide access to justice for all, and build effective, accountable, and inclusive institutions at all levels
- *Goal 17*: Strengthen the means of implementation and revitalize the global partnership for sustainable development

Question 10: Should a Social Change or Social Action Department Be Established in an Organization, or Should Some Other Approach Be Used to Institutionalize Social Change Efforts?

There is more than one way to establish a structure to support social change goal implementation in an organization. One way is to unbundle specific efforts to support a change (such as technology, training, communication, and others) and then establish a company task force, council, or steering committee to oversee all the individual change efforts. That is called the *shadow organization approach.* A second approach is to embed social change goals into every manager and every worker's Key Performance Indicators (KPIs) and job descriptions. That is called an *embedded change approach.* A third approach is to create a so-called dream team composed of representatives from distinct levels on the organization chart and different silos or functional areas from the organization chart. (A *dream team* usually consists of high-potential workers from different departments and various levels on the organization chart.) A fourth approach is to hand off the change effort to a DE&I department or an OD department. There are other approaches. The real question is this: *What approach to institutionalizing corporate culture change is most likely to work in your organization?*

Question 11: How Should Social Change Efforts Be Evaluated?

Social change efforts, when adopted by an organization, should be managed like any organizational effort. The *measurable* goals for the change effort should be established and then used to guide project goals for social change efforts. The UN goals have targets, and they can be helpful in establishing organizational, departmental, and individual social change goals.

Question 12: How Do Advocates of Organizational Social Change Efforts Answer the Common Objection of Business Leaders that "the Purpose of a Business Is to Make Money for the Owners and/or Shareholders"?

According to Murphy, Murry & Kvilhaug (2022), organizations should pursue social change objectives because:

■ Employees are empowered by social responsibility to use the corporate resources at their disposal to do good.

■ Being a socially responsible organization can improve an organization's corporate brand image and its employment brand.

■ Social responsibility initiatives can raise employee engagement in the workplace and lead to increased productivity, which affects the company's profitability.

- Social responsibility activities implemented by organizations can boost consumer, customer, or client retention and loyalty.
- Companies that are socially responsible have an advantage over their competitors because they create superior and good brand perception.

Question 13: What Is Meant by the Term a Values-based Balanced Scorecard, and How Can It Factor in Social Change Efforts Mounted by Organizations?

The Balanced Scorecard (BSC) is a strategic planning and management method. Organizations use BSCs to (1) Communicate their goals; (2) Align the day-to-day work that everyone does with strategy; (3) Prioritize initiatives, products, and services; and (4) Track and measure progress toward strategic goals. While the typical four quadrants of the BSC are customer, financial, business operations, and learning and growth, organizations can use organizational values as the foundation for their BSC. Values express what is most important to the organization. They can focus on business goals—or can include social goals.

References

Murphy, C., Murry, C., & Kvilhaug, S. (2022). Why social responsibility matters to business. *Investopedia*. See: https://www.investopedia.com/ask/answers/041015/why-social-responsibility-important-business.asp#:~:text=Businesses%20that%20implement%20social%20responsibility,superior%20and%20positive%20brand%20recognition.

17 UN SDGs. (2015). Transforming our world: The 2030 agenda for sustainable development. *United Nations*. See: https://sdgs.un.org/2030agenda

Index

Printed in the United States
by Baker & Taylor Publisher Services